PLACE AND DISPLACEMENT IN JEWISH HISTORY AND MEMORY

Place and Displacement in Jewish History and Memory

Zakor v'Makor

Editors

**David Cesarani,
Tony Kushner and Milton Shain**

VALLENTINE MITCHELL
LONDON • PORTLAND, OR

First published in 2009 by Vallentine Mitchell

Suite 314, Premier House,
112–114 Station Road,
Edgware, Middlesex
HA8 7BJ, UK

920 NE 58th Avenue, Suite 300
Portland, Oregon,
97213-3786, USA

www.vmbooks.com

Copyright © 2009 Vallentine Mitchell

British Library Cataloguing in Publication Data

Place and displacement in Jewish history and memory : zakor v'makor
1. Jews - Identity - Congresses 2. Jewish diaspora - Congresses
I. Cesarani, David II. Kushner, Tony (Antony Robin Jeremy)
III. Shain, Milton
305.8'924

ISBN 978 0 85303 950 1 (cloth)
ISBN 978 0 85303 940 2 (paper)
ISSN 1368-5449

Library of Congress Cataloging-in-Publication Data:

A catalog record has been applied for

This group of studies first appeared in a special issue of *Jewish Culture and History*,
Vol. 9 No. 2-3 [ISSN 1462-169X]
published by Vallentine Mitchell & Co. Ltd.

All rights reserved. No part of this publication may be reproduced, stored in or introduced into a retrieval system, or transmitted, in any form or by any means, electronic, mechanical, photocopying, recording or otherwise, without the prior written permission of the publisher of this book.

Printed by the MPG Books Group in the UK

Contents

Preface and Acknowledgments   vii

Introduction   **David Cesarani, Milton Shain and Tony Kushner**   1

PART I: PLACE, DISPLACEMENT AND BELONGING

Foreigners in their Own City: Italian Fascism
and the Dispersal of Trieste's Port Jews   **Maura E. Hametz**   15

'Lost Worlds': Reflections on Home and Belonging
in Jewish Holocaust Survivor Testimonies   **Michele Langfield**   29

Constructing a Usable Past: History, Memory and
South African Jewry in an Age of Anxiety   **Richard Mendelsohn and Milton Shain**   43

Comparing the Jewish and Irish Communities in
Twentieth Century Scotland   **William Kenefick**   53

PART II: RACE, PLACE AND PERIPHERY

On Burial, Boundaries and the Creolisation of the
Surinamese Jewish Community   **Wieke Vink**   71

Memory, Place and Displacement in the Formation
of Jewish Identity in Rangoon and Surabaya   **Jonathan Goldstein**   88

Jews of Algiers   **Moshe Terdiman**   99

Jewish Identity in Two Remote Areas of the Cape Province:
A Double Case Study   **John Simon**   114

PART III: PLACE, MIGRATION AND MEMORY WORKS

Migration, Location and Memory: Jewish History
through a Comparative Lens   **Nancy Foner**   131

Putting London Jewish Intellectuals in their Place   **David Cesarani**   141

Memory at the Margins, Matter out of Place:
Hidden Narratives of Jewish Settlement
and Movement in Britain   **Tony Kushner**   154

'A Slice of Eastern Europe in Johannesburg':
Yiddish Theatre in Doornfontein, 1929–49   **Veronica Belling** 169

Abstracts   181

Notes on Contributors   185

Index   187

Preface and Acknowledgments

The 12 essays in this collection originated in an international conference on 'Place and Displacement in Jewish History and Memory – Zakor v'Makor', held at the University of Cape Town in January 2005. It was organised by the Kaplan Centre for Jewish Studies and Research in association with the Parkes Institute for the Study of Jewish/non-Jewish relations at the University of Southampton. This conference, which brought together 30 academics from across the world, reflected the cooperation between the two centres in Cape Town and Southampton, especially in relation to the study of the concept of the 'Port Jew'. Earlier conferences in Southampton (2001) and Cape Town (2003), and their associated publications, developed this concept in both time and place, expanding the chronological and geographical range. The 2005 Cape Town conference went further. Whilst the 'Port Jew paradigm' was not abandoned, the emphasis was widened to place identity as a whole in the Jewish experience from antiquity onwards. This was the final conference in the series linked to 'Port Jews' which was part of the AHRC Parkes Research Centre's activities on this theme under the direction of David Cesarani. It was not, however, the end of the research that has been stimulated by this project which continues in many academic institutions. Moreover, the collaboration between the Kaplan Centre at Cape Town and the Parkes Institute at Southampton has now been formalised and further conferences have taken place ('Jewish Journeys', Cape Town 2007) or are planned 'Jewish Families and Migration', Cape Town 2009) which have their origins in the earlier gatherings. In all these conferences it has been extremely gratifying to witness the mixing of young scholars alongside those who are more established as they have grappled together with the complex issues of Jewish identity in relation to space and place. These conferences have also provided a shared forum for those inside and outside 'Jewish studies'. It has enabled a helpful dialogue, bringing together specialist and general expertise. The 2005 Cape Town conference was no exception to this pattern and the contributions to this volume reflect its intellectual dynamism and geographical diversity.

We would like to take this opportunity of thanking all those that took part in the conference and to those who made it possible – on the organisational level, Janine Blumberg, administrator of the Kaplan Centre, and Steve Taverner, administrator of the AHRC Parkes Research Centre, and for their financial support, the Kaplan Kushlick Foundation, the AHRC and the British Academy.

DC, TK and MS

Introduction

DAVID CESARANI, MILTON SHAIN and TONY KUSHNER

Part 1: Place, Displacement and Belonging

Places do not simply exist as physical manifestations, they are creations of the mind. People give meaning to what is otherwise an abstract location, a point on a map, a structure at the intersection of coordinates, random space. But people do not simply invest a place with significance: the process is reciprocal, with place becoming a part of the identity of those who interact with it. A place may be deemed secure and pleasant, it may be perceived as fitting for those who inhabit it. Or it may represent danger and the territory of another people who are held in low esteem, disliked, or feared. Human geographers have shown how places can be infused with social status, gendered, and ethnically specific.[1]

But what happens when people whose identity is bound up with a place leave it, voluntarily or under duress? How does the memory of place operate then? And what happens when the process of mental mapping is fundamentally refigured so that a place that once had one meaning acquires another that is very different? How do the sense of place and the sense of belonging interact during periods of upheaval and social transformation?

The four chapters in this section all explore these questions using a rich variety of case studies. In her evocative exploration of Trieste, Maura Hametz shows how the identity of the Triestine Jewish community was initially bound up with the city's self-consciously fashioned image as a bustling, pragmatic, mercantile, cosmopolitan free port serving a great, multi-national empire.[2] The Jews had been welcomed during the era of Habsburg Enlightenment and their talents, as well as their diasporic connections, were deemed well suited to the prevailing ethos of economic liberalism. They, in turn, felt that they fitted in. They were comfortable with an identity that blended loyalty to Jewish tradition with fealty to the Emperor, and a fierce local pride.

By the end of the nineteenth century, however, there were clouds on the horizon. Nationalism within the empire and Italian revanchism placed a question mark over cosmopolitan merits. Socialist and labour movements in the city challenged the unrestrained pursuit of profit as a civic virtue. When Trieste was incorporated into Italy after the First World War, the world of the Triestine Jews threatened to collapse. Economic and technological changes affecting the seaport, the loss of its freeport status and the amputation of its hinterland plunged the region into crisis.

Hametz reveals how the Jewish community reacted to this massive change and adapted rather well. They 'recast' themselves as stalwarts of the Italian bourgeoisie. They rebalanced their business activity, focusing more on financial services and insurance. Indeed, until the late 1930s they continued to prosper.[3] Their nemesis was the hard-edged fascism of Achille Starace, Roberto Farinacci, and Giuseppe Bottai who had pressed for measures against the Jews long before Italy's alliance with the Third Reich became a factor in domestic policy. The cosmopolitanism of the Triestine Jews, which was once perceived as an asset, now became a liability. Nevertheless, the community bravely succoured German and Austrian Jewish refugees seeking safety south of the Alps or making their way to more reliable havens further afield. Their loyalties as Jews to other Jews became more pronounced. Ultimately, it was their diasporic connections and their cosmopolitanism that saved many of them. After the introduction of the racial laws in 1938 young Triestine Jews emigrated to Palestine, North and South America (especially Argentina). Hametz remarks dryly that 'The chosen people became a seafaring people.'

For the Triestine Jews who were fortunate enough to make new lives on distant shores, the city in which they had grown up remained a part of their identity. One who had transplanted himself to Argentina remarked that 'As a good Triestine, [I am nostalgic] for Trieste more than for Italy. We Triestines are parochial to the hilt. That is, first Triestine, then Italian, and then in the end Jewish.' His sense of self was so bound up with place that it remained part of his identity even decades after forced emigration.

Michele Langfield found very similar sentiments amongst the Jewish survivors of Nazi persecution and genocide who ended up in Australia. Drawing on oral testimony she observes that refugees and survivors did not restart their lives after 1945 simply as displaced persons. They drew on a rich store of memories of place that helped them to adapt, and even to shape their new surroundings to evoke in some small measure the familiar environment of the old country. The very act of congregating in certain cities and neighbourhoods was part of this process. Langfield, who makes sensitive use of the work by human geographers, points out that 'A sense of place is not only associated with place, but with people and communities.' Thus the survivors reconstituted communities, stamped their mark on the suburban landscape and so gave locations in an entirely alien setting new meaning that reflected their histories and backgrounds, the places from which they had been so cruelly uprooted.

Langfield necessarily situates this adaptation within the social and cultural history of Australia and Australian Jewry. It was possible for Australian places to change their meaning partly because the country transited from a predominantly Anglo-Saxon European settler population to a multi-cultural society that welcomed diversity.[4] The Jews of Australia were allowed a more expansive identity, one better able to accommodate the experiences of the refugees and survivors. Over the course of four decades the policies of assimilation gave way to the politics of remembrance. The memories of refugees and survivors were publicly transposed onto Australian places, reshaping their meaning in ways that everyone could understand. Events that had occurred thousands of miles away and 60 years ago came to lend a distinctive hue to the neighbourhoods where displaced Jews had clustered and where their children and grandchildren now lived.

INTRODUCTION 3

But what happens to a Jewish population that stays in place while the meaning of place changes around it? In modern times the sense of self is not just inscribed upon and engraved by place as an immediately experienced location, a locality. People learn to imagine geographies, to imagine communities that dwell within far-flung boundaries, and to develop a sense of belonging to a place that is an abstract concept, a set of fabricated meanings mapped onto an actual landscape.[5] In times of upheaval these meanings may change fundamentally. Between 1930 and the post-apartheid era, the territory inhabited by the Jews of South Africa went from the domain of the white minority to being a country that revelled in multi-culturalism. South African Jews had to relocate themselves, metaphorically, from fitting into the Afrikaner hegemony to dovetailing with the new, rainbow republic.[6]

Richard Mendelsohn and Milton Shain use a study of historiography, how South African Jews chronicled their past, to show how they accomplished this transformation. The first communal histories, appearing in the 1930s, were Anglo-centric, whiggish and ended before the era of mass immigration of East European Jews. They screened out the impact of the new immigrants whose cultural specificity, religious leanings, social position and political radicalism were the cause of much anxiety to the established Jewish population that was straining to prove its good credentials in the face of mounting anti-semitism. During the years of National Party rule Jewish authors liked, on the one hand, to cloak themselves in the approbation of Afrikaner political leaders while, on the other, disavowing any collective Jewish interest in politics. They played down anti-Jewish sentiment, ignored Jewish socialists, marginalised Yiddish and Hebrew cultural activity, and stressed the community's own brand of nationalism, Zionism, over ideological rivals.

However, with the end of apartheid in 1994 and the advent of Nelson Mandela that history had to be rewritten. It was now appropriate to emphasise the role of Jews in the anti-apartheid struggle; their disproportionate involvement in socialist and communist movements; the struggle of poor, immigrant, working class Jews; the pluralism, even conflict, within the Jewish population; and in the light of Israel's unpopularity with many Black South Africans, the non-Zionist strands of Jewish identity. Thus Mendelsohn and Shain illustrate how South African Jews learned to live in a new place, and to evolve a new sense of belonging. The landscape was the same, but its meanings were vastly changed. Sadly, many young Jews have found a place that once connoted safety, prosperity and pleasure turned into one of insecurity, struggle and danger. The high rate of Jewish emigration suggests that the transformation of place can be so deracinating that even those who are indigenous feel they no longer belong.

By complete contrast, the Jews of Scotland have experienced two centuries of continuity and stability.[7] While the Strathclyde region has been utterly transformed economically and socially, Glasgow's Jews have experienced a gentle upward social progression represented geographically by the move from the inner city to the suburbs. The complete erasure of the Gorbals, site of first settlement, is an ironic comment on their journey. Yet the past has not been consigned to oblivion. William Kenefick uses a strong collection of oral histories to reconstruct the Jewish experience and, in particular, the pattern of relations between Jews and non-Jews in the twentieth century. He notes the overwhelmingly benign depiction of these relations by Jews. These oral histories testify to improvement and progress, unimpeded by prejudice and unmarked by anti-semitism. This is very much the collective memory of a Jewish community that experienced unmitigated success once it started to escape the trammels of poverty, economic exploitation, and the casual racial abuse that merged into the background experience of daily struggle. It resembles the whiggish collective memory of Jews under apartheid.

Fortunately, Scottish Jews have never been forced to revise this version, unlike Catholics and Protestants, whose relations have been reworked dramatically over the same period. It remains to be seen how Jews will fit into a Scotland that is more nationalistic and may soon embark on the road to independence. Historical experience does not bode well. But nationalism changes, too. A more inclusive civic nationalism may triumph in Scotland, so reversing the trend that has been marked in other great port cities with Jewish populations such as Odessa, Salonika and Trieste that 'changed management' after the end of empire. However, as is observed in the next section of this introduction, the timing of migration and settlement, as well as changing demographic realities, were as important as political change and shifting religious currents in determining the conditions and the identities of Jewish communities.

Part 2: Race, Place and Periphery

In their dispersion at the frontiers of the Jewish world, Jews balanced an identification with the wider Jewish diaspora together with evolving identities, the latter informed by prevailing conditions, including demographic realities and ethnic divides, economic opportunities, and the attitudes of the dominant host society. Within these peripheral communities, there was invariably a contestation of identities, more often than not revealing fissures within the community that focused on differences between the 'natives' or earlier arrivals and the outsiders or newcomers.

Surinam provides a fascinating case in the early modern period and reveals starkly the ways in which group boundaries were created, negotiated and recreated. Wieke Vink traces these developments, with a special focus on the shifting position of 'Coloured' Jews within the Jewish community. Founded in the mid-seventeenth century, Surinam Jewry comprised both Ashkenazi and Sephardi Jews. It was very much an outpost community, far removed from its roots and yet substantial in numbers. To be sure, throughout the eighteenth century Surinam Jewry was among the largest communities in the New World. It was five times the size of the Jewish community of mainland America. Significantly, it was a product of cross-cultural processes, including what Vink describes as the 'creolisation' or localisation of the community or 'the process of becoming local'.

Vink's innovative study examines the changing style of gravestones and debates around burials. The gravestones, she maintains, are the sites of collective memory or 'places where notions of collective identities are located, constructed and changed'. Issues 'related to burial rites, gravestones, and cemetery space', explains Vink, reflected 'the changing notions of Surinam Jewish identity or, at the very least, can be read as a contemporary critique of the dominant notions of Surinam Jewish identity at a certain moment of time'.

In addition to clear divisions between the Portuguese and High German Jews, the community, notes Vink, also distinguished between members with only limited rights (known as *Congregants*) and fully fledged members of the community, the *Yachidim*. An even greater fissure surrounded the question of the offspring of non-Jewish (African) mothers. In this regard ideas changed over time. Vink shows that 'Jewish mulattoes' were part of 'a socially defined Jewish community' in the seventeenth and eighteenth centuries. Here she supports Jonathan Schorsch's wider study of Jewish attitudes towards blacks in the early modern world.[8] Colour clearly attenuated the connections of mulattoes with the mainstream Jewish community. But in line with developments in wider Surinamese society, colour gradually lost its boundary function. Thus in the nineteenth century new boundaries based on *halakha* evolved. A Jewish mother became the arbiter of 'the religious community of the Surinam Jews', writes Vink.

Vink demonstrates these fascinating changes and shifting attitudes by sensitively examining cemetery spaces and debates within the community dealing with burials. 'Apart from their function as *lieux de memoire*', she contends that 'the Jewish cemeteries of Surinam can be used as a cultural doorway for understanding some of the underexposed aspects of Surinamese Jewish history' such as the history of the coloured Jews or the Ashkenazi account of Surinam Jewish history.

Intermarriage also operated in Burma and in the Dutch East Indies, but seemingly without the same tensions and complications as in Surinam. In eighteenth and nineteenth century Rangoon (Burma) and Surabaya (Java), explains Jonathan Goldstein, Jewish identity was contested but untouched by the phenomenon of 'creolisation'. Nonetheless, these were multi-ethnic Jewish communities: Rangoon Jewry included Marathi- and Malayalam-speakers from the Bene Israel and Cochinis communities of India, Arabic-speakers from Baghdad, Syria and Yemen, and Central and Eastern Europeans; Surabaya Jewry included Baghdadis, Dutch and German Jews. While Baghdadis became dominant in both settings, the cultures within which these Jewish communities operated were markedly different: British Burma was dominated by Buddhists and Surabaya by (Sunni) Muslims.

Goldstein lays much emphasis on the importance of memory in identity formation, noting in particular the way in which Baghdadis identified with their suffering co-religionists left behind in Iraq. In the relatively tolerant atmosphere of Rangoon there was much intermarriage and occasional – and sometimes even bitter – communal division. But common connections to the Zionist idea served to unify the community. Burma and Israel were both founded in 1948; both faced strife, and Burmese Jews ultimately all went to Israel.

Surabayo's Dutch Jews rapidly assimilated and intermarried from the eighteenth century. By the twentieth century the more ritually observant Baghdadi and Adeni Jews – who had followed the European Jews – comprised the majority of the community. In the case of the Baghdadis, memories of persecution – as was the case for Rangoon's Baghdadis – informed a powerful identity. In effect the Baghdadis founded the community and laid the basis for a powerful, albeit contested Zionism. Japanese occupation during the Second World War was harsh and 'put a halt to Zionist and indeed all Judaic activity in Surabaya'. After the war most Jews went to

Israel, encouraged by Sukarno's hostility to the Jewish state and discrimination against Judaism.

Communal divisions are also the focus of Moshe Terdiman's study of the Jewish community of Algiers in the seventeenth and eighteenth centuries. Terdiman demonstrates how major fault lines were evident between the Livorno Jews – welcomed for their trading and financial acumen – and the 'native' Jews of Algiers who had lived in the city for centuries. As traders, Livorno Jews were well connected to Europe's Jewish communities; the 'native' Jews on the other hand were *dhimmis* – non-Muslim subjects of the Islamic state – of lower standing and often engaged in lesser occupations, such as goldsmiths, tailors, artisans, peddlers. During the Turkish period, these *dhimmis* were subject to substantial humiliation and often treated with contempt. This led to a number of conversions to Islam, especially among the better off.

Predictably, power and wealth operated when it came to leadership of the community. Livorno Jews served as *muqaddams* (lay leaders of the Jewish community) throughout the eighteenth century until the French occupation of Algiers. Many were wealthy and dictatorial; they effectively bought their positions. Families maintained intricate trading connections. While Livornese Jews would on occasion serve as scapegoats for domestic problems, the head of the palace (the *dey*) by and large appreciated their contributions. Some were even appointed diplomatic emissaries.

Notwithstanding class and other differences, the Jewish community of Algiers maintained a distinctive coherence, this despite Livorno Jews setting their sights on Europe and never fully developing an Algerian identity. Terdiman shows how differences were strengthened by the special conditions under which Livorno Jews lived. These so-called 'Christian or European Jews' were the beneficiaries of *Musta'min* regulations granted to all foreigners. They could, writes Terdiman, 'leave the country whenever they wished as long as they did not leave debts behind them'. In addition, notes Terdiman, 'they lived outside the Jewish quarter, even in the upper city, the Muslims' residence. They could wear whatever they wished'.

Given these special opportunities, the Livorno Jews maintained a distinctive identity: they married within their own community and not with native Jews and they sent their children abroad to study. They did not even mingle socially with native Jews. Nevertheless, they shared communal services, facilities and communal life with the natives.

Jews also experienced divisions at the tip of Africa, usually between the established and more acculturated Anglo-German Jews and the Eastern European newcomers who entered the country in the wake of diamond discoveries in the 1860s and gold discoveries two decades later. But these divisions were usually short-lived and seldom split the Jewish community. In the case of small communities far removed from the mainstreams of Jewish life, they hardly mattered. Communal size appears to have been the key factor, as evident in John Simon's examination of two Jewish trading communities: in the shipping and mineral Namaqualand region of the north-western Cape, and in the ostrich feather and tobacco region of Oudtshoorn in the southern Cape.

In the remote and arid Namaqualand region the isolated and very tiny Jewish communities were fairly homogenous. In the main they were made up of Yiddish-speakers from Eastern Europe. Those of English origin shared more in common with their co-religionists than differences. To be sure, small numbers precluded division; communal institutions and communal life was never divided. Synagogues and Zionist societies gave a sense of meaning and connection with larger Jewish centres in South Africa such as Cape Town. The multi-ethnic character of the wider population and the fundamental divides around colour in a colonial framework appear to have enhanced Jewish identity. There was little out marriage and (to use Vink's term) hardly any instances of 'creolisation'. Relations between Jews and their (white) mainly Afrikaner neighbours were – other than in the 1930s and early 1940s – cordial. Business ties and symbiotic trading relations enhanced and smoothed contacts. One of the region's major towns (Springbok) even boasted a Jewish mayor, Joe Jowell, for 30 years.

Outdshoorn in the southern Cape had far more Jews and a more vibrant Jewish life than that experienced by the Jews of Namaqualand. Known as the 'Jerusalem of Africa', the Jews of Oudtshoorn were largely involved in the ostrich feather business which enjoyed its heyday before the Great War in Europe began in 1914. Most of the settlers came from the two small Lithuanian towns of Shavel and Kelm, ensuring a sense of community, rooted in common memories. Significantly, there were divisions between the members of the so-called *Anglisher Shul* [English shul], comprised of members of Anglo-German background, and the newcomers from Eastern Europe, the so-called *Greuners*. But these divisions, writes Simon, were probably more a product of increasing numbers than of serious ideological differences.

By 1904, the Oudtshoorn's Jews comprised about 15 per cent of the white population, which made up about half the total population of the town. Although some tensions relating to issues of credit were evident with their Dutch-speaking farming neighbours at this time, relations between Jew and non-Jew were in the main cordial. As was the case in Namaqualand, Jews were very much part of the white community, with Max Rose, the 'Ostrich King', attaining fame equivalent to that of Joe Jowell in Springbok. Miscegenation was exceptionally rare and never emerged as an issue as it had in Surinam.

It would seem that the timing of settlement in southern Africa – much later than in Surinam – meant colour lines were more rigid. Certainly the Jewish community identified with the white population which enjoyed substantial advantages in a colonial setting. There was, to be sure, no 'mulatto' problem. As John Simon explains, the 'melting pot syndrome' was absent. Ultimately, these small towns witnessed substantial Jewish emigration to the larger cities where Jewish life was more vibrant and fulfilling.

It is apparent that the behaviour, condition and identities of Jewish communities in far-flung outposts related very much to the timing of settlement, to demographic realities and to the dominant political and religious culture. Algiers in particular left its Muslim imprint on Jewish life, while in Surinam, colour and class substantially informed divisions. This was more so the case for communities founded in the nineteenth century at a time of burgeoning colonialism and the emergence of scientific racism. While place of origin remained a potent dimension of identity, divisions were invariably minimised over time or ignored when necessary.

Part 3: Place, Migration and Memory Works

In their 'exhibition in a book', *Art Works: Place* (2005), Tacita Dean and Jeremy Millar argue that 'Place can be difficult to locate.' They note that Aristotle, responding to the question 'what is place?', concluded that it 'presents many difficulties'. Since the Greek philosopher's intervention, over two millennia of engagement with the term 'place' have only served to show the limitations of our understanding of the concept, especially within recent scholarly discourse from an increasingly wide range of disciplinary perspectives.[9] Even then, the complicating factor of migration has rarely been factored into considerations of 'place'.

The geographer Yi-Fu Tuan has argued that 'if we see the world as process, constantly changing, we should not be able to develop any sense of place'.[10] For those on the move, or of recent settlement, the necessity of creating a sense of place is, on the one hand, crucial, and, on the other, fundamentally difficult as a result of their perceived or experienced rootlessness. Nancy Foner's contribution to this volume starts by acknowledging it is clear that 'place or location matters in understanding the immigrant experience'. Nevertheless, the complexity of the term 'place' is immediately recognised by Foner: 'What is not so obvious ... is just how it matters.' Migrants move from one place to another, and rarely in a straightforward manner. Journeys are often broken, for shorter or longer periods, and the 'final' destination may not turn out to be the one initially intended, or indeed final. As a result, the concept of 'home' and 'belonging' is rarely straightforward for any migrant – it is multi-layered and continuously negotiated through the processes of memory relating to places past and present, 'there' and 'here'. And memory, as James Fentress and Chris Wickham remind us, 'is a complex process, not a simple mental act; even the words we use to describe the act (*recognize, remember, recall, recount, commemorate* and so on) show that "memory" can include anything from a highly private and spontaneous, possibly wordless, mental sensation to a formalized public ceremony'.[11] The four articles in this section of *Zakor v'Makor* confirm that variation in memory work (including the equally complex processes of forgetting), spanning between its expression at an individual and collective level. They also explore the relationship between culture and politics in both public and private expressions of memory.

All four case studies of Jewish immigrants (and their children), place and memory are from (at least partly) English-speaking urban settings – New York, London, Johannesburg and Southampton. Each experienced, to a greater or lesser degree, a sizeable East European Jewish influx at the turn of the twentieth century. Yet it is also the dissimilitude of these cities, and the dominant memory work within them, that makes comparison between them so rewarding. It confirms Foner's analysis, following that of Nancy Green, that 'what is especially useful about comparisons is that as they bring out *both* the similarities and the differences between migrations to different places', and they then force us to account for the variations.[12] It should be added here that the revealing nature of an openly comparative approach is as true of the *memory* of these migrations as the migrations themselves.

The examples in this section vary from New York, perceived as the 'immigrant city' par excellence, to Southampton, which is normally, if at all, seen as a place of embarkation to new worlds rather than a place of settlement in itself. Myth and reality, however, are not always directly related and a close reading of Southampton's history from its Roman roots onwards reveals a port that has always relied on newcomers to provide the labour, goods, enterprise and culture to ensure its continuity and success. In New York, in spite of the huge number of immigrant groups making it their new home, it is *Jewish* immigration from Eastern Europe that still dominates the memory work of the city. In contrast, whilst in reality the 'peopling of London' represents 'Fifteen Thousand Years of Settlement from Overseas',[13] the unwillingness to acknowledge that England has always been a place attracting those from overseas hinders acceptance that its capital is a city of migrants and their descendants. David Cesarani's subtle comparison between New York and London Jewish intellectuals indicates the greater marginality of the latter, noting that, for them, it 'would not be until the 1990s that place and ethnicity were associated and celebrated'.

In any settlement, numbers, as Foner emphasises, 'make a real difference'. The sheer scale of New York's Jewry, but also its political and cultural influence in the city, inevitably helped the processes by which the Jewish memory of migration, especially in relation to the Lower East Side, became dominant. This dominance was not only in the city itself, but, as Hasia Diner has shown, within American Jewry as a whole – Jews whose ancestors had not lived in the Lower East Side still identify it as *the* original place of settlement in the USA.[14] For Britain, even London, where at least two-thirds of the Jewish population has been concentrated since readmission in the mid-seventeenth century, no such prominence, let alone dominance, was possible in constructing national or even local identities. Nevertheless, in a country collectively in denial of its diverse past, certain places, such as the East End of London, are allowed exceptional status. These, however, are limited in number: to acknowledge too many places of migration would disturb the comforting mythology of past homogeneity. Thus, as Kushner's contribution argues, there is no place in either the collective memory of the port of Southampton, or within British Jewry, to enable a recognition of the way in which Jews of East European origin impacted on the town (and in many others across the country) in the first half of the twentieth century. It has been left to individuals whose lives were shaped by that (relatively brief) Jewish migrant presence to rescue them from total obscurity. As a result, it is only in privately published memoirs or fleeting references in oral history projects that the 'cosmopolitan' nature of inter-war Southampton is acknowledged and in which the Jewish presence is particularly noted. Yet outside this marginalised memory work, Jewish (and other) migrations are generally forgotten in Southampton, a pattern of amnesia that is replicated at a local level across Britain. In contrast to the recognition of London's East End, there is no space in Southampton's collective memory for its special place of past diversity and migrant settlement. Here, the comments of historical geographer Doreen Massey are particular pertinent: 'The identity of places is very much bound up with the *histories* which are told of them, *how* those histories are told, and which history turns out to be dominant.'[15]

There is, taking the three case studies considered so far, a clear pecking order in the memory of Jewish migration, starting at the top with New York, and in a category of its very own, and then with London and Southampton having equally large gaps between them. The absence or presence of memory relates obviously to the scale of Jewish migration and the subsequent size of Jewish presence in these urban settings. Nevertheless, the partial or total denial of that migrant past cannot be explained by smaller numbers alone. If the dominant culture is antipathetical to the recognition of diversity – past or present – then minorities will struggle to gain a status in collective memory even if they are numerically large. Alternatively, and equally damaging, if the dominant culture is dismissive towards minorities, it may well replicate such negative attitudes in collective commemoration. Raphael Samuel and Paul Thompson emphasise how 'national myths and the sense of national history which they help to build ... raise fundamental questions of just who belongs and who does not. Time and again, in rallying solidarity they also exclude, and persecute the excluded.' They add that it this is 'why for minorities, for the less powerful, and most of all for the excluded, collective memory and myth are often still more salient: constantly resorted to both in reinforcing a sense of self and also as a source of strategies for survival'.[16] The power relations with regard to place identity and belonging have thus to be taken into consideration before any consideration is given to the construction of specific Jewish memories of migration. But, whilst the wider context cannot be ignored, it also has to be recognised that Jewish communities and their associated memory work are neither homogeneous nor free of internal conflict. Veronica Belling's contribution to this section shows the marginalisation that can occur within an ethnic grouping itself.

Carrying out research on the Yiddish theatre in Johannesburg, the focus of her contribution, was no easy matter. Sources are thin, reflecting marginality in several ways. First, little material produced by those involved survives, an archival absence that itself shows that those involved were (literally) acting on the margins of both Jewish and general society – indeed, much was destroyed by the South African state after 1945 as part of an intolerance towards anything perceived as politically progressive. Second, most contemporary South African Jewish organisations were hostile to Yiddish and Yiddish culture and thus tended to ignore those promoting its theatrical expression. Belling's narrative works at three levels. First, in rescuing a rich but neglected aspect of the Jewish experience. Second, in explaining how it was subsequently forgotten and 'erased from the collective memory of South African Jewry'. In these respects, her work, whilst geographically distant from Kushner's, follows a similar pattern. But Belling adds a third element to the study of place, migration and memory – how the promotion and preservation of Yiddish language and culture acted as a bridge between 'old' world and 'new'. Until the end of the Second World War, the Dramatic Section of the Johannesburg Jewish Workers' Club produced plays of an overtly political nature which was 'Marxist, anti-religious and anti-Zionist'. Plays and other related activities focused on class exploitation, Nazism and anti-semitism. Whilst those involved in the Jewish Workers' Club were a tight-knit local group, their activities revealed an engagement with the global and the strength of alternative Jewish diasporic networks. Not surprisingly, with its anti-Zionist and anti-religious slant, its activities found little support amongst official South African Jewish organisations at either a national or local level. It was only after the war, argues Belling, that the promotion of Yiddish culture became consciously nostalgic with special efforts to keep the language alive. Before then, its theatrical promotion in Johannesburg reflected a politicised form of memory work in which Jewish identities in relation to place, migration and settlement were negotiated and dominant Jewish narratives challenged.

David Cesarani's contribution takes us from the first to the second generation of Jewish migrants. His study of six Jewish intellectuals, all born in London's East End, reveals the care required when identifying the precise nature of individual place identity. All six reveal similar tendencies – the importance of family home and beyond it, what belonged and what was perceived as the hostile world beyond. Mental maps, often made explicit by the use of postcodes, helped create for these individuals in their writings 'geographies of ethnicity and genealogies of migration'. A positive sense of place, of belonging, 'was literally assembled out of sights, sounds, smells and feel'. It went alongside other areas, sometimes adjoining, that were constructed as dangerous and not 'Jewish'. What was perceived as 'Jewish' (or not) in the autobiographical writings of these intellectuals was not straightforward and often rested on an engagement with secular culture – pubs, cafes, cinemas, dance halls, etc. could be labelled as one thing or another. Yiddish, as was the case in Johannesburg, divided not only Jew and non-Jew, but first- from second-generation migrants. For these intellectuals, place, whether the East End or resettlement in the suburbs, mattered and it was interpreted through a strong sense of Jewishness. In the dominant cultural milieu, however, Cesarani concludes that this ethnic focus condemned them to careers 'in the margins'. The 'celebration' of ethnicity in late twentieth century Britain came too late and by then the Jewish East End had largely vanished. As in post-war Johannesburg and the attempt to keep Yiddish culture afloat, Cesarani suggests that for the East End and the memory of Jewish migration, 'nostalgia [was] the only mode in which it could [now] be explored'.

Yi-Fu Tuan notes that 'Home is an intimate place'.[17] In the Jewish experience, migration, whether forced or voluntary, has made the need to establish a 'sense of place' an essential feature in everyday life. The 12 essays, cutting across history and memory, geography and chronology, show the complexities and intricacies involved for a wide range of Jewish communities and individuals in constructing and reconstructing their identities (and challenging others) in relation to ideas and understanding of 'place'. The time span, focusing on the early modern era onwards, is, of course, far from complete. Similarly, whilst the essays cover Africa, the Americas, Europe and Asia, there are, inevitably in a collection of this size and pioneer status, communities and regions that still remain neglected. Nevertheless, the richness of the case studies that follow reveal the potential of inserting the concept of 'place' into our understanding of the Jewish experience and, more generally, in understanding the complex web of Jewish/non-Jewish relations. It is to be hoped that others will be inspired by these essays both to fill chronological and geographical gaps and develop further the concepts that have inspired them.

NOTES

1. For an excellent selection of case studies and theoretical discussions from the perspective of humanist geography see Paul C. Adams, Steven Hoelscher, Karen E. Till, eds., *Textures of Place. Exploring Humanist Geographies* (Minneapolis: University of Minnesota Press, 2001).

2. The definitive study of how the port city and its Jews grew together is Lois Dubin, *The Port Jews of Habsburg Trieste* (Stanford, CA: Stanford University Press, 1999).
3. The most engaging portrait of Italian Jews under fascism is still Alexander Stille, *Benevolence and Betrayal* (London: Cape, 1992). The emergence and role of racism and anti-semitism is discussed in R.J.B. Bosworth, *Mussolini's Italy* (London: Allen Lane, 2005), pp.243–4, 415–21.
4. See Suzanne Rutland, *Edge of Diaspora. Two Centuries of Jewish Settlement in Australia* (Sydney: Brandl and Schlesinger, 1997).
5. Kenneth R. Olwing, 'Landscape as a Contested Topos of Place, Community and Self', in *Textures of Place*, ed. by Adams *et al.* (see note 1), pp.93–117.
6. The most recent overview of the 'before' if not the 'after' is Gideon Shimoni, *Community and Conscience. The Jews in Apartheid South Africa* (Hanover: University Press of New England, 2003).
7. The definitive communal history that is more than just a one city, one century story is Ben Braber, *Jews in Glasgow 1879–1939. Immigration and Integration* (London: Vallentine Mitchell, 2007).
8. J. Schorsch, *Jews and Blacks in the Early Modern World* (Cambridge: Cambridge University Press, 2004).
9. Tacita Dean and Jeremy Millar, 'Entrance: Place, The First of All Things', in *Art Works: Place*, ed. by Tacita Dean and Jeremy Millar (London: Thames & Hudson, 2005), p.11.
10. Yi-Fu Tuan, *Space and Place: The Perspective of Experience* (London: Arnold, 1977), p.179.
11. James Fentress and Chris Wickham, *Social Memory* (Oxford: Blackwell, 1992), p.x.
12. Nancy Green, 'The Comparative Method and Poststructural Structuralism – New Perspectives for Migration Studies', *Journal of American Ethic History*, 13 (Summer 1994), 3–22.
13. Nick Merriman, ed., *The Peopling of London: Fifteen Thousand Years of Settlement from Overseas* (London: Museum of London, 1993).
14. Hasia Diner, *Lower East Side Memories: A Jewish Place in America* (Princeton, NJ: Princeton University Press, 2000), chapter 1, and more generally, Hasia Diner, Jeffrey Shandler and Beth Wenger, eds., *Remembering the Lower East Side: American Jewish Reflections* (Bloomington: Indiana University Press, 2000).
15. Doreen Massey, 'Places and their Past', *History Workshop Journal* 39 (Spring 1995), 186.
16. Raphael Samuel and Paul Thompson, 'Introduction', in *The Myths We Live By*, ed. by Raphael Samuel and Paul Thompson (London: Routledge, 1990), pp.18–19.
17. Tuan, *Space and Place* (see note 10) p.144.

PART I:
PLACE, DISPLACEMENT AND BELONGING

Foreigners in their Own City: Italian Fascism and the Dispersal of Trieste's Port Jews

MAURA E. HAMETZ

Port Jews in Trieste as Exemplars of the 'Social Type'

The experience of Jews in eighteenth- and nineteenth-century Trieste served, to a large extent, as an inspiration for David Sorkin's model of port Jews as a 'social type'.[1] Sorkin traced the origins of modern Jewry to the experiences of Jews in the early modern period that engaged in European, Near Eastern, and Atlantic trade networks. Assimilation and acculturation contributed to the evolution of a 'segmental Jewish life and identity', and in Jewish faith and practice played a role alongside secular education and engagement in commercial and cosmopolitan societies.[2] Certainly, as Sorkin suggested, the Jews of Trieste were characterised by their links to migration and commerce. By the mid-nineteenth century, the 'valuation of commerce' was a hallmark of the entire population of the Adriatic city 'dear to Mercury', as Camillo Boito, one of Italy's best known art historians and architects of the time, described it.[3] Lois Dubin ably demonstrated that Trieste's Jews, immersed in the cosmopolitan port atmosphere, enjoyed legal privileges and freedoms and utilised their wealth and connections to become leading figures in Trieste, contributing to the development of both the local Jewish and secular communities.[4] The identity of Triestine Jews prior to the First World War was, no doubt, tied to their loyalty to the monarchy and their recognition of the advantages afforded by Habsburg rule.

The development of the modern city, the emergence of nation states in the wake of the collapse of empires, and the decline of commercial ports and maritime transport in the twentieth century inevitably affected the role and status of port Jews throughout Europe. However, the demise of Trieste's Jewish community and along with it the Triestine port Jew did not come as a direct result of these economic upheavals. Rather, it was a consequence of political transformations in response to the national disillusionment, political upheavals and economic disappointments of the inter-war period. In 1920, Triestine Jews rejoiced at the opportunities offered by annexation to liberal Italy in the wake of the Habsburg collapse. But, over the 20-year period of fascist rule, changing notions of the role local Jews played in society and changing expectations of loyalty and definitions of Italian allegiance forced the re-interpretation of Jewish status and national belonging. Jews negotiated and re-negotiated their position as unrelenting ethno-nationalist fascist agendas reified national identity in Italy, transforming ethnic association into a racial identity. By 1938, great expectations turned to despair. The fascist racial laws of 1938 set Jews apart, defining them as 'distinct from the Italian–Fascist–Catholic entity regime–state–people–nation and hostile to it'.[5] Although the racial legislation persecuted all of the Jews in Italy, it specifically targeted Jews of 'foreign' origin. The community of port Jews in Trieste, by nature a transient and cosmopolitan population, included many of foreign origin and even foreign citizenship. The laws of 1938 not only excluded these Jews from the Italian nation, they subjected them to expulsion from Italian territory. Trieste had attracted Jews from the far reaches of the empire and the territories of the empire's trading partners. The cosmopolitanism of the Jewish community, prized by the Habsburgs and early fascist regime as a benefit to international trade and expansion of overseas influence, became a liability after 1938. It served as a justification to question the loyalties of all of Trieste's Jews, including the Jewish port elite.

The Roots of Jewish 'Foreignness'

Economic liberalism provided the foundation for port life in Habsburg Trieste. The north-eastern Adriatic Jewish community began to flourish in the early eighteenth century with the Habsburg introduction of free port privileges. Vienna's experimentation with liberal Enlightenment policies designed to promote the expansion of trade included granting liberties to Jews.[6] By the late nineteenth century, the Jewish port population formed part of the flourishing cosmopolitan Central European culture of the fin-de-siècle. In some cases ethno-nationalist or religious networks were maintained through familial arrangements, but privileged Jews also aligned with economic peers. Trieste's commercial relationships with Central Europe and the Near East, in which Jews took a leading role, promoted a cosmopolitan outlook on the part of those engaged in port society. Here, cosmopolitanism referred to interactions born of 'cross-cultural exchange' characteristic of liberals rather than internationalist 'dialogue' typical of socialists.[7] For Jews in Trieste, this cosmopolitanism grew naturally out of currents of assimilation and acculturation fostered by Enlightenment-inspired policies introduced over the course of more than a century.

Cosmopolitanism also contributed to the development of the Triestine Jews' unique version of the 'tripartite' identity characteristic of Jews living throughout the Cisleithanian or Austrian part of the Habsburg empire after 1867. Even assimilated Jews understood themselves as part of a distinct group. Unique in that it did not constitute one of the empire's recognised nationalities, Jewishness allowed for concurrent Austrian political loyalty including support for the monarchy, affiliation with a national culture (generally German in the case of Austrian Jews), and association with a Jewish ethnic identity.[8] For Triestine Jews, cosmopolitanism served as a counterweight to nationalist particularisms that threatened imperial institutions, structures, and commercial arrangements by the end of the nineteenth century.

At the turn of the twentieth century, Habsburg commitment to the expansion of Austrian trade through Trieste continued, despite the rescinding of free port privileges in 1891 as part of an attempt to counter nationalist threats and increase central power. Liberals favoured free trade regardless of ethno-nationalist orientation and lobbied for freer commerce, communication, and transport. Together, members of the commercial urban population of all faiths negotiated challenges to liberal networks and the stability of the empire by internationalist as well as nationalist interests.[9]

The rising tide of socialism, particularly evolutionary socialism that sought cooperation with Austrian institutions and appealed on economic grounds to populations across the empire, was one of the liberal order's chief concerns. Labour demands for social reform and calls for state intervention in the economy threatened liberal structures predicated on principles of the free function of the international market. Nationalist politics also threatened to tear the Habsburg empire apart. The empire witnessed the rise of pan-Germanist politics and pan-Slavic discontent fuelled by the compromise of 1867. A host of groups sought increased autonomy on nationalist grounds. For Triestines, the unification of Italy and development of an Italian state after 1870 had particular salience due to the heavy influence of the Italian language and the cultural ties of the city. Italian irredentism, in particular, became important on the local political landscape. Strong ties to Venetian Jews and the preponderance of Italian commercial elements (or at least those speaking Italian) in Trieste's Jewish community attracted Triestine Jews to the Italian cause.[10] Italianness could be considered the dominant nationality of the upper Adriatic coastland, particularly as Jews in the empire tended to favour 'historic' nationalities like that of the Italians over 'peasant nationalities' like Slavic, Slovene, or Croatian identities.[11] Italy offered an alternative to decidedly anti-semitic pan-German political currents emanating from Vienna. In Trieste, as Felice Venezian, a lawyer and leader of the National Liberal Party sympathetic to Italian nationalism explained in 1902, anti-semitism was 'a recent phenomenon ... It ha[d] not gotten visible teeth yet, but ha[d] begun to bite just the same'.[12]

The relative absence of anti-semitism and wide acceptance of Jews as part of the port population allowed port Jews to flourish, to participate as equal members of a secular commercial society. Participation in secular society and cultural sympathy for Italy did not, however, extend to participation in political institutions. Port Jews tended to remain aloof from political concerns. Through skilful use of their influence and wealth, they became members of a 'hegemonic' class of port elites whose power permeated political circles.[13] Civil service was generally left to professionals who formed part of the rising middle class. They would eventually provide the bridge to integration into Italian frameworks for port Jews when Austrian imperial oversight gave way to Italian state control.

In addition to the changes in the political and national landscape in the empire, traders in Trieste, including Jews, faced challenges related to the technological developments in transportation, communication, and financing in the late nineteenth century. The 'industrialisation of shipping' and modernisation of port cities in the last decades of the nineteenth century disrupted liberal port life and institutional structures throughout the European and Atlantic world. New economic arrangements and technological advances in transportation and communication eliminated the need for traders as middlemen. Commercial ports became transit centres. In addition, labour relations changed with the rise of socialism and working class militancy. In 1907, the year during which Austria adopted universal suffrage, strikes crippled Trieste. Labour actions, anathema to commercial elites including port Jews, had become endemic in port communities.[14]

Although Trieste's fate was not dissimilar to that of other ports, the instability of the Habsburg empire compounded the city's difficulties. Clearly, in Trieste, port elites were feeling the pinch of technological and political change by the turn of the century.[15] By the end of the First World War, Triestine trade had all but collapsed, and the elimination of Central European market networks had cut the city off from its hinterlands. In addition, the rise of nation states on former imperial territory meant that ports in new, self-interested states now competed with Trieste for Balkan and Eastern European trade that had been protected for Trieste by Habsburg subsidies and special trade arrangements.

Despite the general collapse of liberal economic structures and the concomitant decline of ports as international centres for trade and commerce and the specific disadvantages facing Trieste in the post-Habsburg order, the Jewish commercial community in the city proved resilient. Annexation to Italy changed the port Jews' political course, but it did not deprive them of their elite status. In other words, the port Jews of Trieste exemplified the 'recast' bourgeoisie of the inter-war period.[16] The regionalised power structure in Italy allowed Triestine liberals, including Jews, to fit into national economic networks. Commercial elites in Trieste saw the city as a natural maritime outlet. They were accustomed to looking at international relationships and commerce from a local perspective of Triestineness or *triestinità*.[17] Nationalists, particularly professionals involved in political circles, helped to pave their way to integration in Italian economic networks.

In the Triestine view, natural proclivities, cosmopolitan sentiments, and residual ties to commercial networks abroad would enable the city to become an important Italian port for Italy. Although port elites tended to overestimate the importance of former Habsburg networks, these links did provide Italy with a pretext for increased intervention in Central Europe and expansion overseas. Pragmatic promotion of their economic utility helped elites to carve a space for themselves in the emerging fascist corporative structure. In particular, the Triestine insurance sector, dominated by two houses of Jewish origin, fared well by serving Central European and international clients despite the port's general decline.[18]

The Jewish community's wealth and influence, particularly in commercial circles, did however feed nationalist resentments and fuel anti-semitism in Trieste. In April 1921, journalist Eugenio Popovich, a fervent irredentist of Triestine origin, blamed sour relations between Rome and Trieste and economic difficulties on a 'Jewish cabal that never does anything except for industrial speculation'.[19] In 1928, an unidentified informant warned officials in Rome of the invidious influence of Jews in Trieste and called the Jewish commercial elites the 'worst scourge of the city'.[20] Mussolini's attitudes towards Jews appear contradictory, but anti-semitism was not endemic and persecution was not a part of official policy prior to 1938.

Authorities on both the local and national levels welcomed the participation of the Triestine commercial community, with its significant Jewish element, in corporatist economic schemes that served Mussolini's international aims, in particular his aspirations to greater influence in the Mediterranean. Fascist acceptance was, however, limited to Italian Jews and Jews judged loyal to Italy.

Mussolini's tolerance did not extend to foreign Jews or Jewish immigrants in Italy, who were often seen as affiliated with Zionism and internationalism. In 1928, Mussolini targeted foreign Jews in an anti-Zionist campaign. He railed against the 'Jewish Masonic international movement' and the insidious influence of international Jewish capital. This perspective on Jewish capital, while not intended at the time to target Trieste's wealthy port Jews (a group seen as involved in furthering Italian interests), revealed an underlying perception that Jewish and Italian interests were antagonistic. In the near future, this perceived antagonism would furnish an excuse and provide a basis for persecution.

Despite the regime's ambivalence, Jews in Trieste remained well integrated in the urban community and in commercial circles. In 1937, the fascist-appointed presidents of seven of the 24 industrial syndicates in the province of Trieste were Jewish. The two major insurance concerns, Assicurazione Generali and RAS (Riunione Adriatica di Sicurtà) remained in the hands of Jewish directors and managers. On the eve of the passage of the racial laws, Jews headed 26 banks and major commercial firms.[21] Clearly, port Jews' 'valuation of commerce' and propensity for acculturation served them well for the first 15 years of fascist rule.

After Hitler's rise to power in Germany in 1933, the contradictions in Italian fascist attitudes towards Jews became more difficult to overlook. Nazi persecution and the emigration of Central European Jews brought the Jewish question to the fore in European politics. Germany's designs on Austria, particularly in the wake of the assassination of Prime Minister Engelbert Dollfuss in July 1934, aroused Italian suspicions and even prompted Mussolini to 'dress in the garb of protector and friend of the Jews' based on his desire to defend Italian interests and borders against what he saw as an aggressive German state.[22] Despite Mussolini's misgivings about foreign Jews, Italy became a haven for Jews escaping anti-semitic persecution.

Italian fascism's initial stance against German expansionism did not allay suspicions of a conspiracy by foreign Jews. Increased Jewish emigration from Central Europe to Trieste alarmed Italian authorities. Immediately following the First World War, in the years from 1919 to 1923, the majority of Jews immigrating to Trieste were of Greek origin and came to the city to escape continuing violence in territories of the defunct Ottoman empire. Many joined relatives who had settled in Trieste early in the century. A smaller number were former Habsburg subjects, of Hungarian or Polish origin, with links to the city. By the late 1920s, Jewish immigration to Trieste had slowed to trickle. In 1929 (the lowest point of immigration in the inter-war period), only two Jewish families or heads of household (including four individuals – one German and three Poles) settled in the city. In 1933, an explosion in the number of immigrants seeking asylum in Trieste testified to the change in circumstances in Central Europe. Twenty-four Jewish heads of household including 51 individuals (16 with German, 29 with Polish, 5 with Hungarian and 1 with Romanian citizenship) established residency in the city. The influx of Central Europeans would continue until the Italian racial laws were promulgated in 1938.[23] Although these numbers were small for the city with a population of approximately 250,000, the visible increase in the number of Jewish migrants passing through the city combined with the settlement of a select few sparked fascist and Italian nationalist concerns.

Persecution and Dispersal

In June 1936, at the request of the Interior Ministry, Triestine officials prepared and forwarded a list of foreign Jews living in the province. Of the 1,349 foreign Jews counted, the largest group was 429 Greeks, the majority of whom had come to the city prior to the First World War. Next on the list were 382 Poles followed by 89 Germans and 75 Austrians, many newly arrived in the city since the mid-1930s.[24] By 1937, a report on the 'Semitic movement in Trieste' forwarded to the minister of the interior referred to some 60 new families 'with numerous children' who arrived in the period from 1935 to 1937. Clearly, this description relied on anti-semitic stereotypes depicting the influx of the unwanted, unworthy, dangerous, and uncivilised 'exotic' Jewish masses. Official figures show that 57 heads of foreign Jewish families did settle in the city over the three-year period. However, this included only 108 individuals, most had come alone or with a spouse. The largest family units were two Polish families that came in 1937, each with five family members.[25]

The perception that poor foreign Jews were overrunning Trieste ultimately served to erode the position of Trieste's port Jews. While wanting for humane reasons to support co-religionists fleeing persecution, local Jews did not want to offer refugees a haven in their own community. Rather, philanthropic efforts aimed to provide services and assistance to Central European Jews intending to settle abroad. Trieste's commercial networks, with a history of assistance to Zionists, were well suited to providing aid to Jews in transit. In fact, Triestine Jews were noted for their philanthropic works for persecuted communities stretching back to the late nineteenth century.[26] While the fascist government welcomed the economic benefits of increased traffic through Trieste's port, it was suspicious of the seeming promotion of the Zionist cause, considered alien and in opposition to the nationalist tenets of Italian fascism. The position of Trieste's Jewish community, wealthy and useful, yet cosmopolitan and exhibiting support for Zionism, attracted the attention of the fascist hierarchy and fuelled attacks against the city on racial grounds.

In 1937, a concerted propaganda campaign against the Jews began in Italy. Giovanni Preziosi's 'Ten Fundamental Points on the Jewish Problem', published in *Vita Italiana* in August 1937 summed up the ways in which Jews, regardless of ethnic background, social status, or political bent were associated with their co-religionists rather than fellow Italians. Preziosi, a long time proponent of anti-semitism and pro-German, warned that Jews loyal to their faith far outnumbered those loyal to the state.[27] At the beginning of January 1938, Minister of State Roberto Farinacci, editor of *Il Regime Fascista* and a virulent anti-semite, attacked Triestines in particular, implying in two editorials that all of Trieste was tainted by the dominance of Jewish, capitalist interests.[28] Preziosi followed up in May, arguing in *La Vita Italiana* that Jews in Trieste supported fascism 'only as far as their politics did not conflict with their conscience as Jews'.[29]

For the most part, prior to August 1938, the fascist regime's anti-semitic activities and actions remained confidential and outside public policy, but, clearly, the regime's stance signalled its intention to initiate an anti-semitic policy (despite protests to the contrary). In early 1938 the official process of identifying Jews in Italy began. In February, Mussolini had military rolls scrutinised, and the presence of Jewish surnames was noted. Members of the public security forces were also sorted by race.[30] In July, a team of Italian 'scientists' published the Manifesto of Fascist Race, and the regime's office on demography and race Demorazza was established.[31]

Some Jews in Trieste, more attuned to the situation in Germany than other Italians and having experienced Germanic anti-semitism first-hand prior to the First World War, seemed to recognise the dangerous turn of Italian policy. Corrado Uberti, an Italian citizen born in Vienna, recalls Mussolini's speech in September 1938 in Trieste as the decisive point for his family. Mussolini carefully differentiated between loyal Italian Jews and foreign Zionist Jews, but his intent with regard to initiating a racial campaign was clear.[32] Uberti's mother, a widow since 1932, having spent her youth in Silesia (Austria), 'knew Jewish history intimately', and by implication the history of Jewish persecution. Uberti suggests, 'She recognised the significance of anti-semitism, she saw it in the ghettos of Cracow, Bohemia, Silesia, Germany'. She had witnessed first-hand the plight of Central European Jewish refugees passing through Trieste after 1933. After Mussolini's speech, the family decided to emigrate and found themselves in Argentina.[33] Geza Müller, of a Hungarian family in Trieste, recounts a similar experience. His mother, like Uberti's, had assisted refugees in the mid-1930s. After 1938, his family too fled to Argentina.[34]

The promulgation of racial laws passed by the Fascist Grand Council in the autumn of 1938 initiated the period of official persecution of those 'of the Jewish race'. The definition of Jews contained in the provisions signified the end of the influence of port Jews in Trieste, and the demise of the port Jew as a social type. The laws ignored previously recognised social and political distinctions and differing levels of religious affiliation and adherence. The reduction of all Jews to the same level, based solely on their origins, came as a social shock to Jews throughout Italy.[35] In Trieste, where port Jews were accustomed to receiving special privileges and exercising economic power in the integrated society, the laws caused a profound sense of social dislocation and provoked schisms that fragmented the Jewish community. Industrialist and financier Salvatore Segrè Sartorio, known for his support for Italian nationalism prior to the annexation to Italy and baptised a Catholic in 1907, did not denounce the legislation per se. Rather he attacked its inclusion of people like himself. Calling his association with Judaism 'a calamity of [his] ancestors', he claimed: 'My position is different from that of the others. ... I am not a profiteer, I am not a Polish Jew, I am not a Jew by confession.'[36] Citing honours bestowed on him by Mussolini and fascism, he sought, unsuccessfully, to establish his position and identity on the basis of previously valued traits characteristic of those in port Jew communities rather than on the racial grounds chosen by the fascist regime in 1938.

Segrè Sartorio was only one of many in Trieste left disoriented and uncertain by the discrimination initiated in the autumn of 1938. The population's strong history of irredentism, feelings of Italianness, and generic and generalised adherence to fascism made the denunciation of Jews hard to comprehend.[37] Jews had been welcomed as full citizens on annexation from the Habsburg empire barely two decades earlier. As a result of the laws, Jews in Trieste, along with those in the rest of Italy, suffered the seizure of property and loss of livelihood. In Trieste, the laws hit the professions and commercial circles hard. Trade on the Triestine stock exchange fell to an estimated 40 per cent of its previous level.[38]

In the years immediately following the initiation of the racial campaign, as much as one-third of Trieste's young Jewish population (33 per cent) left the city. In this respect, the experience of the Jews of Trieste was not in line with that of the Jews in the rest of Italy. Approximately 6,000 of 45,000 (or approximately 13 per cent) of registered Jews in Italy emigrated over the period from 1938 to 1941. Of the 36,000 to 37,000 Jews considered ethnically Italian, only about 3,000 (or 8 per cent) chose to emigrate.[39]

Trieste's history as an international port where Jews from all over the Habsburg empire had settled exacerbated the problems arising from increasing anti-semitic sentiment and official adoption of anti-semitic policies. The Manifesto of July 1938 called for the expulsion of foreign Jews, excluding those who were older than 65 or had married an Italian prior to 1 October 1938.[40] In mid-July 1938, the prefect of Trieste and the minister of the interior initiated proceedings to expel Austrian Jews living illegally in Italy. Several were effectively stateless, having never legalised their status after the official transfer to Italian sovereignty in 1921. By October, the prefect sought permission to accompany Polish Jews, stranded in the city and unable to renew their Polish passports, to the Italian–Yugoslav border to 'leave them at their own peril and responsibility'.[41]

The threat of expulsion in Trieste was not limited to stateless Jews or those holding foreign citizenship. Legislation of 7 September 1938 revoked the Italian citizenship of Jews who had obtained it after 1 January 1919. It required those affected by the statute to leave Italy within six months.[42] In the transient and highly mobile commercial port society within the confines of a city officially annexed to Italy in 1921, all Jewish citizens were subject to close scrutiny. According to the prefect's calculations, a total of 722 individuals faced loss of citizenship.[43] In July 1939, the prefect of Trieste reported that of 112 heads of families deemed Jewish and foreign, 46 still had not requested permission to stay in Italy and had no right to remain.[44]

However, in many cases, leaving Italy was not easy. Anti-semitic policies adopted by governments throughout Central Europe made it difficult. At nearby border stations, Yugoslav officials proved particularly vigilant, stopping those without transit visas at the border. Yugoslav, Czech, German, and Hungarian authorities invalidated or refused to issue transit visas to Jews being sent back to their countries of origin in Eastern Europe.[45] The prefect of Trieste reported to the interior minister in November 1938 that several foreign consulates had become involved in illicit trade and trafficking in the granting of passport visas to foreign Jews. Argentina and Bolivia demanded as much as 3,000 lire per person.[46] Given that in the mid-1930s, a skilled male factory worker earned between 300 and 400 lire per month, the exorbitant sum was far beyond the reach of most.[47]

Some departed Trieste for Paris or London, hoping to continue on to the United States. These emigrants, who tended to be from upper or upper-middle class families, often had a long wait. US quotas set in 1924 severely restricted Italian immigration.[48] Beginning in the autumn of 1939, French diplomatic representatives forced the Italian Minister of the Interior to investigate the Italian border authorities' complicity in efforts to smuggle Jews through the north-western Italian province of Imperia into France.⁴⁹ In June 1940, with routes for expulsion blocked, the Italian government resorted to the internment of foreign Jews. Men were sent to concentration camps, and their families were moved to the interior of Italy. The majority were Jews who had recently arrived from Central Europe.⁵⁰

Further complicating the situation in Trieste was the mixed ancestry that characterised port Jews. Centuries under the multi-national empire followed by only a short two decades in Italy made ascertaining the official national affiliation and citizenship of some Triestines difficult. The case of Geza Müller is instructive. After the promulgation of the citizenship laws his father, born in Hungary, lost his Italian citizenship. He had to travel to Hungary to get passports for himself and his wife, of Slovene birth, in order to gain permission to emigrate. Müller himself, born in 1910 in Trieste, went to Zurich to ask for an Italian passport. As a minor in 1921, he had not been old enough to exercise his rights as a native-born Triestine. He succeeded in gaining an Italian passport in Zurich only because the Italian official 'thought it absurd that anyone's Italian citizenship could be taken away'.⁵¹ The passports and contacts abroad enabled the family to leave Trieste, their home for nearly three decades, and to emigrate to Argentina.

With the passage of the racial laws in 1938, involvement in international commercial networks and association with foreign traders and foreign markets became a liability, marking Jews as irrevocably 'foreign', part of a racial tribe dedicated to furthering its own interests rather than those of Italy. Yet, for some Triestine Jews, ties that served as a marker of foreignness provided the path to salvation. Jews involved in commercial networks escaped or emigrated along well-worn commercial paths to find shelter in ports overseas. Involvement in international economic networks and ties to finance abroad proved particularly useful. In an attempt to facilitate expatriation, from 1938 to 1940, fascist authorities tended to overlook or assist wealthy Jews who sought to transfer capital and property abroad, despite the statutory limits on such exports.⁵² 'Friends in Trieste have all dispersed', opined Triestine Jewish poet Umberto Saba in a letter written to a friend in October 1940.⁵³

According to Triestine writer Alma Morpurgo, herself an exile to Chile for 16 years, 'The chosen people became a seafaring people'.⁵⁴ Morpurgo's statement regarding the chosen people is particularly poignant in the context of the consideration of the position of the cosmopolitan port Jews. 'Navigatori', the word she used to connote seafaring, can also imply, as 'navigato' or 'navigata', worldly-wise. Clearly, 1938 represented a loss of innocence for many. Morpurgo and her mother and sister went to Chile. Giorgio Voghera, a former employee of RAS and Federico Levi, a dismissed editor of *Il Piccolo*, went to Palestine.⁵⁵ Palestine and North and South America were the principal destinations for Jewish emigrants embarking from Trieste, but some found refuge as far away as Australia and Shanghai.⁵⁶ Argentina was a relatively popular destination. As many as 1,000 Jews emigrated from Italy to Argentina in the years between 1938 and 1943.⁵⁷ Bankers, for example, at least in certain circumstances, found a haven in South America. Local contacts and relationships formed the basis for continued employment and links to Italian banks. In areas of South America, on the periphery and far from the centres of European racial policy, accommodations were made and compromises reached that allowed Jews to continue in their posts and live their lives relatively unmolested.[58]

Emigration was not the only avenue Trieste's Jews sought to escape persecution. Nor was it the only means by which the Jewish community was dispersed. Some chose to distance themselves from the Jewish community through abjuration (official renunciation) of Judaism or conversion to Catholicism. In the secular port society, this seemed for many a less extreme and more viable response than emigration. Many, particularly in the assimilated upper classes, were of mixed descent. The inter-marriage rate in the 1920s had been over 50 per cent.[59] In 1937, the Triestine Jewish Community recorded 20 abjurations. Only 15 were recorded over the previous three-year period from 1933 to 1936. In November 1938, the number skyrocketed, with 177 people abjuring in Trieste, the highest number in any Jewish community of Italy. In 1938 and 1939, respectively, 761 and 313 Jews in Trieste converted to Catholicism.[60] This was in spite of the fact that the racial legislation defined Jews based on blood lines in a manner similar, although not analogous to, the Nazi legislation, and did not recognise the validity of conversions of those of mixed ancestry after 1 October 1938.

Some of Trieste's wealthy Jews chose to remain in the city due to family ties or community attachments. Other relied on their connections and history of loyalty and applied for special exemptions from persecution available to individuals through petition to the Interior Ministry's Commission for Aryanisation in Rome.[61] Generally, the port Jews of Trieste responded with pragmatism, seeking roads of escape along several lines at once. Nicola Ginzburg, for example, after being relieved of his post with Assicurazione Generali in 1938, sought special dispensation, which he was granted by authorities. He chose to emigrate with his family to the United States in September 1939. By the end of 1941, he and his wife had purchased a house, signalling their intention to settle permanently there.[62]

Effectively, by 1941, persecutory policies blocked all channels for Jewish emigration, trapping remaining Jews in Italy.[63] Some from Trieste fled and sought concealment in the relative anonymity of larger cities or perceived safety in the south or interior of the Italian peninsula. In September 1943, the Italian Armistice with the Allied powers and the collapse of the German–Italian relationship led to Italy's dismemberment. The trajectory of Nazi policy was clear. Some, like Luisa and Silvia Zaban, escaped to the south just as the city came under Nazi control. Their mother, Elena Morpurgo, a native Triestine who had experienced Austrian anti-semitism of the Habsburg period, sent them to the interior of Italy on the last train before the German transit visas were required.[64] Others were smuggled, in dangerous and clandestine operations, over the border to Switzerland, where ironically, wealthy Triestines including Jews had sought a refuge during the First World War.

Trieste became the capital of the Nazis' Adriatic Littoral operation zone. Jews in Trieste became subject to Nazi racial policies. Estimates suggest that 2,500 of the population of 5,400 Jews remained at the time of German occupation.[65] Some 546 Jews arrested in Trieste were deported, the second largest number arrested in an Italian locality, after Rome where 1,680 arrested were deported.[66] By June 1945, the once thriving community of more than 5,000 was reduced to a scattering of fewer than 500. The Shoah claimed 7,700 to 7,900 victims of the 43,000 persons classified as Jews in central and northern Italy in September 1943.[67]

Anti-semitic measures had a devastating impact on Italian Jewish communities. Of 87 Italian Jewish communities existing in 1840, only 22 remain today.[68] The destruction of these communities can in part be attributed to the forces of modernisation, acculturation and assimilation that accelerated the breakdown of traditional communities. Conversions and intermarriages were of great concern to Jewish communities even prior to the First World War. However, anti-semitic fervour, fascist racial campaigns and legislative persecution of the 1930s and 1940s accelerated dispersal of communities even in areas where populations were not subject to Hitler's 'final solution'.

Jewish migration of the late 1930s from Italy differs significantly from most Italian emigration of the earlier part of the century. Most Italians living in diaspora communities established between 1910 and 1880 were migrants seeking to improve their lot. They participated in the 'voluntary diaspora' of the turn of the century. The Jews who left Italy after 1938 were part of a 'victim diaspora' created by racial policies. They emigrated to escape political, religious and cultural persecution.[69] This made their return problematic.

Although laws passed in the aftermath of the Second World War offered recourse to victims of racial persecution, Jews had difficulty returning to communities they had left or been forced to leave. Family and friends were absent. Homes were occupied, and property liquidated or dispersed. As Ilaria Pavan has shown, civil cases were not easy to win. Of 85 cases brought by Jews from 1945 to 1964, including 136 individual sentences – several having passed through various levels of jurisprudence – only 52 per cent of verdicts were handed down in favour of the complainant. Forty-eight per cent went against.[70]

Corrado Uberti's experience of emigration illustrates the legacy of the racial laws for Italian Jews and the laws' effect on Jews who were accustomed to assimilation in the cosmopolitan Adriatic city. After his emigration from Trieste to Argentina in 1939, Uberti did not return to Italy until 1962. He tried to resettle his family, with his wife and three children, in Rome and then Milan, not in Trieste. The attempt to repatriate was a 'grave error'. His wife did not take to Italy, and he admitted, 'despite my profound desire to reintegrate myself in Italian life, it was also difficult for me'. By 1962, Uberti and his family had 'become Americans, with a different attitude, a different way of thinking and a different vision of life'. They left Italy to return to Buenos Aires.[71] The adaptability that had served the port Jews of Habsburg Trieste well had helped the subsequent generation to adapt to forced resettlement and to acculturate once again in response to fascist racial policies.

The localised brand of urban cosmopolitanism characteristic of the Triestine port Jew community did survive in a particular devotion to *triestinità*. For port Jews, attachment to the local community transcended national engagement. Tito Kohner, who arrived in Argentina in January 1939 from Trieste, summed up this attitude years later. When asked about his nostalgia for Italy, Kohner replied, 'As a good Triestine, [I am nostalgic] for Trieste more than for Italy. We Triestines are parochial to the hilt. That is, first Triestine, then Italian, and then in the end

Jewish'.[72] The attitude of the port Jews left as its legacy a kind of provincial cosmopolitanism in which Jewishness played a critical role, yet lay in the background, a nearly invisible thread in the fabric of port Jews' identity.

NOTES

The author would like to thank the participants at the Place and Displacement Conference in Cape Town, South Africa in January 2005 for comments and insights, which proved invaluable in the preparation of this article.

1. In his seminal article on port Jews, David Sorkin acknowledges the role of Lois Dubin and her work on Trieste in the conceptualisation of the 'social type'. David Sorkin, 'The Port Jew: Notes Toward a Social Type', *The Journal of Jewish Studies*, 50.1 (1999), 87–97 (p.88 n.7).
2. Ibid., pp.96–7.
3. From Camillo Boito, *Gite di un artista* (Milan: Hoepli, 1884) quoted in Lina Gasparini, ed., *Impressioni su Trieste 1793–1887* (Trieste: Zibaldone, 1951), p.105.
4. Lois Dubin, *The Port Jews of Habsburg Trieste: Absolutist Politics and Enlightenment Culture* (Stanford, CA: Stanford University Press, 1999).
5. Michele Sarfatti, *Gli ebrei nell'Italia fascista:vicende, identità, persecuzione* (Turin: Einaudi, 2000), p.165.
6. Museo della comunità ebraica di Trieste 'Carlo e Vera Wagner', *Trieste: la porta di Sion: Storia dell'emigrazione ebraica verso la Terra di Israele 1921–1940* (Florence: Alinari, 1998), p.7, offers a brief history. On the importance of Enlightenment policies to the growth of the Jewish community in Trieste see Dubin, *The Port Jews* (see note 4).
7. Malachi Haim Hacohen, 'Dilemmas of Cosmopolitanism: Karl Popper, Jewish Identity, and "Central European Culture"', *The Journal of Modern History*, 71 (1999), 105–49 (p.107).
8. Marsha Rozenblit, 'Sustaining Austrian "National" Identity in Crisis: The Dilemma of the Jews in Habsburg Austria, 1914–1919', in *Constructing Nationalities in East Central Europe*, ed. Pieter Judson and Marsha Rozenblit (New York: Berghahn Books, 2005), pp.178–9.
9. Hacohen, 'Dilemmas' (see note 7), pp.108–10.
10. On Italian influence, see Anna Millo, *L'élite del potere a Trieste: una biografia collettiva, 1891–1938* (Milan: Franco Angeli, 1989).
11. Anton Pelinka, 'Anti-semitism and Ethno-nationalism as Determining Factors for Austria's Political Culture at the Fin de Siècle', in *Liberalism, Anti-semitism, and Democracy*, ed. by Henning Tewes and Jonathan Wright (New York: Oxford University Press, 2001), pp.63–75 (p.64). Pelinka does suggest that Italianness, as an identity of the periphery, was not as acceptable as Germanness to Jews in Vienna, Prague and other urban centres.
12. Millo, *L'élite del potere* (see note 10), p.66.
13. The presumption of the power of a 'hegemonic' class derives from interpretations of Gramsci and his observations on the role elites played in Italian society. On distinctions between the 'corporate class' and the 'hegemonic class' in Grascian thought see, Christine Buci Glucksmann, 'Hegemony and Consent: A Political Strategy', in *Approaches to Gramsci*, ed. by Anne Showstack Sassoon (London: Writers and Readers, 1982), pp.119–21.
14. See Josef Konvitz, 'The Crises of Atlantic Port Cities, 1880–1920', *Comparative Studies in Society and History*, 36.2 (1994), 293–318 (pp.293–4, 307–8).
15. Millo, *L'élite del potere* (see note 10), traced the beginnings of the decline of Triestine commercial elites' power to the early 1890s.
16. On the post-First World War bourgeoisie see Charles Maier, *Recasting Bourgeois Europe: Stabilization in France, Germany and Italy in the Decade after World War I* (Princeton, NJ: Princeton University Press, 1975).
17. On *triestinità* and the commercial community, see Millo, *L'élite del potere* (see note 10), p.232; and Giulio Sapelli, *Trieste italiana: mito e destino economico* (Milan: Franco Angeli, 1990), p.157.
18. See Sapelli, *Trieste italiana* (see note 17). Insurance companies did not rely on trade in commodities that was rendered obsolete by the new environment of the transit port. Rather, insurance companies were part of the tertiary sector, furnishing services to facilitate financing and transport, those sections that flourished in the 'transit' environment.
19. Trieste, Archivio diplomatico (Biblioteca civica), Tamaro Papers, Correspondence received, Eugenio Popvich to Attilio Tamaro, 10 April 1921.
20. Millo, *L'élite del potere* (see note 10), p.339.

21. Ellen Ginzburg Migliorino, 'Jewish Emigration from Trieste to the United States after 1938', *Studi emigrazione*, 28.103 (1991), 369–78 (pp.371–2); and Silva Gherardi Bon, *La persecuzione antiebraica a Trieste* (Udine, Del Bianco, 1972), p.58.
22. Furio Biagini, *Mussolini e il sionismo* (Milan: M & B, 1998), p.122.
23. Archivio centrale dello stato, Ministero Interno, Pubblica Sicurezza (1930–56), hereafter ACS, MI, PS (1930–56), A16, b. 16, n.86 Trieste, 'List of Foreign Citizens with Jewish Heads of Household who Entered the Realm after 1 January 1919'. The list covers the years 1919 to 1939.
24. Ibid., list, 8 June 1936.
25. Ibid., list, 1 January 1919.
26. The Jewish periodical of Trieste *Il corriere israelitico* carried articles throughout the 1880s and 1890s referring to efforts on behalf of Romanian and Greek Jews (in Corfu) subject to pogroms.
27. Enzo Collotti, *Il fascismo e gli ebrei: le leggi razziali in Italia* (Rome: Laterza, 2001), pp.50–51.
28. Silva Bon, *Gli ebrei a Trieste 1930–1945* (Gorizia: Goriziana, 2000), pp.39, 46–7.
29. Giovanni Preziosi, 'Il ghetto di Trieste e l'Anschluss', *La Vita Italiana: Rassegna Mensile*, 32 (1938), 664–6 (p.666).
30. Sarfatti, *Gli ebrei* (see note 5), pp.139–40.
31. Collotti, *Il fascismo* (see note 27), pp.58–9.
32. Benito Mussolini, *Opera Omnia XXIX (1 ottobre 1937–10 giugno 1940)*, ed. by Edoardo Susmel and Duilio Susmel (Florence: La Fenice, 1959), p.146.
33. Eleanora Maria Smolensky and Vera Vigevani Jarach, *Tante voci, una storia: Italiani ebrei in Argentina 1938–1948* (Bologna: Il Mulino, 1998), pp.150–51.
34. Ibid., pp.185–6.
35. Mario Toscano, 'L'emigrazione ebraica dopo l'avvio della persecuzione', *Nuova storia contemporanea*, 19 (1988), 1287–314 (p.1289).
36. Millo, *L'élite del potere* (see note 10), pp.66, 336.
37. Bon, *Gli ebrei* (see note 28), 171.
38. Ibid., pp.99, 129, 180.
39. Sarfatti, *Gli ebrei* (see note 5), pp.208–9.
40. Michele Sarfatti, *Mussolini contro gli ebrei: cronaca dell'elaborazione delle leggi del 1938* (Turin: S. Zamorani, 1994), p.188.
41. ACS, MI, PS (1930–56), A16, b.16, n.86 Trieste, various correspondence, Prefect of Trieste to Minister of the Interior, 15 October 1938.
42. For a full text of the statute, see Sarfatti, *Mussolini* (see note 40), p.185.
43. ACS, MI, PS (1930–56), A16, b.16, n.86 Trieste, undated list.
44. Ibid., report, 18 July 1939.
45. Ibid., report, 15 October 1938.
46. Ibid., correspondence 13 November 1938 and 5 December 1938.
47. Statistics cited in Maria Sophia Quine, *Italy's Social Revolution: Charity and Welfare from Liberalism to Fascism* (Hampshire: Palgrave, 2002), p.119.
48. Migliorino, 'Jewish Emigration' (see note 21), pp.374–5.
49. ACS, MI, PS (1930–56), A16, b.11, f.38 Imperia, various correspondence, Minister of the Interior and Head of the Security Police, Ventimiglia.
50. See various orders dated June and July 1940 in ACS, MI, PS (1930–56), A16, b.16, n.86. The first list of internees sent to the Interior Ministry on 22 June 1940 included eight Germans (from Austria and Germany), two Hungarians, one Romanian, and one stateless Jew born in Danzig. By 3 July, the fourth list was sent. It included four Germans, three stateless (born in Polish/German territories), three Polish, one Czechoslovak, and one Hungarian Jew.
51. Smolensky and Jarach, *Tante voci* (see note 33), p.186.
52. Toscano, 'L'emigrazione ebraica' (see note 35), pp.1291–2.
53. Robert Deidier, ed., *Umberto Saba: lettere a Sandro Penna, 1929–1940* (Milan: Archinto, 1997), p.41.
54. Alma Morpurgo, *L'esilo 1939–1955: ricordi dal Cile* (Udine: Campanotto, 1997), p.12.
55. For more on anti-semitism in Trieste and exile, see Maura E. Hametz, 'The Ambivalence of Antisemitism: Fascism, Nationalism, and Racism in Trieste', *Holocaust and Genocide Studies*, 16.3 (2002), pp.376–401.
56. Museo della comunità ebraica, *Trieste* (see note 6), p.21.
57. Smolensky and Jarach, *Tante voci* (see note 33), p.25.
58. Roberto Di Quirico, 'La Banca e la razza: Riflessioni sulle conseguenze del varo delle leggi razziali sull'attività delle banche italiane all'estero', in *Gli ebrei in Italia tra persecuzione fascista e reintegrazione postbellica*, ed. by Ilaria Pavan e Guri Schwarz (Florence: Giuntina, 2001), p.70.
59. Arthur Ruppin, *The Jews in the Modern World* (New York: Arno, 1934), p.320.
60. Migliorino, 'Jewish Emigration' (see note 21), pp.370–71.
61. On exemptions, see Sarfatti, *Mussolini* (see note 40), p.188.

62. Elle Ginzburg Migliorino, 'Dopo le leggi razziali. Gli ebrei italiani in America: prime impressioni', http://www.sissco.it/attività/sem-set-2003/relazioni/Ginzburg.rtf (accessed 18 April 2005), pp.2, 8.
63. Sarfatti, *Gli ebrei* (see note 5), p.171.
64. Elena Morpurgo, Luisa Zaban and Silvia Zaban, *Guerra, esilo, ebraicità: diari di donne nelle due guerre mondiali* (Ancona: Lavoro editoriale, 1996), pp.85–6.
65. Bon, *Gli ebrei* (see note 28), p.343.
66. Liliana Picciotto Fargion, *Il libro della memoria: Gli Ebrei deportati dall'Italia (1943–1945)* (Milan: Mursia, 1991), p.29.
67. Sarfatti, *Gli ebrei* (see note 5), pp.271–2.
68. Smolensky and Jarach, *Tante voci* (see note 33), p.45.
69. Donna Gabaccia, *Italy's Many Diasporas* (Seattle: University of Washington Press, 2000), p.6, draws the distinction between the two types of emigrants and diasporas.
70. Ilaria Pavan, 'Gli incerti percorsi della reintegrazione. Note sugli atteggiamenti della magistratura repubblicana 1945–1964', in *Gli ebrei in Italia* (see note 58), p.108.
71. Smolensky and Jarach, *Tante voci* (see note 33), pp.153–4. He notes that all of his children have married Catholics and follow the Catholic faith.
72. Ibid., p.114.

'Lost Worlds':
Reflections on Home and Belonging in Jewish Holocaust Survivor Testimonies

MICHELE LANGFIELD

Introduction

In 1933, Jews in Australia numbered approximately 26,500.[1] Most were Anglo-Australians 'of the Jewish faith'.[2] In the aftermath of the First World War, the *Jewish Herald* proclaimed 'We Australian Jews in this remote outpost of the British Empire are Britishers to the backbone and spinal marrow'.[3]

Despite waves of Jewish immigration to Australia from Germany, Russia, and Poland, the Anglo-Australian Jewish establishment was not successfully challenged until the arrival of 7–8,000 refugees from Nazism (predominantly German and Austrian) in 1938–39, and some 17,600 Holocaust survivors (broadly defined) from Central and Eastern Europe between 1945 and 1954. Of the pre-war intake, 80 per cent settled in the two port cities of Melbourne and Sydney, which had established Jewish communities. Of the post-war arrivals, about 60 per cent, largely Polish Jews, settled in Melbourne and 40 per cent in Sydney.[4] W.D. Rubinstein suggests that 'post-war Melbourne may have had proportionately the highest percentage of Holocaust survivors of any diasporic Jewish community'.[5] About 230 before the war and 130 after the war also settled in Perth.[6] The Australian Jewish population rapidly became very diverse in terms of national and cultural backgrounds, and notions of Jewishness.

European anti-semitism, the rise of Nazism culminating in the Holocaust, and the establishment of Israel, redefined and reinforced Jewish identities.[7] For those who escaped Europe before and after the Second World War, their identities were reshaped by individual experiences and influences in their adopted countries. This article explores the interaction between place and displacement in the formation of local, Jewish and ethnic identities, drawing upon a selection of oral and video testimonies, the former collected by the author, the latter held in the Jewish Holocaust Museum and Research Centre in Melbourne. As these testimonies were conducted several decades after survivors arrived in Australia, the article also addresses issues of remembering and forgetting and, in particular, the ways in which the personal experiences of the interviewees have affected their notions of 'home' and 'belonging'.

Substantial sections of these testimonies relate to childhood experiences and lives before the Holocaust. Thus one theme explored here involves an examination of how views about places of origin change throughout the course of a lifetime.

How do place and identity interrelate? Several interviewees have made return visits to former homelands both immediately after the war and much later in life, prompting different emotions and responses. What were their reasons for returning or not returning? Many former Jewish homelands, along with families, communities and cultures, no longer exist and memories of them are inseparable from feelings of grief and loss. Places of former close association have become tainted, owing to the traumatic events that occurred there. The corollary, then, is the place of refuge, the place of adoption. For Jews escaping Nazism or its aftermath, the process of relocation was unlikely to be completed in a direct move from one country to another. More often, it involved several attempts to escape, followed by a circuitous route over many years, and a series of temporary stays in different places. Their ultimate destinations were the result of luck, opportunities that arose, or family members or acquaintances already settled in a particular place, rather than any conscious decision-making about where to go.[8]

The notion of 'home' is full of contradictions and ambiguities, and linked with the memory – or forgetting – of origins. It is closely associated with ideas of 'belonging' and concepts of the 'exile', 'alien', 'stranger' and 'outsider', not only in the political form of citizenship – formal inclusion and exclusion – but also in the more intangible *sense* of belonging as Jews in Europe prior to migration and in Australia after migration. A sense of belonging is not only associated with place but with people and communities. For some, the existence of pre-established Jewish communities and precincts in Australia facilitated settlement and encouraged a sense of belonging on arrival; for others, it was largely irrelevant.

The theme of place and displacement lends itself to such investigations, especially how Jews, once *dis*placed, rebuild their sense of place, home and belonging and either maintain or relinquish their cultural identification in different local and regional community settings. The memories and life stories of Jewish Holocaust survivors in Melbourne offer a rare opportunity to explore these themes.

Childhood and Identity Formation

Much has been written about the meaning and significance of 'home'.[9] Peter Read, a specialist in place studies, writes that 'homes, like other places, are mentally constructed'.[10] He cites sociologist Doreen Massey, who argues that the social relations of 'home' go well beyond the actual physical space and that there is a constant tension between 'the role of consciousness in creating meaning and the role of structural forces in shaping consciousness'.[11] Read emphasises the close relationship between home and belonging and argues that 'belonging embraces the intellectual, emotional, physical and metaphysical dimensions of the human psyche'.[12] The meaning of home is therefore conceptual as well as physical.

> Home may be memories of activities, or a satisfaction in simple living, or an absence of negative emotions, or the joy of being in or cultivating a garden, of children growing up, memories of particular trees or shrubs, associations with particular people or special sites. Some of these elements are not portable because they are conceptual or intangible.[13]

How do individual refugees, displaced persons and migrants perceive the notion of 'home'? For Jews arriving in Australia before and after the Second World War, what role did their place of birth, the place they first called home, have on their identity formation? When did their places of birth and upbringing cease to be 'home'? Did they see their relocation as temporary or permanent? At what point did they substitute another place as 'home' in the physical and cultural sense, and in their deepest consciousness? Were their later views of 'home', including the idea of Israel as home, different from those held earlier in their lives? If so, in what ways did these meanings shift?[14]

Lisa, born 1922, and Anne, born 1925, were daughters of a well-to-do Czech engineer and his Viennese wife. They were 80 and 77 years old respectively when interviewed in Melbourne in 2001. Until March 1938, they lived a culturally rich, non-religious lifestyle in Austria. They left school when their parents decided to emigrate shortly after the Anschluss, undoubtedly a turning point in their lives. Responding to a warning, they narrowly avoided a Nazi round-up of Czechoslovakian Jews. They fled immediately, masquerading as holidaymakers in order to cross the Austrian border. Jewish Welfare, Geneva, organised for the family to be billeted on a Swiss farm for three months after which they travelled to Liverpool and thence to Melbourne in December 1938.[15]

Anne recounts in detail the home in which she lived until aged 13:

> It was an apartment opposite a park, on the first floor. I remember very well, not only the interior of the house, of course, because if I was naughty I'd race into the middle of the flat where the dining room was, so mother couldn't catch me. Walk round and round the table. My sister and I shared the bedroom and it was designed by an interior architect and it was rather nice. I do remember all the furniture and dad's lounge had leather covered lounge chairs. They were pretty well worn and could have done with restretching or something. The view from the first floor was over the park. After school, which usually finished at one o'clock, I'd go down and play with the boys if I could. Marbles, all kinds of funny games we had and I remember them well and enjoyed it thoroughly. It wasn't a Jewish school; we were agnostics and religion never came into it.
>
> [Father] played the violin and mother played the piano and often took us out to the museum. Also the holidays were exciting because mother introduced us to a love of nature and there were times when she rented a house during the school holidays and other friends too near Vienna, where we'd pick blueberries and wild strawberries, all these lovely, yummy things. Mother created a very nice home for us which later, when we migrated to Australia, she did the same and the house was always full of people, young people. It was good fun, happy. It was a very happy childhood. Dad encouraged us to be creative, mother too, both my sister and I in different ways. In my case it was drawing and painting and [for] my sister [it] was literature, which she studied later on. I remember Dad, Sunday mornings, we were allowed to hop into his bed and we could choose three objects or things in the house at random which he would weave into a fairy tale story. When we migrated we fled to Switzerland and my sister wrote the best of the stories down into a sort of book and I illustrated. I went to a school in a country town, Gentod, near Geneva.

Lisa also had positive memories of her early years. 'I had a very, very nice childhood.' Both sisters emphasised the happy, almost idyllic, cultured, *and non-Jewish* nature of their childhood, their 'normal' school life and the importance of close family relationships for their sense of home and well-being.[16] As Joan Bryans notes, 'feminist philosophy emphasises the importance of family and friends in a person's life. ... Without them we lose track of who we are and where we belong in the world'.[17]

Marianne was another pre-war Jewish refugee from Nazism, interviewed in 1996 in Melbourne, aged 76. Born in Oppeln, a small town near Breslau in Upper Silesia in Germany, she came to Australia in May 1939. Before leaving she was studying for her matriculation at a German Jewish school in Berlin. Marianne's father was a university professor and her mother a musician. She too had a very cultured home life. Her parents loved music, philosophy and the sciences and were very religious. Her father belonged to B'nai B'rith and was highly regarded in the local Jewish community. Marianne recalls her childhood:

> I had a brother one year younger ... we had lovely games together, outings together. These were the happy years of my childhood where I can only remember good friends, good food, good company, didn't matter if you were Jewish or not, but we kept all the Jewish festivals. When Hitler came to power, we could see there was a different atmosphere, different wind blowing.[18]

Like other women, Marianne describes her childhood home minutely: a second floor apartment in a five-storey block, 'a very nice dining and sitting room'. Her father had his own study lined with books, there was a maid's room, kitchen and bathroom, and she and her brother had their own bedrooms. They frequented the opera and theatre and had private tutors for music and French.

These pre-war refugees were fortunate enough not to see what became of their homes during the war. In their narratives, 'home' is closely linked with identity. As Fiona Allon notes:

> People invest places with a host of social and cultural meanings that reflect their cultural histories and backgrounds, including of course a worldview shaped by experiences of ethnicity, race, gender and class. These cultural conversations demonstrate how various forms of belonging are articulated, how individuals fashion cultural difference and identity into manners and ways of living and being and how memory and desires and yearnings for belonging are made manifest and get inscribed, physically and materially within place.[19]

Marianne was proud to be Jewish, emphasising that she felt 'more a Jew than a German'.[20] Her father, however, according to her brother Hans, was a staunch German nationalist of Jewish origin and religion – German first then Jewish – who did not believe in a Jewish state.[21] Their parents argued about the need to emigrate after 1933, their mother keen to leave, their father reluctant, even though he had the chance to go to South America. The themes and emphases placed on particular events and responses to them differ in the testimonies of brother and sister. As Oren Stier reminds us, 'memory is about the presentation and representation of past events, not the events themselves'.[22] Nonetheless, both Hans and Marianne identify

Kristallnacht (9–10 November 1938) as the turning point for the family. Non-Jewish colleagues warned their father not to remain at home that night. Marianne was left with the maid while her mother, father and brother walked for three days and nights from one relative to the next. Her father eventually gave himself up to the authorities but was allowed to return home. Five weeks later he fell ill with a stomach ulcer and died. Hans was sure this was the result of *Kristallnacht*. The family was forced to sell their furniture 'at a ridiculous price' and move into a two-roomed flat, their standard of living already reduced by the anti-Jewish laws of the 1930s. In 1939, Hans' mother arranged for him to go to London on the *Kindertransport*; he was eligible because he was a 'half-orphan' and not yet 17. He left in April, a month before Marianne was sponsored to Australia by a second cousin in Melbourne. Hans was interned on the Isle of Man, then released on war work grinding lenses by day and studying to be an optometrist at night. In the internment camp and at a Jewish hostel in England, he practised his Jewish traditions and became an orthodox Jew but later reverted to liberal Judaism. Meanwhile, their mother, left alone in Germany in a worsening situation for Jews, twice attempted suicide, was transported to the Warsaw ghetto and finally 'disappeared' somewhere in Poland. Hans always expected to return home but having lost most of his family, decided to accept Marianne's offer of sponsorship to Australia in 1949. His identity had undergone a number of changes during this traumatic period. At the time of his 1996 interview, he considered himself Jewish in an ethnic but not a religious sense and was studying comparative religions.

Floris was a child survivor who spent the war years in hiding. She was born in Brussels in 1934 and had a sister five years younger. Her parents were Polish but had migrated to Belgium in 1929. She knew no other family until after the war. Although her first language was Yiddish, she 'had no idea about being Jewish'.[23] Her parents were secular Jews, atheists: neither they nor their friends observed Jewish festivals and they were active members of the Bund, a Jewish socialist party. As a young child, Floris was conscious that: 'there was something about us, a feeling that you musn't go out ... and I knew that the Germans were there, we were under occupation and there was something scary in the air but I didn't particularly relate that to being Jewish'.[24] At the cinema one day, an anti-Jewish propaganda cartoon aroused her awareness. She felt uncomfortable and wondered what she really had to do with those kinds of people. She knew she was Jewish but it meant little to her, 'nothing concrete, nothing positive'. In May 1940 the family moved to a village in Brittany; on the way there her father was conscripted into the Polish army. She had no idea where he was, nor was it discussed. Soon after their arrival, the Germans invaded and in November, they went back to Brussels and her father returned. His homecoming was a major event for Floris.

In July 1942, Floris' mother took her two daughters to a holiday camp and left them there. While Floris did not witness the terrible happenings around her, she felt she was not living a 'normal' life because she was not at home. She spent the rest of the war in a series of foster homes, feeling neglected, hungry and lost. For a short time she returned to her family while they rented two rooms in a house with a hidden basement. 'Life revolved around this hiding routine – it was a way of life. There was a sort of alarm system set up. They had strings going everywhere with bells. It was a very tense time'. She had nightmares about trying to escape. Her mother was 'wrapped up in her own problems and very self-absorbed' while her father was 'a very distant person and children were not his concern'.[25]

Floris relates her childhood experiences during the war with considerable emotion, visibly distressed during her videotestimony and rarely looking at the camera. She confides that she had recently received counselling and the unhappiness and lack of warmth in her upbringing 'had come out'. At one stage after living with a Christian family, she wanted to be baptised but her parents opposed it. With the constant moving from place to place, she never knew what was expected of her, and was continually trying to please, unable to express her feelings. 'I think I would have done anything if it would have produced a loving reaction'. Above all, she wanted to belong. During her time in hiding her mother visited frequently to pay for her care but the time she spent with her was 'minutes, as I remember it, minutes. It would just go so quickly and on one occasion I really just broke down and cried and I said to her, "this war will never ever end"'. Floris only saw her sister once during her years of hiding. Her ability to speak Yiddish disappeared, overtaken by French and Flemish. Unlike other respondents, Floris remained in her own country during the war but her experiences constantly destabilised her sense of home. So affected was she that later in life, she was determined that her own children would not be brought up as she was, without warmth and affection, communication or encouragement.

Returning Home after the War

Returning to former homelands immediately after the war was often traumatic. Floris was reunited with her family soon after liberation.

> My expectations of that homecoming must have been something incredible! Everything would be made good, everything would turn to warmth and joy and happiness. Well, it was a great disappointment. I remember that feeling of disappointment and I remember crying and my mother said 'Why are you crying' and I felt very bad because, why was I crying? Here we were, we were together and things were happy – or they were meant to be happy but they weren't happy – and then it was the same thing, of finding out what was expected, of finding out how we were going to live. I didn't really remember what things were supposed to be like. So it was strange. It was not the happy relief, put it that way.[26]

Alexander A., born in Bialystock, Poland in 1915, returned home in 1948 after four years in Israel. 'I found very little. I couldn't recognise the place where I was born. Everything was in ruins.'[27] Isaac, born in Moldavia in 1932, travelled mostly on foot back to his hometown after the Russian liberation and found 'everything destroyed. Our house wasn't there. Nothing was there ... Wasn't much happiness when we came home'. In the centre of the town there were a lot of abandoned houses and he settled in there. 'There was great hunger, people died, starved to death.'[28] Alexander B., a Czech, born in 1925, returned after the war to his village near the Hungarian/Slovakian border to find his home occupied by a non-Jewish peasant family.

> The dog bit me. They were reasonable to me. They let me stay in the house. I had no feeling. I must have been sad. My worry was how to get some money and get on with my life. I inquired if any of my people [Jews from the village] came back. I was told that one man came back and I went to see him. He gave me money. I went to see an aunt. I stayed with her for a while. Then after, I was just going from place to place.[29]

Reconstructing Homes

Peter Read has highlighted the shift in theorising by sociologists over the last half century about the process of belonging for migrants and refugees in a new country. Earlier linear models of naturalisation, adaptation, absorption and acculturation, of gradual Australian identification or melting of old and new cultures,[30] have been replaced by an increasing acceptance of cultural pluralism and individual difference. Migrants understandably seek to re-establish their old countries in the new, and minority cultures can remain resistant to outside influences.[31] It is now acknowledged that attitudes to cultural retention can change over the space of a lifetime, especially as people age and wish to renew or resolve their attachments with their homelands. Identity is always evolving. The death of parents in the old country and the birth of children in the new are often important turning points in the process of cultural reorientation.[32] Conversely, later generations often seek to regain the language and culture of parents and grandparents. Some who have moved from one place to another, however, never feel that they really belong anywhere.

Lisa emphasises her mother's practicality in establishing the family in Australia.

> Mother was setting up home. She got Anne into RMIT[33] and then she started doing things. She started cooking for single people who came every day to pick up the food. She started making little cheeses in little tubs and sold them ... she did all sorts of things like that to help.[34]

Even those who were not religious accessed the established Jewish communities in Sydney and Melbourne:

> The liberal Jewish community had Temple House in Alma Street and this is where we met a lot of other young people, a social club. Yes, we did meet there quite a bit in the early days. I didn't go to religious things but I went to the social club. We did not go to the Temple because we had no affinity; well it just wasn't our scene.[35]
>
> Gradually we met people and some of them were Jewish and some of them were not. I think there were more Jewish ones than not.[36]

On the other hand, Jewish organisations could be exclusive. Doris, who was born in Germany and came to Australia as a refugee in 1939, was excluded from Temple Beth after several years because she married a Christian.[37] Paula, who arrived under similar circumstances, found the Australian Jewish community uninviting. 'We were not accepted. You had to go [to school] on the tram if you were orthodox and we were made to go to schule and we resisted it. We held our own services when we didn't go.'[38] Similarly, Marianne relates that 'The Australian Jewish people had no understanding of us of any kind. They were so antagonistic. The Australian Jews felt more English than the English and had no sympathy for a refugee's needs'.[39] For most Jewish pre-war refugees such as Paula, Marianne, Lisa and Anne, their acceptability and sense of belonging in Australia were challenged once war began. As Anne recalls: 'We had to report every fortnight. We were friendly aliens as Czech citizens whereas the Austrians were enemy aliens, so called or considered.'[40] And Marianne confirms: 'When war broke out, I had to have a permit to go from one suburb to the next. I was fingerprinted. Many Jews were interned.'[41]

After the war, Sydney attracted the more assimilated German, Austrian and Hungarian Jews whereas the majority of Polish Jews settled in Melbourne, encouraged by the established leadership and *Landsmanschaften* [mutual aid organisations]. Post-war Jewish migration not only greatly enlarged the Jewish populations of both cities but also changed their character, reviving existing institutions, such as the Kadimah, and forming new ones.[42] In this way, Jewish identities were reinforced, particularly by the Jewish day school system, which emphasised survival and opposed assimilation.[43]

After the war, Floris attended school in Brussels, went to Yiddish Sunday school and joined a youth group of the Bund to which her parents belonged. However, she found it difficult to make friends, and always felt insecure; it was years before she developed any self-confidence, especially with non-Jewish friends whom she liked but with whom she felt there was an absolute gulf: 'It was something that could not be overcome.' After a period when her father was unemployed, the family left for Australia in May 1949 to make a fresh start. Floris was 15 and ready for a change. Many of their acquaintances were migrating and an uncle and aunt were already there. Melbourne was a port city and she loved the sea. They believed it would be economically beneficial and there was a whole social milieu in Melbourne with which they could identify.

After coming from a socialist background, Floris gained a strong sense of Jewish identity in Australia. This came to her through her children. Her oldest daughter began attending a synagogue Sunday school and one day urged that they light Sabbath candles, have wine and say the blessings. She also wanted to do Bat Mitzvah. This was strange to Floris at first and her parents' resistance had to be overcome. She now attends services at the liberal synagogue and finds it meaningful and satisfying. She became a member of the board, studied Hebrew at University, and connected with Jewish spiritual values. Her children have visited Israel and now keep kosher homes.[44] Thus, over her lifetime, Floris, like Hans, has experienced significant changes in her identity as a Jew.

Return Migration

Examining patterns of return migration is another way to explore understandings of home, place and belonging. Migration is rarely a one-way or irreversible movement. Indeed, significant numbers of migrants return permanently to their place of origin or make frequent visits home.[45] The permanent return rate for immigrants to Australia between 1870 and 1914 was 40 per cent and for British migrants in the late

1940s it was 25–30 per cent.[46] For British immigrants, the rate of return increases as they reach retirement age.[47] Such figures are difficult to quantify and vary over time and for different types of migrants. In addition, the factors influencing return migration, both permanent and temporary, are many and varied.

There are obvious differences between migrants and refugees in relation to return migration. For Jewish refugees who arrived in Australia before the Second World War, and Jews who arrived after the war as displaced persons, there were particular reasons why, for many years, returning home was either impossible or undesirable. Significantly, survivors rarely mention homesickness in their testimonies, at least in terms of place, although a sense of nostalgia is often evident.[48] This indicates that their relationships with their former homelands have been drastically affected and, in contrast to 'ordinary' migrants, their family connections often no longer exist or exist in diasporic communities rather than in their countries of origin.

From 1947 to 1953, approximately 180,000 displaced persons came to Australia. An assimilationist policy was in place, the economy depressed, conditions in migrant hostels dire, and housing limited.[49] The desire and ability for these migrants to return home was affected by past experiences and post-war conditions in their countries of origin. Traumatic personal and psychological factors influenced the way Holocaust survivors viewed their former homelands; many wanted to be as far away from Europe as possible.[50] The establishment of communist states, such as East Germany and Czechoslovakia, made return impossible for some. They became exiles.[51] Their highest priority in Australia was to get on with their lives and many made no attempt to return home until much later in life. They then found that they did not belong.

Those who arrived before the war sometimes had more positive experiences. After Anne's father died in his early 60s, her mother returned to Europe several times before she died, aged 83. Anne has also returned home.

> Well, my husband didn't want to go at all at first. He lost both his parents. For me it wasn't as personal as for Bill. I wanted to show him where I lived and the area where the school was. Vienna is a beautiful city and the countryside is glorious, no doubt about it. My grandmother and my father's brother and family were caught up in the Holocaust. My grandmother on mother's side escaped with her sons to Panama of all places. Well, I suppose it was the only place that welcomed migrants at the time. They weren't called migrants then, they were 'bloody refugees'. My mother's brothers then went to America, to New York, and grandmother came to stay with my parents.
>
> Last year, we took our family, that's children and grandchildren and husbands, to Europe to show them where my husband lived, his first ten years in Czechoslovakia on a country estate, farm, mixed farm, and where I lived in Vienna. Then we took them to show them Salzberg and the Magic Flute Puppet Theatre and the marvellous music to go with it, wonderful, and the Dolomites, which my husband adores because he was a great mountaineer and to a small place in Czechoslovakia to see some of the style of architecture and countryside. It was truly a successful trip. I hope it's going to be a nice memory for the

children and grandchildren when we're gone.

Anne's sister, Lisa, has also frequently returned, but for her Vienna holds no special significance.

> It's just like going anywhere, going to Paris or anywhere else. I've got no feelings for it as home or anything like that, none at all, nothing. It's a long time ago. It really is and I mean, I go back there and this friend of mine said something like, 'You are a Viennese'. and I said, 'I'm not a Viennese. I'm an Australian'. and she said, 'Are you really?' I feel very strongly that I am. I'm just grateful. You have no idea the difference it made when you suddenly got to a country where you could say what you wanted to. If you wanted to say, 'The Prime Minister is an idiot', nobody cared.

With mixed feelings, Floris visited Brussels in 1978 after 29 years. She contacted people she knew and returned to places where she had lived. She does not feel she belongs there now and believes she has acquired something valuable by migrating to Australia.

Doris explained her views about returning to Germany:

> The first time it was actually a business trip for my husband and we flew in from London and I really hadn't thought at all how I would react when I got to Germany. I didn't want to get out of the plane, I couldn't get out. ... That was Hamburg because he had business in Hamburg and it was our first stop in Germany ... He had to practically drag me out of the plane and then I spat on the ground. Then the strange thing was that every elderly German I saw, in my mind, was in a Nazi uniform. ... That was the reaction. I don't mind young people and I've met some very nice young German people but the older generation, you inevitably look at them and think, 'What did you do? Where were you?' So that's how it was when you go back.
>
> Some people go back and have school reunions. I haven't done that and I wouldn't know who with. Also, the little town where my grandparents had the factory and where my aunts and uncles lived, I went there and saw their homes but there was nobody left I could contact and I didn't even want to.[52]

Marianne reacted similarly. Her trip to Germany was sponsored by the city of Berlin.

> I never wanted to go back to Germany. I hated the country and I hated what they had done to my family and I never wanted to see the country again. My male friend asked me to go to Berlin with him. At least I would see my father's grave. We were a group of Jewish people from all over the world. The Germans couldn't have treated us better. This was in 1995. My [non-Jewish] school friends made a reunion for us. One of my classmates looked at me and said 'you know other people had suffered too'. They didn't ask me too many questions. The feeling of anti-foreigner is strong there. It was so good to come back to Australia.
>
> In one way it was good that I saw it, that I saw my father's grave and the department store that I used to shop in with my mother. [But] I was so affected by it mentally and physically, that I was very sick and glad to get out of Germany, glad to come back to Australia and have a normal life, and it took me one year

to get over that physical disability. The nicest people were the young people; the people my age I didn't trust. That says enough, doesn't it? I knew the young people had nothing to do with it, to me they are just like my children or anybody else's children. They are young people born after the war who had nothing to do with this gruesome politics.[53]

Although Hans took several years to get used to Melbourne and thought it very provincial after London, he is now happy that he emigrated. He has been a member of B'nai B'rith for 40 years and is president of one of the lodges.[54]'When I am with non-Jews, I always tell them I am German Jewish', he says. 'I never fail to mention the Jewish part.' He felt very bitter against Germany during the war and while he is emotionally attached to his first name, has since anglicized his surname. When he visits Germany, he makes sure that he does not mix with anyone from his own generation 'so as not to bump into any old Nazis'.[55]

Many like Alex have never returned. Born in Poland in 1913, he now says 'I can't say I'm Polish'.[56]

Memory, Meaning and the Construction of Personal Narratives

What is the role of memories in constructing these life stories and personal narratives, and how do they give meaning to individual lives?

> Migrants [and refugees], perhaps more than many people, are made by their memories of their birthplace, their homeland, those left behind – interruptions in their life narratives that require resequencing, remodelling and reinterpreting as the newcomers incorporate and surpass their pasts.[57]

Interview structures tend to follow a similar pattern, beginning with family background, then moving to lives before the war, the early effects of Nazism, escape if relevant, experiences during the war, descriptions of deportation, life in the ghettoes and camps, the fate of family members, liberation, return home in search of loved ones, migration, and finally subsequent lives.[58] Survivors are encouraged to describe their lives before the Holocaust, to enable them to reconnect with their origins, their pre-war cultures and identities, as well as to recount their later experiences.[59] Phillip Maisel, co-ordinator of the Testimonies Project at the Jewish Holocaust Museum and Research Centre in Melbourne notes that 'each of them had different realities depending on their place of birth, background, places they had been'.[60] Maisel became interested not only in what the survivors told him but how they described it. These testimonies thus shed light on ways of thinking and the impact of past events on individuals, as well as the events themselves. In addition, Maisel writes:

> It was important not only for the individual stories to be told, but also to build up a picture of communities which had once existed in Europe, but have since disappeared. Traditions were described and information given on lost worlds. Events of the Holocaust are already well documented; it is the individual stories which can help to counteract the growing trend of revisionism and anti-Semitism.[61]

Because of the value placed by the institution on gathering information on life before the Shoah, on 'lost worlds' as Maisel describes it, ideas of home, place, identity and belonging are often related in great detail, especially by women. At the end of the videotestimonies, survivors are encouraged to leave a message for future generations. Many make the simple plea, 'Don't forget you are Jewish'. But Floris goes further, advising, 'Do what you feel is right for you, in the sense of how you belong, how you want to be Jewish, what sort of values you have in your life'.

The excerpts used here demonstrate the importance of the past in shaping Jewish identities, especially the significance of childhood homes and relationships in the early lives of the survivors.[62] Identity formation is not only associated with place but even more importantly perhaps, with people, families, communities and the intangible values they share. All the interviewees used in this article have made Australia their home, and their identities have been remoulded by their displacement from Europe and their subsequent lives. Their memories are continually being re-examined and revised as they reflect upon their experiences and attempt to create meaning for themselves and future generations.

NOTES

My thanks go to Pam Maclean, Donna Frieze and Janette Sato for their valuable advice.

1. W.D. Rubinstein, *The Jews in Australia. A Thematic History*, vol.2 (Melbourne, 1991), pp.36–77, cited in Judith E. Berman, *Holocaust Remembrance in Australian Jewish Communities, 1945–2000* (Perth: University of Western Australia Press, 2001), p.5.
2. Suzanne D. Rutland, *Edge of the Diaspora: Two Centuries of Jewish Settlement in Australia*, 2nd edn (Sydney: Brandl & Schlesinger, 1997), p.xii; Hilary L. Rubinstein, 'From Jewish Non-distinctiveness to Group Invisibility', cited in *Jews in the Sixth Continent*, ed. by W.D. Rubinstein (Sydney: Allen & Unwin, 1987), p.22, in Malcolm J. Turnbull, *Safe Haven, Records of the Jewish Experience in Australia*, Research Guide, No.12 (Canberra: National Archives of Australia, 1999), p.9.
3 *Jewish Herald*, 21 March 1919, in Turnbull, *Safe Haven* (see note 2), p.9.
4. Rutland, *Edge of the Diaspora*, pp.254, 288, cited in Berman, *Holocaust Remembrance* (see note 1), p.5. Of 85,000 Jews in Australia in 2004, Sydney and Melbourne each exceeded 40,000. South African Jewish Museum, Cape Town.
5. Rubinstein, *The Jews in Australia* (see note 1), p.77, cited in Berman (see note 1), p.6.
6. Berman, *Holocaust Remembrance* (see note 1), p.6.
7. Turnbull, *Safe Haven* (see note 2), p.10.
8. Hans explains: 'It was not Germany who would not let us out, it was the others who would not let us come in.' Similarly, Marianne comments: 'We were in a spider's web. Who would take us?' Videotestimonies by Hans, 17 November 1996, and Marianne, 7 August 1996. Videotestimonies cited are held at the Holocaust Museum and Research Centre, Melbourne.
9. See Doreen Massey, 'A Place called Home', *New Formations*, 17 (Summer 1992), 3–15; J. Macgregor Wise, 'Home: Territory and Identity', *Cultural Studies*, 14.2 (2000), 295–310; Peter Read, *Belonging: Australians, Place and Aboriginal Ownership* (Melbourne: Cambridge University Press, 2000); Loretta Baldassar, *Visits Home: Migration Experiences between Italy and Australia* (Melbourne: Melbourne University Press, 2001); Mandy Thomas, *Dreams in the Shadows: Vietnamese-Australian Lives in Transition* (Sydney: Allen & Unwin, 1999), pp.xiii–xiv; F. Anthias, 'Metaphors of Home: Gendering New Migrations to Southern Europe', in *Gender and Migration in Southern Europe: Women on the Move*, ed. by F. Anthias and G. Lazaridis (Oxford: Berg, 2000); Eric Hobsbawm, 'Preface', in *Home: A Place in the World*, ed. by Adrien Mack (New York: New York University Press, 1993); David Fitzpatrick, ed., *Home or Away? Immigrants in Colonial Victoria. Visible Immigrants: Three* (Canberra: Australian National University, 1992).
10. Peter Read, *Returning to Nothing: The Meaning of Lost Places* (Melbourne: Cambridge University Press, 1996), p.101.
11. Doreen Massey, cited in ibid., p.125.

12. Peter Read, 'Leaving Home', p.1, Australian Public Intellectual Network Archives: *Journal of Australian Studies* 61, http://www.api-network.com/cgi-bin/page?archives/, accessed 4 November 2004.
13. Ibid.
14. Questions inspired by Paul Bourke, 'Foreword', in *Home or Away?*, ed. by Fitzpatrick (see note 9).
15. Interview with Anne, 12 December 2001. Audio tapes are held by the author.
16. On childhood memories, see Michele Langfield and Pam Maclean, '"But Pineapple I'm Still a Bit Wary Of": Sensory Memories of Jewish Women Who Migrated to Australia as Children, 1938–39', in *Speaking to Immigrants. Oral Testimony and the History of Australian Migration. Visible Immigrants: Six*, ed. by A. James Hammerton and Eric Richards (Canberra: Australian National University, 2002), pp.83–109; and on Jewish identity formation see Pam Maclean and Michele Langfield, '"Tinged by the Holocaust": Gender, War and Jewish Identities', *Australian Journal of Jewish Studies*, XVII (2003), 88–111.
17. Joan Bryans, 'How to Survive in the West, Young Woman', in *Canadian Migration Patterns from Britain and North America*, ed. by Barbara Messamore (Ottawa: Ottawa University Press, 2004), p.145.
18. Videotestimony by Marianne.
19. Fiona Allon, 'Translated Spaces/Translated Identities: The Production of Place, Culture and Memory in an Australian Suburb', p.2, Australian Public Intellectual Network Archives: *Journal of Australian Studies*, 72, http://www.api-network.com/cgi-bin/page?archives/, accessed 4 November 2004.
20. Videotestimony by Marianne.
21. Videotestimony by Hans.
22. Oren Baruch Stier, *Committed to Memory, Cultural Mediations of the Holocaust* (Amherst and Boston: University of Massachusetts Press, 2003), p.2.
23. Videotestimony by Floris, 30 November, 1 December 1995.
24. Videotestimony by Floris.
25. Videotestimony by Floris.
26. Videotestimony by Floris.
27. Videotestimony by Alexander A., 25 June 1993.
28. Videotestimony by Isaac, 14 October 1997.
29. Videotestimony by Alexander B., 31 March 1998.
30. See, Ronald Taft, *From Stranger to Citizen* (Nedlands: University of Western Australia Press, 1965); Phillip Kunz, 'Immigrants and Socialisation: A New Look', *Sociological Review*, 16.3 (November 1968), cited in Read, *Returning to Nothing* (see note 10), pp.27, 41.
31. Read, *Returning to Nothing* (see note 10), pp.27–8.
32. Ibid., p.33.
33. Royal Melbourne Institute of Technology.
34. Interview with Lisa, 23 December 2001.
35. Interview with Anne.
36. Interview with Lisa.
37. Interview with Doris, 22 October, 2001.
38. Videotestimony by Paula, 3 June 1996.
39. Videotestimony by Marianne.
40. Interview with Anne.
41. Videotestimony by Marianne.
42. Berman, *Holocaust Remembrance* (see note 1), pp.5–6.
43. Rubinstein, *The Jews in Australia* (see note 1), 15, cited in Berman, *Holocaust Remembrance* (see note 1), p.6.
44. Videotestimony by Floris.
45. Bourke, 'Foreword' (see note 14); Eric Richards, 'Return Migration and Migrant Strategies in Colonial Australia', in *Home or Away*, ed. by Fitzpatrick (see note 9), pp.64–104.
46. Alistair Thomson, 'Voices we Never Hear: The Unsettling Story of Postwar "Ten Pound Poms" who Returned to Britain', *Oral History Association of Australia Journal*, 24 (2002), 52.
47. Graeme Hugo, 'Migration between Australia and Britain: Past and Present', in *Immigration and Integration: Australia and Britain*, ed. by David Lowe (London: Menzies Centre for Australian Studies, 1995), p.53, in Thomson, 'Voices we Never Hear' (see note 46), p.52.
48. On homesickness, see M.A.L. von Tilburg, A.J.J.M. Vingerhoats and G.L. Van Keck, 'Homesickness: A Review of the Literature', *Psychological Medicine*, 26 (1996), 899–921, in Carole Hamilton Barwick, 'Emigrant Women A Study of The First Generation of Postwar British Women Migrants To Australia 1947–1957' (Ph.D. thesis, LaTrobe University, 2005); and Bryans, 'How to Survive in the West' (see note 17), pp.153–5.
49. Thomson, 'Voices we Never Hear' (see note 46), pp.52–3.
50. Read, *Returning to Nothing* (see note 10), p.29. This is confirmed in many Holocaust testimonies.

51. Ibid., pp,28, 36–7.
52. Interview with Doris.
53. Videotestimony by Marianne.
54. B'nai B'rith is an international fraternal society formed in 1843. Many Jewish organisations and institutions work under its auspices. Berman, *Holocaust Remembrance* (see note 1), p.235.
55. Videotestimony by Hans.
56. Videotestimony by Alex B., 24 September 1996.
57. Mary Chamberlain and Selma Leydesdorff, 'Introduction. Transnational Families: Memories and Narratives', in *Transnational Families: Memories and Narratives in Global Networks*, ed. by Mary Chamberlain and Selma Leydesdorff, Special Issue, *Global Networks*, 4.3 (July 2004), 228.
58. Stier, *Committed to Memory* (see note 22), pp.75–6.
59. Berman, *Holocaust Remembrance* (see note 1), p.113.
60. Philip Maisel, 'First Hand: The Holocaust Testimonies Project', in *Reflections, 20 Years: Jewish Holocaust Museum and Research Centre*, ed. by Stan Marks (Melbourne: Jewish Holocaust Museum and Research Centre Inc., 2004), p.73.
61. Ibid.
62. Alexander B comments: "The past has not shaped me; I was shaped by my upbringing as a child.' Videotestimony by Alexander B.

Constructing a Usable Past:
History, Memory and South African Jewry in an Age of Anxiety

RICHARD MENDELSOHN and MILTON SHAIN

Between 1930 and 1955 three seminal histories were published which played a formative role in the self-definition of South African Jewry in the Apartheid era: *A History of the Jews in South Africa* by Louis Herrman, published in 1930 in London and republished in Johannesburg and Cape Town by the South African Jewish Board of Deputies in 1935; *The Birth of a Community* by Israel Abrahams published in Cape Town in 1955; and *The Jews in South Africa. A History*, edited by Gustav Saron and Louis Hotz and published in Cape Town in 1955.[1]

The works of Herrman, a Cape Town intellectual, Saron and Hotz, respectively a Jewish communal official and a journalist, and Abrahams, Chief Rabbi of the Cape Province and of South West Africa, became standard texts, providing the received version of the South African Jewish past. The image they collectively present is of an industrious, upwardly-mobile, respectable, classless, civic-minded, loyal and uniformly Zionist community, contributing energetically to the commonweal, and generally welcomed by the host society.[2] Written out of these accounts or minimised (and consequently obscured or ignored in popular consciousness) are anti-semitism, class struggle within the Jewish community, non- and anti-Zionism, the struggle between Yiddishists and Hebraists, and Jewish criminality. A whiggishness and presentism pervades these histories, each palpably informed by contemporary needs and by the search for a usable past.[3]

Louis Herrman (1883–1980) was born and educated in Southampton where he qualified as a schoolmaster at the Hartley University College. He came to Cape Town in 1907 to take up a position as vice-principal of the Hopemill Hebrew Public School. After Hopemill closed, he taught English at Cape Town High School. He obtained an MA (with distinction in Zoology) at the University of Cape Town in 1928 and his doctorate at London University in 1932 for research into the Genetic Status of Intelligence in Twins. Between obtaining these degrees he published *A History of the Jews in South Africa*. He went on to become principal of Cape Town High School, retiring in 1943. Louis Herrman was a prolific writer, broadcaster and lecturer, and intimately connected with Cape Town's intellectual elite.[4]

A History of the Jews in South Africa began as an enquiry into the history of the Cape Town Hebrew Congregation, the mother congregation of South African Jewry established in 1841. The study was originally undertaken at the behest of the synagogue committee and despite its broadening out beyond Cape Town, retains all the hallmarks of a congregational history writ large, a fact acknowledged and defended by the author. The story of Cape Town Jewry, he writes, 'for the greater part of the nineteenth century is the story of South African Jewry. All the other congregations during that time were its daughters'.[5] The proportions and emphases of the book reflect these priorities.

Herrman devotes approximately one-third of the book to the remote origins of the community, including Jewish involvement in the Portuguese voyages of discovery (where Abraham Zacuto, the Astronomer Royal, acted as adviser to Vasco da Gama) and in the Dutch East India Company, which officially excluded non-Protestants from its possessions, but which, according to Herrman, nevertheless employed baptised Jews. This opening section also deals with early Jewish arrivals at the Cape under British rule from the beginnings of the nineteenth century. The next third of the book is built around the establishment and early years of the Anglo-Jewish Cape Town Hebrew Congregation, the mother congregation of South African Jewry. The final third briefly introduces the discovery of diamonds and gold – the mineral revolution central to both South African and South African Jewish history – and then tersely essays, in a mere nine pages, the reasons for the Eastern European migration in the last decades of the nineteenth century, before returning to the Cape Town Hebrew Congregation and its initial difficulty in assimilating the alien and more observant newcomers. 'The "Russian" Jew', writes Herrman, 'looked upon the English as heathenish and ignorant, considered parts of Jewish ritual that others considered trivial, and trivial what others thought weighty.'[6]

Herrman's periodisation is revealing, particularly the year he chooses as the terminal date of his history of South African Jewry. The choice of 1895, the year in which a new minister is appointed to the Cape Town Hebrew Congregation, smacks of the parish pump rather than the national experience. After all, at that time Johannesburg was already beginning to dominate South African Jewry, with a Jewish population of 6,253 in the inner city.[7] By Herrman's own admission, this abrupt and arguably arbitrary ending excluded those major developments which shaped the South African Jewish world at the time of writing. But for all this, in line with Croce's dictum, his history was deeply informed by contemporary events.

The reader of Herrman's history is thus subtly presented with a portrait of a Jewish community deeply rooted in the (white) South African past, led by an acculturated Anglo-Jewish establishment, situated in Cape Town and committed to liberal values, which included civic virtue and enterprise. It cannot be coincidental that this book was conceived and written at the very time that Eastern European Jews had come to define all Jews in South Africa and were increasingly deemed unassimilable and a threat to the Nordic character of (white) South Africa. Their outward appearance, it was argued, reflected an inherent or biological essence putting paid to nineteenth century expectations of acculturation and assimilation.[8] Herrman could not have been unaware of the calls in the 1920s to curtail the influx of Eastern European Jews into South Africa. The *Cape Times* in particular, under the editorship of the public-school educated Englishman B.K. Long, persistently called for curbs on undesirable immigration from countries where democratic ideals were unknown and 'western concepts of morality are quite unappreciated'.[9]

Herrman's depiction of South African Jewry and its liberal and Anglo-Saxon antecedents would have served to counter this. His affirmative message was assimilated and succinctly captured in a review by the distinguished South African historian, Sir George Cory, who noted that it 'is not sufficiently realized what a very prominent part the Jews, from the very earliest times, have played in the industrial and other growth of this country. They have to their credit the fruits of adventure, enterprise and the successful development of the natural resources of the land'.[10]

Unsurprisingly then, Herrman's history was republished in 1935, this time in South Africa, by the South African Jewish Board of Deputies, the representative voice of South African Jewry since its establishment in 1912. Ostensibly re-issued 'in response to a specific demand in South Africa for lower priced copies of the book',[11] Jewish communal leaders considered it a weapon in the arsenal of the community's self-defence against burgeoning anti-semitism that included the emergence of far-right radical organisations, inspired by Nazi forms and rhetoric.[12] Other than the addition of a number of illustrations and appendices, the new edition was essentially unchanged with only, as the author put it, 'trifling' changes to the text. The most telling of the additions was the inscription on a tablet erected by the Jewish Guild War Memorial Association and the United Hebrew Congregation of Johannesburg commemorating the 118 South African Jews who died during the Great War, an event well beyond the chronological scope of the book but a useful reminder to non-Jewish readers of Jewish patriotism. Further thought was given by the Board of Deputies the year after re-publication to an extended edition, which would bring the Jewish South African story closer to the present and would emphasise 'especially those aspects of their internal life and organization which would illustrate their qualities of citizenship, humanitarianism, culture and general worthiness and value as human assets of the country'.[13] However, this further edition never materialised.

Twenty years after the South African edition of Herrman's *History*, Saron and Hotz's *The Jews in South Africa* and Abraham's *The Birth of a Community* were published. The former was a multi-authored volume, substantial in every sense and much of it informed by original research, conducted under the auspices of the South African Jewish Sociological and Historical Society, founded in 1947.[14] The editors' 'directives to writers' indicated that the 'essays are intended to be a serious contribution to Jewish and South African history. Wherever possible, original sources are to be consulted and observation and comment to be based on factual material'.[15] Although contributors were specifically warned that it was 'not intended to be a volume of Jewish apologetics in the sense of highlighting Jewish achievement',[16] they were also told that 'implicit throughout the volume should be: the Jewish community illustrating the principle of cultural pluralism, i.e. a community which, while preserving and fostering its own culture and way of life was at the same time fully integrated into the life of South Africa, making its due contribution to the progress and development of this country'.[17]

To understand the editors' somewhat contradictory instructions one must appreciate the context within which the volume was conceived and produced. Jews had recently experienced the National Party's advent to power in 1948 and were in the process of establishing a *modus vivendi* with a ruling party that had harboured extreme anti-Jewish sentiments in the 1930s and early 1940s and had opposed the war against Hitler. Although relations between Jews and Afrikaners had improved, Jews still felt at risk, though significantly less than in the recent past.[18]

Though the book was not, as the editors assert in the preface, 'an official publication of the Board of Deputies', the contributors were mainly communal notables[19] – attorneys, educators, journalists and rabbis – all seemingly sensitive to potential Jewish vulnerability under National Party rule and all apparently eager to present the Jewish community in the most favourable light and in a way that would be appreciated by the new rulers.[20]

Thus *The Jews in South Africa* focused on the deep-rootedness of the community; its enterprise and contribution; and its supposedly apolitical character, at least in a formal sense. 'Jews as a group, as opposed to individual Jews, have played no part in politics', explained the editors in the introduction. 'Whatever political causes individual Jews espoused, they acted as individuals, giving expression to their personal beliefs and convictions, and not as representatives of the Jewish group.'[21] The editors' disclaimer, which echoed the official mantra of the South African Jewish Board of Deputies, was an unabashed response to mounting accusations that Jews were disproportionately represented in the radical organisations opposing the Apartheid order in the 1950s.[22] The publication of the book ironically coincided with the adoption of the Freedom Charter, secretly drafted, as we know today, by a Jew.[23]

The intended chronological boundaries of *The Jews in South Africa* were not much broader than those of Herrman's history. The Saron and Hotz volume was originally planned to terminate before the Great War[24] Somewhere between conception and publication, the editors rethought this rather premature ending and decided to add an epilogue, authored by Gus Saron, the intellectual force behind and instigator of the project. (Saron, a lawyer by training and a one-time lecturer in classics at the University of the Witwatersrand, was the General Secretary of the Board at the time of writing.)[25] The entire period of South African Jewish history between 1910 and 1955 is encapsulated in a mere 30 pages – 'a rapid survey', in the words of Saron – out of a grand total of 400 pages.

Saron's epilogue reinforces the message of the volume's introduction: that Jews had 'become ever more integrated into the life of South Africa in all its aspects, economic, civic, cultural, artistic, political and recreational'; had 'never acted as a group' on 'general political issues'; and on 'racial questions' acted 'in terms of their personal outlook and convictions'. While noting that a 'few Jews' had 'been among the militant supporters of the campaign for non-European advancement', Saron insisted that 'the majority inclined to moderate, middle-of-the-road policies which avoid the extremes both of the left and of the right'.[26] Significantly, Saron added a last-minute 'postscript' to his epilogue, quoting at length generous praise of the Jews by the prime minister, Dr D.F. Malan, reported in the *S.A. Jewish Chronicle* in June 1955. The Jew, explained Malan, had identified 'himself with the country' and had 'become a good national as well as a good Jew ... a good South African as well as a true son of Israel'.[27]

This message, that Jews were fully integrated into the wider society while maintaining a distinctive identity, was largely affirmed in the press reviews of *The Jews in South Africa*.[28] The critical response to the volume was in the main what the editors would have hoped for. W.A.P. Phillips, a lecturer in public administration at the University of the Witwatersrand, writing in the *Rand Daily Mail*, the leading

Johannesburg daily, noted the balance between 'assimilation' on the one hand and the 'preservation of Jewishness' on the other.

The degree of success attending the efforts of South African Jewry to integrate into the general life of South Africa, whilst maintaining its specific cultural characteristics is of great interest to the world at large. For the problem of interracial communal living is one of the most critical facing us to-day. And it is in the Union, with its six main races (if we include the Jews) that the most complex experiment in this field is being made. *The Jews in South Africa* provides some hope that the experiment stands a chance.

By contrast, the review in *Die Burger*, the Cape mouthpiece of Afrikaner nationalism, was more ambivalent – and a reminder of the underlying tensions and concerns which had subtly informed the book.[29] While extravagantly praising *The Jews in South Africa* as 'a valuable addition to our historiography' and one that 'will be regarded for many years throughout the world as the authoritative history of the Jews in South Africa', it lamented the book's treatment of the vexed Jewish–Afrikaner relationship during the 1930s and 1940s, asserting that the 'facts have been concealed'.

It is a pity that a work which will be regarded as authoritative on the Jews in South Africa should be so misleadingly superficial about Jewish–Afrikaans relations. It is a pity, too, that in a period in which so much is being done to foster better relations, evidence should be provided in this manner that the more official Jewry, to be distinguished … from the 'Jew in the street', has still found so little connection with the Afrikaner.

Tellingly, Chief Rabbi Israel Abrahams' *The Birth of a Community*, published in the same year as the Saron and Hotz volume, also opens with a laudatory preface by Dr Malan about South African Jewry. The Jews in South Africa, he approvingly noted, had managed to maintain a distinctive 'racial' identity while contributing significantly to the society at large. They could, he argued, serve as a model for a complex 'multi-racial country' like South Africa.[30] In turn the author expressed his thanks for 'the deeply significant words of this great Elder Statesman of our country' that he was sure would 'long be remembered as a notable contribution to better race relations, among all sections of the population'.

By his own acknowledgement Abrahams' book (which was published by the Cape Town Hebrew Congregation) was simply an expanded version of his contribution on Western Province Jewry between 1870 and 1902 in the Saron and Hotz volume. Abrahams also acknowledged his heavy indebtedness to Herrman's pioneering study, some of which Herrman had himself recapitulated in a chapter in Saron and Hotz. Like Herrman, Abrahams centres his history upon the Cape Town Hebrew Congregation, the pulpit he had occupied since his arrival in South Africa in 1937 from Britain where he had trained at Jews College, London, and had served congregations in London and Manchester.[31] Abrahams structures his narrative around the ministries of his predecessors and, like Herrman, does not traverse into the more controversial and conflict-ridden twentieth century.

Thus all three books under consideration are of a piece. All three helped to define the received history of South African Jewry.[32] All helped towards a self-definition of a community increasingly dominated by South African-born Jews looking for a usable and respectable past under National Party rule. Shaped in significant measure by these texts, a collective memory emerged which incorporated a questionable understanding of the community's origins, development and character. Critical dimensions of the South African Jewish experience were ignored or distorted in their drive towards acceptance and respectability. For example, Jewish radicalism – an important component of the South African Jewish past which had become an embarrassment in an increasingly authoritarian and anti-communist Cold War milieu – was minimised.[33] Similarly, anti-Jewish sentiment and legislation were downplayed and explained away as an aberration, resulting from short-term and transient conditions in the 1930s and early 1940s.[34] Acceptance and accommodation by the host society was instead emphasised. The collective memory, like the historical texts upon which it drew, especially singled out the Afrikaners for their recalled kindness and courtesy towards the 'people of the Book' in the early years of immigration.[35]

Communal victors write and define communal history in accord with contemporary needs. The collective memory, heavily informed by the seminal texts, was largely oblivious through the Apartheid era to earlier struggles within the community. It was not only the radical left and Jewish trade unionism that were written out: with Zionism hegemonic and nationalist Afrikanerdom hugely sympathetic to the Zionist enterprise,[36] the struggles between Yiddishists and Hebraists,[37] Zionist and non-Zionists,[38] were relegated to obscurity. At a time when the Jewish community was prospering within the Apartheid economy and respectably middle class,[39] collective memory had little place for social (as for political) deviance. The underbelly of the South African Jewish experience was simply ignored: criminality and the seamier side of some immigrant Jewish behaviour – prostitution and pimping, and illicit liquor dealing – were expunged and formed no part of the collective memory.[40] Class divisions within the community were similarly ignored.[41]

Since the collapse of Apartheid in 1994 Jewish collective memory has been duly modified. In the Apartheid era, the Jewish collective memory, moulded by the seminal texts of Herrman, Saron and Hotz and Abrahams, had promoted a usable past which encouraged conformism to the racial social order, political quietism, and a myopic focus on entrepreneurship. Predictably, new circumstances after the collapse of Apartheid have necessitated the re-formation of South African Jewish collective memory. What was formally disquieting or even taboo has now been recovered, valorised and often proudly publicised. Thus, for example, Jewish radicalism, once embarrassing to the community and requiring explaining away, has now been given pride of place.[42] Such is the nature of collective memory, serving as it does changing needs and circumstances.

NOTES

1. Louis Herrman, *A History of the Jews in South Africa from Earliest Times to 1895* (London: Victor Gollancz, 1930); Israel Abrahams, *The Birth of a Community: A History of Western Province Jewry from Earliest Times to the End of the South African War, 1902* (Cape Town: Cape Town Hebrew Congregation, 1955); Gustav Saron and Louis Hotz, eds., *The Jews in South Africa: A History* (Cape Town: Oxford University Press, 1955).

2. The authors' emphasis on Jewish contribution is also noted by John Simon. See 'Towards an appraisal of South African Jewish historiography', in *Festschrift in Honour of Frank R. Bradlow*, ed. by Pieter E. Westra and Brian Warner (Cape Town: Friends of the South African Library, 1993), pp.19–30.
3. These works grew out of a new South African Jewish historical self-awareness, first manifested in a Year Book published in 1929 by the newly-established South African Jewish Historical Society and which included a range of historical contributions as well as a communal directory and who's who. Like the histories under consideration here, the Year Book was a product of contemporary needs. It was informed, at least in part, by an anxiety about the place of Jews in South Africa and a determination to embed the Jewish community in the wider culture and to ward off those characterising Jews as outsiders. The editor, Morris de Saxe, succinctly captured these anxieties in his introduction when he alerted his readers to the threat posed by the misinformation informing attitudes towards Jews in South Africa at the time. Beyond the Jewish community, he contended 'such information as generally obtains is usually so inaccurate as to be worse than misleading; it frequently becomes a positive source of danger to Jews'. *The South African Jewish Year Book* (Johannesburg: The South African Jewish Historical Society, 1929), p.6.
4. Biographical note, Louis Herrman Papers, BC 695: Manuscripts and Archives, University of Cape Town Library. Among those Herrman befriended were the distinguished authors, Olive Schreiner, whom he described as an 'exceedingly vivacious little old lady', and Sarah Gertrude Millin, the artists Irma Stern, Moses Kottler and Wolf Kibel, and the historians George Cory and Eric Walker. See Baruch Hirson, *The Cape Town Intellectuals. Ruth Schechter and her Circle, 1907–1934* (Johannesburg: Witwatersrand University Press, 2001); and M.E. Katz, 'Dr. Louis Herrman at 96', *Jewish Affairs*, 35.2 (1980), 27–9.
5. Herrman (see note 1), p.9.
6. Ibid., p.263.
7. Z.A.R. *Johannesburg Gezondheids Comite Sanitare Departement Census* 15 July 1896. By contrast, the Jewish population of the whole Cape Colony in 1891 was 3,009. See the *Census for the Cape Colony*, CCP 4/11/4, Statistical Register for 1891 and 1904.
8. 'Unassimilability' had become the new catchword, an idea influenced directly by nativist literature from the United States as well as by a new domestic segregationist discourse in which race and culture were conflated. See Saul Dubow, 'Race, Civilization, Culture: The Elaboration of Segregationist Discourse in the Inter-war years', in *The Politics of Race, Class and Nationalism in Twentieth Century South Africa*, ed. by Shula Marks and Stanley Trapido (London and New York: Longman Group, 1987), pp.71–94; and Milton Shain, *The Roots of Antisemitism in South Africa* (Charlottesville and London: University Press of Virginia, 1994), chapter six, *passim*.
9. *Cape Times*, 16 August 1921. The *Cape Times* was imbued with an exaggerated fear that British subjects were being replaced by aliens who were 'from racial stocks which experience has shown to be unsuitable to the peculiar conditions of this country'. In the *Cape Times*' view (29 October 1927), a reasonable proportion of foreigners was acceptable; when that proportion rose beyond a certain point 'there was a real risk of endangering the continuity of the development of those broad ideas, upon whose conservation and general acceptance throughout the British Commonwealth the health, the solidarity and the prosperity of the Empire alike depend'.
10. *Cape Argus*, 30 September 1930. Ironically, in the very year that *A History of the Jews in South Africa* was published, the South African government introduced a Quota Act which effectively precluded the entry of Eastern European Jews into the country. See Shain (note 7), pp.137ff. and Edna Bradlow, 'Immigration into the Union, 1910–1948: Policies and Attitudes' (unpublished Ph.D. thesis, University of Cape Town, 1978), pp.215–49.
11. Herrman (see note 1), p.9.
12. Gideon Shimoni, *Jews and Zionism: The South African Experience 1910–1967* (Cape Town: Oxford University Press, 1980), p.150. For the radical right and anti-semitism in the 1930s, see Patrick J. Furlong, *Between Crown and Swastika. The Impact of the Radical Right on the Afrikaner Nationalist Movement in the Fascist Era* (Johannesburg: University of Witwatersrand Press, 1991). See also the exchange between Furlong and Hermann Giliomee, a leading authority on Afrikaner history: Hermann Giliomee, 'The Making of the Apartheid Plan, 1929–1948', *Journal of Southern African Studies*, 29.2 (2003), 373–92; Hermann Giliomee, *The Afrikaners. Biography of a People* (Cape Town: Tafelberg, 2003), pp.417–18; Patrick Furlong, 'Apartheid, Afrikaner Nationalism and the Radical Right: Historical Revisionism in Hermann Giliomee's *The Afrikaners*', *South African Historical Journal*, 49 (2003), 207–22.

13. South African Jewish Board of Deputies, minutes of meeting of deputies, Johannesburg, 26 April 1936 cited in Shimoni, *Jews and Zionism* (see note 12), p.150.
14. The South African Jewish Sociological and Historical Society was established in Johannesburg with the support and sponsorship of the South African Jewish Board of Deputies. It sought to conduct research and establish an archive, and to stimulate public interest in the South African Jewish past. In his opening address to the Society, its first chairman, Chief Rabbi Louis I. Rabinowitz (who was also Professor of Hebrew at the University of the Witwatersrand) indicated that among its purposes was to increase 'our own self-respect' and to 'know thyself'. See L.I. Rabinowitz, 'Preserving the Record', *Jewish Affairs*, 2.4 (1947), 46–8 (p.47). For the work of the Society, see also Naomi Musiker, 'The South African Jewish Sociological and Historical Society and the SAJBD Archives', *Jewish Affairs*, 59.3 (2003), 89–94.
15. Folder C1. 181-C1.190, Louis Herrman Papers, BC 695: Manuscripts and Archives, University of Cape Town Library.
16. Despite these intentions the editors initially commissioned a chapter specifically concentrating on 'major benefactions' made by Jews to South African causes. For this chapter, which was never delivered, see correspondence between Dora Sowden and Hilda Purwitsky in files of South African Jewish Sociological and Historical Society, South African Jewish Board of Deputies Archives, Johannesburg.
17. This echoed the views of the American Jewish social theorist Horace Kallem who earlier in the century had developed the concept of cultural pluralism in opposition to the notion of the 'melting pot'. See Howard M. Sachar, *A History of the Jews in America* (New York: Alfred A. Knopf, 1992), pp.426–7.
18. See Gideon Shimoni, *Community and Conscience. The Jews in Apartheid South Africa* (Hanover and London: University Press of New England, 2003), pp.11–17 and 25–6.
19. Deborah Abelson, journalist; Israel Abrahams, rabbi; Abraham Addleson, attorney; Jack Alexander, former secretary of the South African Zionist Federation; George Aschman, journalist; Max Geffen, attorney; Chaim Gershater, editor of the *Zionist Record*; Louis Herrmann, retired headmaster; Louis Hotz, journalist; Myer Pencharz, accountant; Louis Rabinowitz, rabbi; Solomon Rappaport, rabbi; S.A. Rochlin, archivist; Eric Rosenthal, attorney and author; Dora Sowden, journalist; Gustav Saron, General Secretary, South African Jewish Board of Deputies.
20. For a similar critique, see Claudia Bathsheba Braude (ed.), *Contemporary Jewish Writing in South Africa. An Anthology* (Lincoln and London: University of Nebraska Press, 2001), pp.xl–xliv. Unlike the authors of this article, Braude goes so far as to indict Saron of 'an active process of historical revisionism' (p.xli) with a view to wooing the Apartheid regime.
21. Saron and Hotz (see note 1), p.xvi.
22. See Shimoni, *Community and Conscience* (see note 18), chapter 2 *passim*. The year after the publication of the Saron and Hotz volume, more than half the 23 whites among the 156 activists arrested on charges of treason were Jews.
23. See Rusty Bernstein, *Memory Against Forgetting* (London: Viking, 1999), pp.145–62 for his role in drafting this historic statement of African National Congress policy.
24. Explaining this decision to end at the First World War, Saron wrote 'we do not go beyond that period as that brings us too close to living personalities and contemporary events' (G. Saron to Chairmen of Regional Committees, 21 May 1951. South African Jewish Sociological and Historical Society file, South African Jewish Board of Deputies Archives, Johannesburg).
25. Unlike Herrman, Saron was South African-born. He was educated at the University of the Witwatersrand and at Oxford. After lecturing in Classics at his alma mater in Johannesburg, he practised at the Bar before becoming Secretary of the South African Jewish Board of Deputies in 1936. His co-editor, the Lithuanian-born Louis Hotz came to South Africa in 1903 as a child, and was educated at the South African College in Cape Town and at the London School of Economics. He was a veteran journalist and experienced social and economic researcher.
26. Saron and Hotz (see note 1), pp.373–5. In this regard, Saron was certainly correct. See Shimoni, *Community and Conscience* (see note 18), chapter 2 *passim*.
27. Saron and Hotz (see note 1), pp.399–400. This was a far cry from Malan's public utterances of the 1930s. 'The Jews did everything in their power to keep the Afrikaners from uniting', he told a Stellenbosch audience in 1937, 'as they feared South Africans would rise from their lowly and insignificant position to save South Africa for the South Africans ... Throughout the world the Jews availed themselves of democratic institutions for their own profit'. Furlong (see note 12), p.65.
28. See 'What the Reviewers Say', *Jewish Affairs*, 11.1 (1956), 26–8.

29. These tensions were also evident at a symposium organised by the South African Jewish Board of Deputies to launch the book. One of the speakers, Professor C.J. Uys of the department of history at the Afrikaans language University of the Orange Free State, caused consternation among his primarily Jewish audience when he called on Jews to 'find salvation' in the Bible and the Synagogue rather than in Communism – 'which was essentially a Jewish conception' – or in capitalism or liberalism. See Atalia Ben-Meir, 'The South African Jewish Community and Politics, 1930–1978 with special reference to the South African Jewish Board of Deputies' (unpublished Ph.D. thesis, University of Natal, 1995), p.201.
30. '... in spite of', wrote Malan, 'the well-known Jewish regard for their own racial and religious integrity, some measure of integration in both respects did in fact occur, in some notable instances to the great advantage of the rest of the South African Community. ... In two important respects the Jewish race is decidedly unique, and such even to an extent bordering on the miraculous. The first is the maintenance of their racial identity for almost two thousand years. ... The second is the amazing adaptability of the Jewish race, which makes it possible for them to fit themselves into the national structure of the various countries in which they happen to live. If properly utilized both of these attributes can not only serve a useful purpose in themselves in our multi-racial country, but can also be of immense assistance in the solution of South Africa's greatest problems. A race-conscious nation like the Jews, proud of their own identity, will the more easily understand and respect the same feeling in the case of every other section of the community.' Foreword to Abrahams, *The Birth of a Community* (see note 1), pp.xii–xiii.
31. The Vilna-born Abrahams was Chief Rabbi of the Cape Province and South West Africa and Professor of Hebrew at the University of Cape Town.
32. This received history is reflected in two major publications produced in subsequent decades: *South African Jewry 1965*, ed. by Leon Feldberg (Johannesburg: Fieldhill Publishing, 1965); and *South African Jewry. A Contemporary Survey*, ed. by Marcus Arkin (Cape Town: Oxford University Press, 1984). Both books essentially conform to the master narrative delineated by Herrman, Saron and Hotz and Abrahams. The Feldberg volume contains substantial articles by Saron on 'The Making of South African Jewry'; by Hotz on 'Jewish Contributions to South African Economic Development'; and by others on the Jewish contribution to law, public life, the arts and trade and commerce in South Africa. Arkin's volume, though drawing on some new research, is still embedded in the established paradigm.
33. For the history of Jewish radicalism in South Africa, see E.A. Mantzaris, 'Radical Community: The Yiddish-speaking Branch of the International Socialist League, 1918–1920', in *Class, Community and Conflict. South African Perspectives*, ed. by Belinda Bozzoli (Johannesburg: Ravan Press, 1987), pp.160–76; Taffy Adler, 'Lithuania's Diaspora: The Johannesburg Jewish Workers' Club, 1928–1948', *Journal of Southern African Studies*, 6.1 (1979), 70–92; Mark Israel and Simon Adams, '"That Spells Trouble": Jews and the Communist Party of South Africa', *Journal of Southern African Studies*, 26.1 (2000), 145–62; James T. Campbell, 'Beyond the Pale: Jewish Immigration and the South African Left', in *Memories, Realities and Dreams. Aspects of the South African Jewish Experience*, ed. by Milton Shain and Richard Mendelsohn (Johannesburg: Jonathan Ball, 2002), pp.96–162; Glenn Frankel, *Rivonia's Children. Three Families and the Cost of Conscience in White South Africa* (New York: Farrar Straus and Giroux, 1999); and Shimoni, *Community and Conscience* (see note 18).
34. For the depth of anti-semitism preceding the 1930s and 1940s, see Shain, *The Roots of Antisemitism in South Africa* (see note 8).
35. By contrast with their experience in Eastern Europe, the newcomers in the late nineteenth and early twentieth centuries did enjoy a degree of affection on the part of their Afrikaner hosts. But relations were not without conflict. Nor indeed were perceptions of the Jew as favorable as those later remembered. See Shain, *The Roots of Antisemitism in South Africa* (see note 8), pp.19–48.
36. In 1953 Prime Minister D.F. Malan had been the first head of a government to visit Israel. His admiration for the new state was shared by many fellow Afrikaner nationalists. See Shimoni, *Jews and Zionism* (see note 12), p.213.
37. For the at times ferocious debate, see Joseph Sherman, 'Between Ideology and Indifference: The Destruction of Yiddish in South Africa', in *Memories, Realities and Dreams* (see note 33), pp.28–49.
38. Besides those on the left ideologically opposed to any form of Jewish nationalism, the mother congregation led by the Reverend Bender only joined the Zionist movement in the wake of the Balfour Declaration of 1917.

39. For an indication of Jewish upward mobility in the Apartheid years, see Antony Arkin, 'Economic Activities', in *South African Jewry. A Contemporary Survey* (see note 32), pp.57–77.
40. For the Jewish demimonde and the seamier side of the South African Jewish immigrant experience, see 'Randlords and Rotgut, 1886–1903' and 'Prostitutes and Proletarians, 1886–1914', in Charles van Onselen, *Studies in the Social and Economic History of the Witwatersrand 1886–1914, volume I New Babylon* (Johannesburg: Ravan Press, 1982), pp.44–162. Although van Onselen first published his findings in the 1970s, these deviant behaviours, as van Onselen shows (pp.84 and 138–9), were well known within the community at the time.
41. See Riva Krut, 'The Making of a South African Jewish Community in Johannesburg 1886–1914', in *Class, Community and Conflict* (see note 33), pp.135–59.
42. Jewish activists are celebrated in the new South African Jewish Museum which opened in Cape Town in December 2000. See Oren Baruch Stier, 'South Africa's Jewish Complex', *Jewish Social Studies*, 10.3 (2004), 123–42 (p.135).

Comparing the Jewish and Irish Communities in Twentieth Century Scotland

WILLIAM KENEFICK

In the late nineteenth and early twentieth centuries Glasgow and its hinterland lay at a great centre of industrial production and commerce: it was these attributes that attracted migrants to the city and the west of Scotland generally. Jews fleeing the pogroms or working to realise their dreams of making it to America disembarked, for the greater part, at Edinburgh's Leith docks – or occasionally, and even mistakenly, Dundee harbour believing that they were in New York, and that they had indeed, after all their exertions, finally made it to the Golden Land[1] They then moved westward and to Glasgow where they 'required no passport, no visa, no documentation' to settle or sojourn a while in Britain's second city of Empire.[2] Glasgow linked Scotland to the rest of the world, and the transmigration west not only provided a means of migration abroad, but access to temporary accommodation, work and even at a basic level some form of support from the established Jewish community at Glasgow. Many of these Jews, although a minority, were to make Scotland and Glasgow their home before 1914.

The modern history of the Jews in Scotland, however, refers mainly to the community that developed in Glasgow after 1914, and who were to make the city their home. Unlike other Jewish communities the pre-1914 community was not so large, being only one-third of the size of Leeds or one-fifth of the Manchester Jewish community, but Glasgow started to attract greater numbers during the inter-war years and in fact peaked at around 15–16,000 during the 1950s. This is in itself an unusual Jewish demographic profile in so far as most communities peaked in Britain in the 1930s and then dispersed, whereas in Glasgow and in the Gorbals area in particular the Jewish community continued to grow.[3]

As Glasgow was a leading cosmopolitan maritime trading centre it attracted many other immigrant groups including the Irish, and it was the relationship between the Irish and Jewish communities there that was the subject of a paper presented at the Second Port Jews Conference in Cape Town, in January 2003, 'Jewish and Catholic Irish Relations: The Glasgow Waterfront c.1880–1914'. This paper considered the settlement of the largely Russian Jewish community in the Glasgow from the 1880s, and the relationship that developed between them and the Catholic Irish from Donegal. They were the two main immigrant groups to settle in the Gorbals, on Glasgow's south side, in an area generally regarded by native Scots as a 'Glasgow Ghetto'. Despite many hardships and considerable poverty, this paper concluded that the relationship between the Jews and the Irish was a good one, and there that was very little anti-semitism experienced by the Jewish community there before 1914.

This article, based on a follow-up paper presented to the 'Third Port Jews Conference' in Cape Town in January 2005, proposes to take the story further and consider the experience of the Jewish community from 1914 onwards. The Third Port Jews conference also extended the range of the previous conference theme to account for the development of the Jewish community beyond the early days of settlement in cosmopolitan maritime trading centres. This study charts the evolution of the Jewish community of the Gorbals and Glasgow, and their relationship with the Irish, and the host community in twentieth century Scotland.

Recurring Themes and Methodology

The evidence used in this article is drawn largely from a collection of 33 oral history transcripts held at the Scottish Jewish Archives Centre, Garnethill Synagogue, Glasgow, gathered to keep a record of the collective memory of the Jewish community of Glasgow. This valuable resource had not until recently been systematically or rigorously examined or evaluated. While this chapter is based on oral evidence drawn from this resource its author was never part of the original project and had no control over the process of collecting these testimonies. The method was largely by interview and not the preferred 'life history' method which allows for the uninterrupted free-flow of memory. It is clear from the tapes and transcripts that interpolation does take place, but this type of interruption is generally rare and where an interview position is adopted the questions asked are essentially non-contentious.

Notwithstanding the problems associated with the method and approach to gathering oral history testimony, there are still problems associated with assessing the validity and accuracy of testimony and the reliability of memory. There is always a potential for distortion but if oral testimony is rigorously evaluated in the same manner as any other form of historical evidence this can be avoided. These testimonies will thus be subjected to a four stage process of evaluation and validation as outlined in an approach promulgated by Dr Murray Watson, an Honorary Research Fellow of the Department of History, University of Dundee: (i) to clearly distinguish between first-hand and secondary knowledge; (ii) to seek internal consistency within individual testimonies; (iii) to verify and corroborate content against other sources (other oral history testimony, documentary sources or newspapers, for example); and (iv) to search and identify recurring themes throughout all the testimonies.[4]

This last stage is important because it is at this point we identify the 'recurrent themes' that form the basic narrative of this chapter and the analysis that emerges from it. Thus we consider among others themes such as childhood; anti-semitism; inter-ethnic relations; life and work in the 'Ghetto'; assimilation and acculturation; poverty, progress and improvement; and the role of place and memory in the formation of ethnic identities. This research also maintains the methodological association with the approach adopted by Maria Vassilikou in her treatment of Greek and Jewish relations in Salonika and Oddessa.[5] Therein she stresses that historians tend to look too fondly through the lens of inter-ethnic conflict and communal violence, rather than search for positive inter-ethnic relations that stress shared values and similarities when looking at immigrant and host communities.

Vassilikou noted that the Greeks and Jews of Salonica and Odessa shared the same social space and 'looked for paths of existence' which would guarantee 'their group survival' and that this in time would favour their 'upwards social mobility'. Importantly, Vassilikou adds, and this holds true for Jews and the Irish of Glasgow:

> Their choices were far from homogenous, but were rather conditioned upon their economic background, social position and ideological legacy. The immediate outcome of this inter-communal fragmentation took the form of social behaviour which cut across their ethnic distinctiveness.[6]

John D. Klier advocates a similar approach, but emphasises cultural developments in the ideology of Zionism, Jewish varieties of socialism, a modern Jewish Press, and the modern Jewish stage: noting the 'novelty and innovation' which marked the Jewish contribution to their new societies. Such cultural determinants were all evident at Glasgow and manifested themselves in various forms, not least the prolific spread of Zionist clubs and societies, groups such as the Workers' Circle, but also the Glasgow Jewish Institute which spawned sports clubs and art and musical societies, and the 'Little Theatre Workshop'. The latter was an offshoot of the Glasgow Jewish Institute Players amateur dramatic society which by the second half of the twentieth century was recognised as an outstanding centre of drama production in West Scotland, and they produced plays for the Jewish and non-Jewish community in the Gorbals (some productions were in Yiddish).[7]

This type of information is scattered throughout the oral histories used for this research and demonstrate the great pride that the Jewish community took in these developments. The Jewish community made a significant contribution not only to the economic well-being of Glasgow but also to social and cultural developments, and the experience of living and working in Glasgow also helped to shape and construct modern Jewish identity in Scotland.[8]

'Are You a Bill or a Dan'? Childhood Memories[9]

As Vassilikou's model suggested, and as previous research findings demonstrated, what we see occurring at Glasgow between the Jews and the Irish was a clear example of good inter-ethnic relations and the identification of shared values and similarities. Living in such close proximity did not lead to the type of conflict and communal violence and discrimination that did occur elsewhere, and most notably – in a Jewish/Irish context – the Limerick pogroms of 1904.[10] Perhaps there was no need for conflict in so far as both the Jews and the Irish were too eagerly involved in the daily struggle for survival. Indeed, this is borne out in some of the oral testimonies consulted in this study when one respondent (born 1908), in answer to the question 'what was your first childhood memory' answered: 'Children going without shoes, bare foot, and women wearing shawls. I remember saying that I didn't want to be an old women and wear a shawl.'[11] Another respondent born in 1914 – within the sounds of the Gorbals Bells – described and defined the Gorbals as a big Jewish area: 'A type of ghetto, full of Jews.' 'We must have had seven synagogues in the area', he noted, and 'Jews mixed quite freely with non-Jews.' In the tenement building in which he lived there were one or two Jewish families to every six or eight apartments on each level of the building:

> So we grew up in a mixed group of Jews and non-Jews. We were all friendly and mixed very well ... and we never had any serious arguments with non-Jews. The boys in the neighbourhood accepted that we had to go to school after school.[12]

Another female contributor (born 1912) could hardly forget the appalling housing conditions that were all too apparent at that time, but suggested that it was mostly Jewish families who lived in her building: 'there were only a few non-Jewish folk there'. She did mix with non-Jewish girls at school and remembered wearing a tartan kilt given to her by an aunt, who referred to the plaid fondly as the Winetrobe tartan (her family name).[13] Others remembered clearly the poverty and problems associated with tenement living, not least the 'one room and kitchen' shared by a large family.[14] For one respondent this equated to a 'hard, hard childhood', but despite not having an inside toilet – 'you went to another building completely out of sight' – and no bath 'mother kept the children clean'.[15]

Maybe it was a question of just accepting each other, for as Ralph Glasser suggested, and in spite of some occasional name-calling, the Irish Catholics of the Gorbals had a better relationship with the Jews than they had with the 'indigenous Protestant' population.[16] And perhaps it is for similar reasons that Scottish Protestants had a good relationship with the Jews in Glasgow. Indeed, according to evidence presented in another oral testimony there is much truth in this. One respondent (born 1903) stressed, in answer to a question on evidence of anti-semitism: 'No, in Scotland we were fortunate. We had very little anti-semitism, very little. It was mostly the Billies [sic] and the Dans [sic], the Catholics and Protestants like.'[17] It was suggested in other testimonies that while anti-semitism was not really a problem in later life, it was at school where children perhaps did come into contact with such sentiments. Asked what they learned at school one respondent (born 1908) was to reply, 'threatened, assaulted, by Roman Catholic children at the accompanying school. They would get hold of you and say "are you a billy or a dan" [sic]'.[18] Depending on your answer you either escaped lightly or you received a 'bit of a thrashing'. Another respondent (born 1912) saw things differently:

> You don't encounter anti-semitism from children, you get that from adults. ... [there was] one day a year – St Patrick's Day, when the Roman Catholics came about and they got at the Protestants. When they were going up to the school, you heard them shouting out, are you a Billy or a Dan? If you say the wrong thing, you get hit on the head. But in those days you didn't – I don't think at school I ever experienced any anti-semitism.[19]

Generally, Jewish kids were seen as 'kind of impartial' and came in for such treatment probably because they went to Protestant schools rather than because they were Jewish. However, there was an element of school name-calling within the Protestant schools that was seen to be particularly aimed at Jews. As one respondent (born 1907) recalled:

> When I was a boy I used to think that most goyim must have been Zionists, because they would say: 'Go back to Palestine.' This was a very common expression. The boys in the school thought that the Jews came from Palestine. There was more anti-semitism when I was a boy than now (late 1980s). Not a great deal of violence. Yes, in school you had to fight, but that was among boys. They wanted to fight for any reason. The Protestants and Catholics were worst against each other. Protestants hated the Catholics more than Jews.[20]

Of the 22 testimonies sampled for this study (there are 33 oral testimonies in all) eight felt the need to mention their school days and mostly in relation to Protestant and Catholic sectarianism. Several respondents made reference to a Jewish majority at some schools, and at one Gorbals school, just after the First World War, one respondent noted there were 'a lot of Jewish children in his class. About fifty per cent'.[21] Another respondent did briefly touch on 'being separated from the non-Jewish boys' when they went to morning assembly, and thought that this was a type of segregation – even if it was only for 20 minutes each day. He was a keen member of the Cub and Boy Scout movement and when considering his out of school childhood activities 'never experienced any religious bias or any anti-Jewish person'. Indeed, the Scout Master of the First Glasgow Scout Troupe – the biggest in Scotland – was Reginald Levy, a dentist and a West End Glasgow Jew.[22]

'I Never Met Any Anti-semitism in Scotland': Jewish and Non-Jewish Relations

It is clear, however, that there were some elements of anti-semitism experienced at school as the following extract seems to suggests, but was this as apparent in later life? Here we find something of a mixed bag:

> People say there was a lot of anti-semitism. I think there is, people are jealous. But I have to say that during my career I can't think of a single incidence where covert anti-semitism has decided against me. I'm sure I have been decided against, but not on anti-semitic grounds. I think that happened at school too. I got on well with people who are not of my faith.[23]

One respondent (born 1892) noted that in inter-war Glasgow there were many Jewish musicians and that most of them came from the Gorbals. Asked if there was any envy on the part of the non-Jewish musical fraternity he replied: 'I never experience anti-semitism. No they accepted us. There may have been one or two – you get one or two – but on the whole, I never found much anti-semitism.' But there is clearly some confusion as to the extent and nature of anti-semitism, for the same respondent then added, 'There was a lot of anti-semitism, it was rife, but it didn't show much'[24] Whether this means that he personally did not experience much himself, or that it existed at a more subtle subterranean level is not clear.

The aforementioned former Boy Scout – who was in fact Jack Elias Miller, who later qualified as a medical doctor in 1943, put it more plainly when he stated: 'Anti-Semitism! Yes it is under the surface but I have experienced very little overt anti-semitism in my life. And I have spent as much time with non-Jews as I have with

Jews.'[25] The boy who remembered being told to 'Go back to Palestine' while at school, recalled as a young man in 1923 one serious episode of anti-Jewish discrimination. He applied for a post in an insurance company, and after his interview his potential employers seemed pleased with his performance. He was then asked his religion and in answering that he was Jewish was told: 'Oh, we only employ our own. We are a family business. We would not employ Jews, although I have not got anything against them.' Prior to attending this particular interview he had considered applying to university to study metallurgy – 'a subject not very popular among Jewish students'. Indeed, later in the 1930s he only knew of one Jew who had a doctorate in metallurgy, and he was chief metallurgist with a leading Glasgow engineering firm. But in 1923 he decided that was what he wanted, and so he made his mind up.

> I had heard about metallurgy and I went to a professor. I told him I was Jewish, but he said that made no difference. And strictly speaking, I do not think it made a difference through my career. Except for instances, but not with the people who owned firms.[26]

He left Scotland for a time but returned to Glasgow just months before the Second World War broke out to work with a leading Glasgow engineering firm. He noted that 'there was no anti-semitism in the firm', and then remembered a Polish Nazi Party member who had been dismissed from the firm for spreading anti-semitism. Ironically, in the firm in which he worked there was an unwritten law,

> ... that no Catholics should hold any post of authority. They did not mind Jews. There were not many, but there were many Catholics. Before the war some companies did not employ Jews, others did not employ Catholics. You saw adverts in the papers: 'Roman Catholics need not apply.' But never Jews!

Another born and bred Gorbals boy stressed he 'wasn't conscious of any real block anti-semitism or hostility', and if it did happen it was more on an individual basis. However, after leaving his Gorbals school – top of his class – to attend the more upmarket Hutcheson Secondary School, he encountered something different:

> I found Hutchy [sic] far more, perhaps dislike on, on the part of the non-Jewish boys than I had experienced in [the] Gorbals. Somehow or other I came to the conclusion that the poorer have greater humanity than the wealthy people have. The non-Jewish boys came from very comfortable families. I wasn't happy there and didn't remain long.[27]

Another respondent also suggested a class dimension to aspects of anti-semitism he encountered:

> The Scots character, particularly the people I know so well. It's not them that are anti-Jewish it's the sort of well-off class. The sort of lawyer class. They have an attitude that is not outspoken but definitely there. I have never met anti-semitism in Scotland they haven't said anything to my face. I was invited to join [the board of a] football club and nothing anti-Jewish there, they knew I was Jewish.

Indeed, this particular respondent was a regular attendee at both Rangers and Celtic football matches and latterly as a guest of the directors. He was in fact a Rangers supporter, although 'the best hospitality was [at] Celtic' and he became friendly with Sir Robert Kelly. Indeed, when Robert Kelly was made a Knight this respondent made a presentation to him 'on behalf of the Jewish community'. But he did have an interesting angle on Jewish football allegiance in Glasgow: 'I used to go to Rangers ... Some Jewish boys were Celtic supporters. Most were Rangers supporters. Maybe because it was blue [sic]? The Jewish prayer shawl is blue. Or just no reason at all.'[28]

Throughout these testimonies constant reference is made to non-Jewish friends and acquaintances – both of Scottish Protestant and Irish Catholic descent. And while the Glasgow Jews seldom – if ever – married outside the Jewish faith, this did not preclude close and long associations with people of the Christian faith. Jews freely mixed with non-Jews in Glasgow and were members of the same political parties and in relation to their cultural lives were often members of the same clubs and associations. One respondent noted that while there had been seven Jewish children in her class at school, 'not one of them was my bosom friend. My bosom friends were non-Jewish girls ... Well I made one Jewish friend, a very strong friend at university, but I mostly mixed with non-Jewish girls'.[29] Dr Friedl Ehrlich Jacob, born 1901, spoke of her close working relationship with a 'very sweet wonderful woman, a Catholic doctor'.[30] Another described how one of her nephews married an Irish Catholic and 'that she was [her] favourite relation', and that another niece married an Irish Protestant.[31] But these examples of marrying outside the faith were later developments and for the most part a phenomenon of the 1970s.

Another respondent, born in the Gorbals in 1914 of Russian parents, stressed that he and his brothers all married Jewish girls. He did note that his first wife's sister did marry out and that her father banished her from the house. But it was well known that when her father was in his workshop she would slip in and visit her mother. He personally reproached her for her actions but 'secretly admired her for having the strength to do what she wanted to do with her life'. Her actions were frowned upon by many but others simply accepted the situation: 'it was a mixed community, mixed in feeling'.[32] Interaction between the Jews and non-Jews was experienced at various different levels. It was noted by one respondent that Michael Simon – one time Glasgow Councillor and Justice of the Peace who in 1905 became Scotland's first Jewish Magistrate – made a personal contribution of £900 some time before 1914 to help with the construction of St Margaret's Catholic Church.[33]

Mrs Lilian Leighton, born in 1907, moved out of the Gorbals with her husband and family sometime in the 1930s, and she quickly realised that while she may have left behind the ghetto, she was also leaving a familiar Jewish community infrastructure that had been built up there. To maintain these links she and her family travelled back and forth throughout the remainder of the 1930s and the war years in order that her children were not 'brought up as non-Jews'. After the war she got together a rather disparate group of former Gorbals Jews in her area with a view to organising a small *cheder*, but they found it difficult to find a regular meeting place. After meeting for some time in someone's spare room they eventually found more permanent accommodation at the local Catholic School. Indeed, Lilian was also a founder member of the Glasgow Jewish Cancer Group and collected much money for that charity – for Jews and non-Jews. In 1988 they collected £22,000, of which £6,000 came from a 'non-Jewish lady': 'She had made the donation because she was fond of the Jewish people. She had been brought up with Jewish people in the Gorbals.' She saw this as an example of the degree of mutual respect that existed between Jews and non-Jews.

It is clear that Lilian Leighton was a quite remarkable woman. When she organised the *cheder* in 1946 her youngest son was already 16 years old, so she did this not for her family but for her community. She also gave her time to work in the wider non-Jewish community and before the start of the Second World War had joined the Civil Defence Corp. During the war she became an Air Raid Warden and Chief Fire Guard with a liaison role with the Police Department centred in the Gorbals. She was in attendance in the aftermath of several bombings in Glasgow, and spoke of the heavy bombardment of Clydebank, adding:

> And for anyone to tell me that the Germans didn't know what was happening to the Jews in Germany, well it's just lies. Because far far earlier than reaching Yoker, you could smell the horrible horrible smell of burning flesh. I'll never forgive it – never forget it.[34]

'They Were All Peddling': Occupational Diversity and Forms of Culture

Most of the respondents' testimonies represented here can be seen as conduits between two and even three generations, and they speak eloquently about families, their fathers and mothers, where they came from, and what they did. Here we see the employment profile of the Jews who were part of the earlier settlement taking shape. It clearly demonstrates that those Jews who settled in Glasgow from the 1880s may have been poor – often the poorest – but they were not bereft of skills. And perhaps this was the main difference between them and the Irish who were overwhelmingly unskilled – a vast army of mostly labourers, dockers and other waterside workers.[35]

By contrast there were many Jews who were woodworkers and metalworkers, tailors, clothes-makers, cutters, hatters and drapers, and a good many were involved in the tobacco trade. There were also various types of shopkeeper, as well as musicians and actors not to mention peddlers, hawkers, and travelling salesmen. Indeed, before 1914 many Jews in Glasgow were peddlers and travellers. This is clear in much of the testimony consulted for this research (usually secondary evidence). One respondent (born in 1897) actually started peddling while still in uniform after the First World War and made a good living from it. But as a child in the early years of the twentieth century he remembered that recently arrived immigrants were met 'by a sort of committee set up to receive them' and that they were directed into the peddling business:

> They were given a pot ... and a bag and told to go peddle. And that was all. There was no real organisation. Nobody of any real wealth in Glasgow among the Jewish people [of the Gorbals]. But they had to do something with the immigrants who were arriving.

He did note that those who had been tailors, cabinet makers, shoemakers, or jewellers – any good artisan – naturally went into those areas of employment in Glasgow. But until they got a position 'they were all peddling'.[36]

It was the same in the 1930s, although by then peddling was not an occupation generally taken up by Jews, and while things did improve for many – and radically so for some families – poverty was still a problem for the majority of Gorbals Jews. The respondent who wore the kilt of the Winetrobe tartan at school, and remembered the appalling poverty of the Gorbals, noted too that in the many and numerous small workshops and factories of the Gorbals conditions were still quite harsh during the 1930s. The poverty experienced by many at that time meant that Jewish boys and girls had to leave school at 14 in order to make their contribution to the family budget: there was to be no university career in law or medicine for them at that juncture.

Indeed, this particular respondent vividly recalled her factory days in the clothing trade, and that in the 1930s they generally only worked for six months and were laid off for the remainder of the year. They would sometimes get work on the north side of the river, and although it was some way distant – the trams run there regularly – they walked there and back in order to save the tram fare. She noted that her dad was a machinist in one of the smaller factories – owned as it happened by a step-grandfather who did not 'give any privileges away' – and that she worked with her father. Her description of the factory gives a real insight into how the garment industry operated:

> There were eight machinists. Four facing each other. One person was in charge of that, my father was in charge of that. There would be another man in charge of his eight, and another in of his ... we had two lots upstairs and six lots down stairs. ... My father was the boss ... then there was the top worker [she] ... knew how to make the whole garment. Then the rest of us did wee bits ... a sleeve, a collar or a pocket. And the top machinist put it all together!

Improvement of a sort did finally come for her family just before the Second World War when her youngest brother got a position in Weir's factory. He became an engineer 'and never suffered the bouts of unemployment associated with the clothing trade'. That last remark spoke powerfully of the precarious nature of the clothing industry and the significant underemployment suffered by those who worked in it.[37]

This study has also unearthed a whole host of occupations and some not perhaps commonly associated with the Jews or forms of Jewish culture. A penchant for promoting boxing matches (licensed and unlicensed) and a love of gambling and card playing among secular Jews – it was stressed that 'religious people' did not gamble – were other themes to emerge from this research. One respondent actually stated 'that at one time I would say that 60 per cent of the bookmakers of Glasgow were Jewish' – 'and very much illegal in those days' – and that many of their customers were Jews: 'Jewish people like to have a bet, like to gamble a little ... they like to play cards.' Indeed, this prompted community leaders to visit many a 'gambling den' to request that the owners refuse to accept further bets from certain individuals. That the bookmakers seemed to acquiesce to these requests suggests that they were fellow members of the Jewish community.[38]

There were also numerous travellers or travelling salesmen and many became quite well-off. These salesmen offered the Scots a vital service as they plied their trade all around Glasgow and the surrounding areas and into the agricultural and mining areas all across Scotland from west to east. But, importantly, they dealt with poor people directly and because they offered payment by instalment and credit were providing a vital service to a working class group who often functioned outside the cash economy. Indeed, there was one example of a salesman who traded in the Highlands of Scotland and in order to ensure the success of his business – which was selling pots and pans – he learned to speak Gaelic. But the emphasis was always on improvement and as one respondent (born 1903) put it, 'My generation ... we learned from our parents, and we learned from our own experiences, and our children benefited from these experiences. You find that with most Jewish Families'.[39]

One highly skilled metal worker, who arrived in Glasgow in 1904, worked for a while with another independent Jewish metalworker who ran his own business, but within a year he too had his own workshop. He started with six men and by the 1930s had 60 men, and by the end of the Second World War they had 500 workers. In this case this man was followed by both his sons into the family business, but both his sons also had good technical college qualifications. Before the Second World War, noted Monty Finneston, there were few Jewish people who were professional, but speaking in the early 1990s he noted that there were many Jewish doctors.[40] But according to Dr Leslie Naftalin between 100 and 150 Jews had qualified as doctors before 1939, and just after the war this quickly rose to around 200. The main difference post-1945 was that these doctors stayed in Glasgow whereas in the inter-war years they more or less left Scotland altogether.

'Jews ... Were More Integrated': Assimilation, Acculturation and Improvement

These oral testimonies therefore demonstrate that this process of improvement was well underway by the inter-war years and some Jews were already leaving the Gorbals behind after less than a generation. This is what happened to the Naftalin family. The father arrived in Glasgow from Lithuania in 1887. He left for the United Stated but returned in 1891 and was married in 1893:

> Over the next twenty-five years he had thirteen children. One died at almost infant age in an accident, but the rest of the family lived on. There were two girls and ten boys. ... I was the youngest boy. ... The remarkable thing is [we were] more or less all professional men. With that family were five doctors, one was a lawyer, one was a dentist, one was an optician, and one was a chiropodist. None of them followed him into business.[41]

Indeed, according to Monty Finneston, one reason that the Jews got on so well in Scotland so quickly was that the Scots were kinder to the Jews – not least in relation to the English:

> I know that prisons in Scotland are worse that prisons in England, I know lots of things happen in Scotland that don't happen in England. But on the whole I

think Scots are much, much better in their acceptance of other peoples and other things than the English. I think they are brought up differently. ... I think the Scots are more prepared to accept a Jewish person more readily.

But for others it was the determination of the Jewish people to assimilate – without giving up their own beliefs and culture – that was most important:

Jews ... we're more integrated, not segregated. Jews do that – they integrate themselves. My father did not speak a word of English, but he went to night school to learn English. ... It did not happen overnight. It took some time. The children of immigrants integrated immediately. We went to ordinary schools.

Assimilation came in many different ways, through music, debating societies, trades unions and political parties, and even through the Jewish Institute, where – according to one regular attendee and former convenor of the Literary Section – 'Mostly non-Jewish people came to speak – about politics, all kinds of subjects'. Indeed, the Jewish Institute had many different sections including those for drama, music and bridge, as well as football, athletic and tennis. Jewish football teams played against non-Jewish sides in a church league, and as a point of interest the aforementioned Dr Naftalin was five times Glasgow tennis champion before 1939.

Politics was another route to assimilation whether it was as socialist or members of the Independent Labour Party or the Labour Party in the inter-war years, or part of a contingent of Jews who left to fight in Spain in the 1930s. Some were fervent socialists or communist and in the Gorbals they shared this attachment with many Irish Catholic and Scottish Protestants. In such cases – whether Jewish or Christian – these political types were usually described as atheists. Many of the educated and middle class Jews also discussed their left-wing leanings. One respondent of the West End Jewish community was interested in socialism and communism when he was at Glasgow University, but he did add, '[it was the] mood of the time ... I think it would be fair to say. ... who didn't go through a socialist or a communist phase ... every student did!'

Some Jewish students did join the CP but most, he noted, supported the Labour Party and a few voted for the Conservatives. But it was less the question of Scottish party politics than the question of Zionism that divided the Jewish community politically. West End Jews in general did not actively support Zionism to anywhere near the extent of the Gorbals Jews, and in the Gorbals there were two main divisions – almost evenly split between Poalei Zion and the general Zionists: 'The community was fairly split in its attachment to Palestine.'[42]

Monty Finneston suggested that in the 1940s and 1950s the great majority of Jews continued to support the Labour Party. According to another respondent, however, by the 1960s onwards 'the majority of Jews were voting Conservative'. But as each new generation improved on the last, and more Jews moved into the professions, or developed independent businesses, so too did more move out of the Gorbals. As one respondent put it, an 'evacuation had taken place from [the] Gorbals. Indeed, with the massive redevelopment of the Gorbals in the 1960s the last vestiges of a Jewish presence in the area finally disappeared. But importantly this process of embourgeoisment had its roots in the inter-war years and within another generation the Gorbals Jews would be more or less a memory.

Such testimony is borne out through these Scottish Jewish oral histories. Jack Elias Miller, himself a medical doctor, argued that there was little anti-semitism and while there was the 'odd anti-semite' it was not overt. As previously noted, he mixed as much with non-Jews as Jews and was elected to high office within the British Medical Association (BMA) and added, 'there is nothing more satisfying ... than to be recognised by your own colleagues ... your peers'. Dr Miller had served on the Glasgow Local Medical Committee, was made a Justice of the Peace in 1962, and elected Assistant Scottish Secretary of the BMA. 'Out of the blue', in 1983, he was awarded an OBE, which he concluded 'was a nice episode in one's career'.

At its height, noted another respondent – although not himself a Gorbals Jew – the Jewish community of Glasgow numbered around 16,000 and at that juncture 90 per cent lived in the Gorbals, and added, 'This was no stigma because that was the centre of Jewish activity ... the groceries and the butchers and small bakers, small jewellers ... they were all there'. But these small family businesses disappeared altogether, he opined: 'the whole face of Glasgow [was] changing'.[43]

It was true that the Gorbals was the centre of Jewish activity – both religious and cultural – but to suggest there was no stigma is to perhaps stretch the truth a little. According to Dr Jack Elias Miller, the south side Jews regarded the West End Jews 'as being rather snobbish, rather stand-offish' and it was often said that if the daughter of a West End Jew married a Gorbals Jew she would be considered as marrying out of her class.[44] The Gorbals was clearly more working class and, as another respondent put it (born in 1933, a convert to Judaism, and unusually for the time the product of a Catholic and Protestant union), 'I suppose they [West End Jews] looked down on it, because it was very slummy'[45]

But it was clear too that when a family improved their position they moved out. Dr Naftalin suggested that the first migration occurred before the First World War – as happened with his family. When conditions allowed others followed in greater numbers in the inter-war years – as occurred with Lillian Leighton's family. But many remained behind in the Gorbals, like the respondent formerly of the Winetrobe family and the Jewish workers employed in her step-grandfather's factory, until after the Second World War. The process of moving may have started in the inter-war years and, according to another respondent, 'the community that was left in the Gorbals were poor'.[46]

By the 1960s and 1970s there were many changes taking place within the Jewish community of Glasgow. As noted earlier, one respondent, 'born within the sounds of the Gorbals bells' in 1914, referred to the Gorbals as a 'type of ghetto full of Jews'. But when he later spoke of the outward migration he noted with some sadness the fact that the 'the ghetto was breaking up ... we all grew up and went our separate ways': 'We were spreading out.'[47] By then the Gorbals was emptied of Jews, and at the same time many of the West End Jews were also moving south of the River Clyde – but much further back from the ghetto to the more salubrious suburbs of Giffnock and Newton Mearns. According to Dr Naftalin, from that time the southward migration gathered pace and by the 1980s up to 80 or 90 per cent of Glasgow's Jewish population lived there.[48]

But there was another effect of this migration south, for as the new Jewish community settled in their new homes more of the next generation were moving away – and some away from the religion. Many respondents born mostly in the first decades of the twentieth century stressed that few Jews of their generation married out, but the following generation did not hold with the same firmness to the religion or the culture. Dr Naftalin, suggested about 25–30 per cent of the children born to his generation had 'married out' – although he suggested a contrary position for his own family, noting that of his parents' '60 grandchildren' only two or three had married out.

To give one of many examples of this phenomenon contained in the oral testimonies, Dr Naftalin cited the case of a prominent Glasgow Jewish woman who became President of the non-Jewish Scottish Boys Club Association. This was a great achievement and a great honour and a further example of how far the Jewish community had come in Scotland. Indeed, she too went on to receive an OBE. But her family was totally assimilated and as a result '[t]hey disappeared. The whole family are no longer Jewish'. Another stressed that his generation 'all grew up with strict Jewish supervision ... [but] the new generation [they] are still Jewish and still strong, but their teaching is not as strong'. There was a cost to assimilation, but it clear that the great majority of those who remained in Glasgow were, as Jack Elius Miller put it, 'still conscious of their Jewishness'.

Conclusion

It was during the inter-war years that the process of improvement was beginning to impact on the Jewish community, and it is ironic indeed that it was at the same time also that the Catholic Irish community – both first and second generations – were experiencing fresh attacks in the shape of the General Assembly of the Church of Scotland, and from two Protestant Political Parties – Protestant Action in Edinburgh and the Scottish Protestant League (SPL) in Glasgow. Indeed, in the 1930s the General Assembly of the Church of Scotland, backed by these two political parties, recommended the repatriation of Irish Catholics, because they were 'a completely separate race of alien origins'.[49] And according to Patrick Reilly 'the government pondered long and hard before rejecting pleas to stop Irish Catholic immigration and to deport as many of the interlopers as possible'. Moreover, both Protestant Action and the SPL secured council seats in both Edinburgh and Glasgow in the early 1930s. Given this ideological climate is it any wonder, argued Reilly, 'that the interwar years were marred by serious sectarian conflict'.[50]

The Jewish community was not perceived as a threat, or as so big a threat, to the Protestant community in Scotland, but the Catholic community was. It is clear from the evidence drawn from this oral history testimony that when we consider the notion of displacement the Jewish experience of settlement in Glasgow was much less problematic than that of the Irish, or Scots Catholics of Irish descent, and that there was relatively less prejudice experienced by the Jews in Scotland because of the great antipathy of the host community towards Catholics. And there is some support for this theory. Aubrey Newman recently stated: 'That there was so many other antagonisms around that people didn't have much time to be anti-semitic: it is blindingly obvious.' Harvey Kaplan, Director of the Scottish Jewish Archives Centre in Glasgow, added that the theory deserved more investigation: 'You get the same feeling if you talk to the small Jewish community in Northern Ireland at the time of the *Troubles*, where they feel there were left alone.' And Dr Joe Bradley, an expert in ethnic and religious identity at the University of Stirling concurred: 'I see this argument as viable. Undoubtedly, though, the most traditional and damaging form of racism has long been anti-Irish and anti-Catholic in nature.'[51] In 1989, the *Observer* newspaper claimed that Scotland was the only country in Europe 'that had in recent, or past times, not shed Jewish blood or persecuted the Jews'.[52] And in 1999, Rabbi David Kunin, speaking of his new community of Jews at San Diego, California, noted with fondness his time in Glasgow and that 'overt anti-semitism was rare in Scotland, although there were some golf clubs which declined to accept Jewish members'. But he noted, rather mischievously, that Conservative Jews in Glasgow generally 'felt greater hostility from the orthodox Rabbis' than they did from the local non-Jewish population.[53]

This period also coincided with the publication of two important books: the first was *Out of the Ghetto* (1998), which charted the emergence of the Catholic community in Modern Scotland; the second, *Scotland's Shame* (2000), which considered bigotry and sectarianism in modern Scotland. The former hoped to more positively consider the contribution of the Catholic community on Scottish cultural and political life, and arguably achieved this end. The latter argued 'that even if anti-Catholic attitudes still flourish in modern Scotland' we had nonetheless witnessed 'a remarkable transformation' when compared to previous generations.[54] As Vassilikou's model predicted, those descendants of the Jews and Irish Catholics in Scotland had ensured 'their group survival', and their experience of life in Scotland did in time 'favour their upward social mobility'. But for the Irish it was some time coming.

NOTES

1. Noted in several oral testimonies used in this study, but refers directly to two testimonies in particular. These oral testimonies are available to the public and the tapes and transcripts are held at the Scottish Jewish Archives Centre, Garnethill Synagogue, Glasgow – the leading interviewer was Ben Braber. The people involved in this project – the interviewees or respondents – could be named, but unless they are well-known public figures their anonymity will be respected here as a matter of course and only their initials will be noted. The reference made here relates to two interviews made in 1988 and 1990 respectively by respondent SM, born in Glasgow 1905, and Dr Jack Elias Miller, born 1918, in Glasgow's West End. They were interviewed by Ben Braber (BB).
2. MG, born 1898 (Interviewed: BB – 1988).
3. This emerged from discussion following the paper presented at the Third Port Jews Conference; 'Place and Displacement in Jewish History and Memory', University of Cape Town, January 2005, and was confirmed later by Nick Evans, Research Institute of Irish and Scottish Studies, University of Aberdeen (also a participant of the 2005 conference), and Harvie Kaplan, Director of the Scottish Jewish Archives Centre, Garnethill Synagogue, Glasgow.
4. For further discussion on methodology, oral history and memory see: M. Watson, *Being English in Scotland* (Edinburgh, 2003); M. Watson, 'The Invisible Diaspora: The English in Scotland 1945–2000' (unpublished Ph.D. thesis, University of Dundee, 2003); A. Portelli, *History, Memory and Meaning of a Nazi Massacre in Rome: The Order Has Been Carried Out* (Basingstoke, 2003); D.L. Schacter, ed., *Memory Distortion: How Minds, Brains and Societies Reconstruct The Past* (Cambridge, MA, 1997); A. Thomson, M. Frisch and D. Short, 'The Memory and History Debates', *Oral History*, 22.2 (1994); and P. Thompson, *The Voice of the Past* (London: Oxford University Press, 1988).
5. William Kenefick, '"We know you are our brothers, but we wish you had not come". The Glasgow Waterfront and Irish and Jewish Relations c.1891–1914', *Port Jews and Jewish Communities in*

Cosmopolitan Maritime Trading Centres, International Conference in Association with the University of Southampton, Kaplan Centre, University of Cape Town, 5–8 January 2003.
6. Maria Vassilikou, 'Greeks and Jews in Salonika and Odessa: Inter-ethnic Relations in Cosmopolitan Port Cities', in *Port Jews: Jewish Communities in Cosmopolitan Maritime Trading Centres, 1550–1950*, ed. by David Cesarani (London and Portland, OR: Frank Cass Publishers, 2002), p.156.
7. Mrs RG in joint interview with Mrs IB, both born in Glasgow Gorbals (Interviewed: BB – 1987).
8. This is a growing area of academic interest and is borne out in an abstract for a PhD thesis by Leora Mandelson, at Tel Aviv University, under the joint supervision of Professors Haim Hazan and Shlomo Sand. The title is 'Constructing Identity and Life Course as Historical Narrative. The Story of Glasgow's Jewish Community between 1920–1950' (Accepted for supervision 29 August 2002).
9. There was a saying in Glasgow that was intended to have an individual identify their ethnic and religious affiliations and it generally went like this: 'Are you a Billy or a Dan or an Old Tin Can'. 'Billy' was a reference to King William (King Billy) of Orange a defender of the protestant Faith, and the 'Dan' referred to Irish politician Daniel O'Connell who fought for Catholic Emancipation in Britain in the nineteenth century. The 'Old Tin Can' was a reference to a Jew and is most probably derives from the stereotyping of Jews as peddlers: see also T.M. Devine, *The Scottish Nation 1700–2000* (London: Penguin, 1999), pp.518–22; and W. Kenefick, 'Jewish and Catholic Irish Relations: The Glasgow Waterfront c.1880–1914', in *Port Jews*, ed. by Cesarani (see note 6).
10. See Dermot Keogh, *Jews in Twentieth Century Ireland* (Cork: Cork University Press, 1998).
11. Hannay Frank Levy, artist and sculptor, born 1908 (Interviewed by her niece Fiona Frank – 1989).
12. RHL, born in the Gorbals, 1912 (Interviewed: BB – 1987).
13. FR, born in the Gorbals, 1922 (Interviewed: BB – 1992).
14. RS, born in the Gorbals, 1897 (Interviewed: BB – 1987).
15. JHG, born in Tradeston on the edge of the Gorbals, 1913 (Interviewed: BB – 1989).
16. Ralph Glasser ('Omnibus' edition), *Growing up in the Gorbals; Gorbals Boy at Oxford; Gorbals Voices, Siren Songs* (London: Lomand Books, 1999), p.22.
17. AF, born in Russia, 1903 (Interviewed: BB – 1989).
18. Hannay Frank Levy, second joint interview with LL (born in the Gorbals, 1912) by BB – 1989.
19. LL (see note 18) (Interviewed: BB – 1989).
20. HC, born in Leith, 1907 (Interviewed: BB – 1988).
21. JHG (see note 15).
22. Jack Elias Millar (see note 1).
23. Monty Finneston, born in Glasgow, 1912 (Interviewed: BB – 1988).
24. LF, born in the Gorbals, 1892 (Interviewed: BB – 1989).
25. Jack Elias Miller (see note 1).
26. HC (see note 20).
27. JHG (see note 15). Hutcheson School was a fee-paying school: see also AF, born in Russia, 1903 (Interviewed: BB – 1989) Hutcheson school? – 'it was one of the best then ... today it's still a very good school'.
28. RS (see note 14).
29. Hannay Frank Levy (see note 18).
30. Dr Friedl Ehrlich-Jacob (nee Ledermann), born in Bernstadt, Silezia, 1901 (Interviewed: BB – 1987).
31. Hannay Frank Levy (see note 18).
32. RHL (see note 12).
33. MG (see note 2).
34. Lilian Leighton, born in Grimsby in 1907, moved to Hull 1909, then the Gorbals via Belfast in 1918 (Interviewed 1988).
35. W. Kenefick, *Rebellious and Contrary: The Glasgow Dockers, 1853–1932* (East Linton: Tuckwell Press, 2000), see chapter five.
36. RS (see note 14); see also LF (see note 24), his father was a peddler 'all his life': 'That's what all Jewish men had to do in those days'.
37. FR, born in the Gorbals, 1922 (Interviewed: BB – 1991).
38. RS (see note 14), and AF (see note 17), and there was one note of a well-known Glasgow Jewish boxer known as Meyer Stinger who one respondent believed turned professional: RC, born in the Gorbals, 1903 (Interviewed by BB – 1988).
39. RC, born in the Gorbals, 1903 (Interviewed: BB – 1988).
40. Monty Finneston (see note 23).
41. Dr Leslie Naftalin, born in Glasgow, 1912 (Interviewed: BB – 1989).
42. Jack Elius Millar (see note 1): see also MS (born in Govan on Glasgow's South Side, 1917), active socialist, member of Poalei Zion and the Women's Movement. He actively campaigned on behalf of the Spanish Government from 1936.

43. SM (see note 1): a figure agreed by Harvie Kaplan (see note 3).
44. As noted in the 2003 paper presented by the author (see note 5).
45. MN, born 1933 – her husband was a West End Jew (Interviewed: BB – 1988).
46. RC – moved from the Gorbals in the 1930s (see note 39).
47. RHL (see note 12).
48. Dr Leslie Naftalin (see note 41).
49. W. Kenefick, 'Irish Dockers and Trade Unionism on Clydeside', *Irish Studies Review*, 19 (1997), p.24.
50. P. Reilly, 'Kicking with the Left Foot: Being Catholic in Scotland', in *Scotland's Shame? Bigotry and Sectarianism in Modern Scotland*, ed. by T.M. Devine (Edinburgh and London: Mainstream, 2000), p.32.
51. *Glasgow Herald*, 17 October 2004: a report on the symposium that took place that day at Garnethill Synagogue, *Jewish Settlement, Development and Identities in Twentieth Century Scotland*, Scottish Jewish Archives Centre, Garnethill Synagogue, in Association with the AHRB supported Research Institute for Irish and Scottish Studies, University of Aberdeen.
53. *Observer*, 12 February, 1989.
54. Donald H. Harrison, 'Come Together. Rabbi at Newly-merged Ohr Shalom Synagogue knows how to build Bridges between Cultures', *San Diego Jewish Press-Heritage*, 17 September 1999.
54. Raymond Boyle and Peter Lynch, eds., *Out of the Ghetto? The Catholic Community in Modern Scotland* (Edinburgh: John Donald, 1988); and *Scotland's Shame*, ed. by Devine (see note 50).

PART II:
RACE, PLACE AND PERIPHERY

On Burial, Boundaries and the Creolisation of the Surinamese Jewish Community

WIEKE VINK

Surinamese Jews, Creole Community

The history of the Surinamese Jews is the story of a small social group in a colonial setting that started in the mid-seventeenth century when – adherent to the then general mania of forming colonies in the New World – Jews started to migrate to Suriname on a regular basis and a Jewish community was established. Early Jewish migration to Suriname was predominantly a Sephardi affair (in Suriname referred to as Portuguese Jews). However, the number of Ashkenazi migrants (referred to as High German Jews) increased rapidly during the eighteenth century. At the turn of the eighteenth to nineteenth century, the Surinamese Jewish community counted an estimated 1,400 individuals, divided over two equally sized communities[1] At this time, the Jewish community of Suriname was among the largest of the New World – five times the size of the Jewish community of the North American mainland.[2]

In the slave economy of Suriname, Jews belonged to the upper strata of colonial whites. Up to the late nineteenth century, they made up about one-half of to one-third of the total white population in Suriname.[3] As planters and – later – colonial officials, Jews played an important role in the colonisation and further development of Suriname as a colony[4] After the notorious financial crisis at the Amsterdam stock exchange in the 1770s, many planters could not settle their debts and had to sell their loss-making properties. At the turn of the eighteenth to nineteenth century, an estimated two-thirds of the Jewish population lived in poverty. The High German Jews had always lived and worked in Paramaribo; now the Portuguese Jews deserted their plantations *en masse* and moved to Paramaribo as well. Both groups tried to make a living in Paramaribo's urban colonial environment. They found employment in (small) trade, craft and craft like professions (goldsmiths, bakers, butchers, carpenters, etc.) and administrative jobs held at the offices of plantation directors, commercial establishments and the colonial administration.

Ever since their first settlement, the migrants were faced with challenges brought about by their new environment: a slave society and a colonial order. A place, moreover, located at the margins of an expanding world. This new cultural context was daily reality to the Jews of Suriname, and forced them to react, to adapt, or at least to assume some sort of position. This colonial context, and more specifically the intersection of the Jewish and African diasporas in Suriname, resulted in specific cross-cultural elements to be incorporated in the Surinamese Jewish communities. Notwithstanding the often one-sided attention to the Sephardi communities of the New World, the development of a creole Jewish community was not limited to Suriname's Portuguese Jews. Both the histories of the Portuguese Jewish community and the High German Jewish community show a creolising cultural identification, especially from the late eighteenth century onwards.

I will use the concept of creolisation to address this process of a changing cultural context and adapting to a new place.[5] In this use of creolisation, 'localisation', i.e. the process of becoming local, is at the heart of the concept. Although generally associated with processes of cultural mixing, in the historical Caribbean context 'creole' referred to something or someone that had become localised in the New World with foreign (normally Metropolitan, but also African) origins.[6] Locally born slaves were referred to as Creoles, as well as locally born whites (so-called white Creoles). Only relatively recently has 'Creole' become a synonym for the black Afro-Caribbean population and Afro-Caribbean culture. I refer to creolisation, then, as the ongoing process of cultural change and/or a changing cultural identity in the context of a process of localisation after an experience of migration or, in a more ephemeral form, the relocation of culture itself. In this conception, creolisation does not centrally refer to cultural mixing – although it is often an important aspect of creolisation – but to the process and affects of adapting to a new environment.[7]

The Cemetery as a *lieu de memoire* and Site of Creolisation

In this essay, I will address some of the critical moments in the process of a creolising Surinamese Jewish community through a case study of the Jewish cemeteries in Suriname. Although cemeteries provide for a fairly practical necessity – the disposal of corpses – they are also places full of meaning. Not just sites for individual remembrance of lost loved ones, cemeteries are powerful monuments for collective memory as well. They are *lieux de memoire par excellence*: places where notions of collective identities are located, constructed and changed. The Jewish cemetery is indisputably an important symbol for the long and troublesome past of the Jewish people. The worldwide interest in Jewish cemeteries is enormous. Interestingly enough this interest is not focused on the burial places of active, flourishing contemporary Jewish communities, but the ones that are long gone and symbolise vanished Sephardi splendour and erased Ashkenazi cultural life.[8]

Likewise in Suriname, the historical site of Jodensavanne (Jewish Savannah, by contemporary Jews simply referred to as 'the Savannah') symbolises the Golden Age of the Portuguese Jewish plantocracy during the eighteenth century, while the ruined remnants of its synagogue epitomises the years of decline thereafter. Located at the Suriname River at ten hours' rowing from the capital city of Paramaribo, Jodensavanne was the place of early settlement of Suriname's Portuguese Jewish community. Only few people inhabited the village on a daily basis, the majority lived on their sugar plantations surrounding the small village. During the eighteenth century, Jodensavanne became the centre of Portuguese Jewish community life. It was the place where the Portuguese Jews grew up and got married; where they shared the latest gossip from Paramaribo, and where they worshipped and buried their dead. When in the late eighteenth century Suriname's sugar industry collapsed, and Portuguese Jewish planters moved away to Paramaribo, the Savannah fell into ruins and became overgrown by forest vegetation. Only during the late twentieth century did Jodensavanne gain a new function. Deeply embedded in Surinamese Jewish historiography and historical consciousness, Jodensavanne now refers to a long gone past that provides the Surinamese Jewish community with an aura of antiquity and the status of an old elite.

In this notion of a fading past, a central role is reserved for the Jewish cemeteries. The *Beth Haim* at Jodensavanne is one of the few tangible remnants of this bygone past and probably no historical figure, monument or building is a stronger symbol for Surinamese Jewish history (although the Nassy family may be considered worthy alternatives).[9] Throughout the twentieth century, several efforts have been made to clear the site of Jodensavanne from its luxuriant overgrowth, but mostly to no avail. The isolated location, the persistent tropical vegetation, and the civil war of the 1980s have undone all previous attempts to renovate the burial grounds. It was not until the late 1990s when, with renewed interest, local enthusiasts and academic researchers discovered the importance of the Surinamese Jewish cemeteries as a source of genealogical information and came to appreciate it as a historical site of great symbolic value. In the year 2000, Jodensavanne was added to the list of 100 most endangered sites by World Monument Watch. Once again, the site was restored and this time also made accessible for visiting tourists. The cemeteries of Jodensavanne were carefully cleaned, tombstones deciphered and listed, and cemetery maps were drawn. Today an excursion to the site of Jodensavanne has become a standard item of any organised tourist trip to Suriname, for both Jewish and non-Jewish tourists alike. Jodensavanne has clearly exceeded its symbolic function for a purely *Jewish* historical memory; the site is now firmly embedded in Suriname's national cultural heritage as well.

Notwithstanding the importance of the cemetery as a place of historical memory, the (Jewish) cemeteries are neither simply nor solely a *lieu de memoire*: the different styles of tombstones and grave markers are also the silent witnesses of a community changing throughout history. During my fieldwork in the archives of the Portuguese Jewish and High German Jewish communities of Suriname and the Dutch colonial archives, I came across several accounts and fundamental conflicts related to burial rites, gravestones, and cemetery space. These discussions reflect the changing notions of Surinamese Jewishness or, at the very least, can be read as a contemporary critique of the dominant conceptions of Surinamese Jewish identity at a certain moment in time. The demarcation between Portuguese and High German Jews, *Congregants* [community members with only limited rights] and *Yachidim* [fully fledged community members], white and coloured Jews, and Jews and non-Jews was constantly performed anew at each burial. Differences were made tangible by gravestones, fences and the location of burial plots.

Seen in this light, the cemetery is not just an icon of a long gone past, but a microcosm of changing and conflicting identifications within the Surinamese Jewish community during the process of localising to the Surinamese environment; in other words, a site of Surinamese Jewish creolisation. In the rest of this essay, I will focus on the shifting position of the coloured Jews in the Surinamese Jewish community as displayed at the cemetery and in cemetery-related stories. First, I will make a short tour along Suriname's Jewish cemeteries. In particular the rise of a specific form of creole sepulchral art at the Jewish cemeteries during the nineteenth century is in line with the argument put forward in this essay. Some of the questions triggered by the cemeteries can be addressed by taking a closer look at the various conflicts related to cemetery space. In the second section of this paper, I will focus on practices of inclusion and exclusion of coloured Jews at the cemetery as displayed in various archived documents.

A Cemetery Tour

Several Jewish cemeteries exist in Suriname. Most are no longer in use and have been transformed into historical sites and tourist sites as well. Three Portuguese Jewish cemeteries are located in or around Jodensavanne; the other cemeteries, including the High German cemeteries, are located in Paramaribo. Two of the gravesites found at, or near, Jodensavanne (the old cemetery near Cassipora Creek and the *Beth Haim* at Jodensavanne) date back to the mid-seventeenth and late seventeenth century, when a Portuguese Jewish community was established in Suriname.[10] In appearance, both the Cassipora gravesite and the *Beth Haim* at Jodensavanne resemble the Jewish burial grounds of the Amsterdam mother community in Ouderkerk aan de Amstel or the sister community at Curacao. Characteristic to these cemeteries are the horizontal graves made from various types of limestone and marble. Some stones are decorated with detailed ornamental engravings, as was customary for seventeenth century Jewish tombstones; the priestly hands of the *Cohen*, the knife of the *Mohel* [ritual circumciser], a cut-down tree symbolizing a life taken before its time, and so forth.[11]

A recent cleaning operation in the cemeteries at Jodensavanne and Cassipora and deciphering of the tombstones (led by architect Rachel Frankel and historian Aviva Ben-Hur) have brought to light some interesting epitaphs that reveal the harsh reality of daily life on the sugar plantations of Jodensavanne. Consider the epitaphs of David Rodrigues Monsanto and Emmanuel Pereyra. Both boys were killed during a *maroon* [escaped slaves] attack. The words on their tombstones express feelings of pain and hatred, and reflect the hazards of those living on the frontier of the slave economy of eighteenth century Suriname. The epitaph (in Portuguese) of David Rodrigues Monsanto reads:[12]

> O Lord God, to whom vengeance belongs; O God, to
> whom vengeance belongs, shine forth!
>
> Tombstone Of the Curtailed
> Young Man David Rodrigues Monsante
> Who Was Killed By the Cruel Uprising Negroes
> On 29 Av the Year 5499 Which Corresponds
> To 4 September the Year 1739
> May His Blood be Avenged

Perhaps the most famous tombstone belongs to David Cohen Nassy, descendant of the famous colonist David de Isaac Cohen Nassy (1615–85), who was the 'founding father' of the Portuguese Jewish community in Suriname. His epitaph is a testimony of his Surinamese Jewish legacy: a mixing of traditional Jewish elements and references to that historically burdened but essential part of colonial Surinamese Jewish history which is slavery. The epitaph (in Hebrew) reads:

> And David rested with his ancestor
> [engraving of priestly hands]
> Tombstone of the burial place of the venerable
> Elderly man, the exalted lord,
> Man of valor, man of many deeds,
> The officer David, son of Jacob
> HaCohen Nassy, whom God took
> with a good name to his world after he returned
> from beating the black slaves on
> the 19th of the month of Kislev [etc.]

These epitaphs are powerful examples of grave markers as silent witnesses of a community's historical experience. The epitaphs tell the story of a colonial Jewish community whose daily life was deeply affected by colonial power relations. Throughout the eighteenth century organised raids by escaped slaves (called maroons) posed a serious threat to Jodensavanne and its surrounding plantations. A Jewish militia was raised to protect Jodensavanne against these attacks. Maroon attacks were often followed by maroon hunting expeditions to avenge the losses. As a captain of the Jewish militia, David Cohen Nassy was notorious for his activities in these expeditions. He died in 1743, at the age of 67.[13]

A third cemetery found at Jodensavanne is the so-called Creole cemetery, which is somewhat of a mystery. For a long time it has been assumed to be a slave cemetery, until recently Rachel Frankel challenged this idea. Frankel argues that the cemetery's early burials are most likely the graves of the free offspring of Portuguese Jewish fathers and African mothers who were not accepted as Jews because their mothers were not Jewish.[14] This assumption might appear logical, especially in the perspective of today's dominancy of *halakhic* notions of Jewish identity, but does not apply to seventeenth and eighteenth century Suriname. Actually, there are numerous examples of children of mixed relationships between Jewish males and female slaves or free coloured women, who became members of the Jewish community even though their mothers were clearly not Jewish. It appears that the *halakhic* factor was not as decisive in determining Jewish identity in seventeenth and eighteenth century Suriname as it would become later. These Jewish mulattoes, as they were called, were buried within the cemetery space of the *Beth Haim* in both the Portuguese and High German Jewish communities, albeit on separate lines designated for the burial of *Congregants*. I will return to this issue later.

Still, the precise status of the Creole cemetery is an intriguing issue. The more recent graves (late nineteenth to mid-twentieth century) with stone tablets and Christian symbols suggest its prolonged use by people living in the neighbourhood long after Jodensavanne had been deserted by the Portuguese Jews. Although there is no evidence that this cemetery was already in use during the eighteenth century, when Jodensavanne still functioned as the centre of Portuguese Jewish community life, the idea of the early Creole cemetery as some sort of mixed Jewish–Afro-Surinamese graveyard is a tempting one. As a matter of fact, the High German community archives mention the existence of a category of Jewish mulattoes 'belonging to *Yachidim*': presumably slaves who – because of their slave status – could not officially become members of the religious community. Yet the High German community did reserve burial spaces at the *Beth Haim* for this group.¹⁵ This may indicate that even though they did not belong to the religious community, they somehow were considered to be part of a socially defined Jewish community. If the High German community did recognize such a group, how far-fetched is it to suppose that the Portuguese Jewish community also assigned burial plots to Jewish mulattoes 'belonging to *Yachidim*'? It may be that the Creole cemetery served this function. This would at least explain the location of the Creole burial site near the *Beth Haim* and the synagogue.¹⁶

Unless some new archival documents are found, the exact use and function of this Creole graveyard will probably remain speculative. For now, I would like to point at the particular style of grave markers found at the Creole cemetery. Immediately eye-catching are the vertical grave markers that are scattered around the burial site: wood carved sticks with round or heart shaped tops. Similar wooden grave markers can be found at several plantation cemeteries in Suriname. Rachel Frankel believes these heart shapes are sankofa symbols, used by the Akan people of West Africa (nowadays Ghana and Ivory Coast: a region that accounts for a large part of the slave trade to Suriname during the eighteenth century).¹⁷ Sankofa (which symbolises the importance of learning from the past; to connect between past, present and future, between ancestors and the living) has now become an often used symbol in the cultivation of African diasporic consciousness. Frankel's view poses some problems though. The import of slaves from Africa to Suriname was not characterised by one dominant group or culture, but by a mix of Africans from various regions. Various studies of creolisation in Suriname have shown that the process of creolisation is too complicated to assume a self-evident connection between numerical dominance and influence on the making of Afro-Surinamese culture. Moreover, the wooden sticks also resemble wooden headboards found on nineteenth century African-American graveyards in North Carolina. As indicated by M. Ruth Little, many wooden markers on African-American graveyards that date from nineteenth century are characterised by gently curving tops: rounded, squared off, or diamond shaped. M. Ruth Little believes these forms to be a mimicry of the bold curves of Baroque headstones popular in the late 1700s and early 1800s.¹⁸

Let us now turn to Paramaribo, place of residence of the Surinamese Jews from the late eighteenth century onwards. Paramaribo houses several Jewish cemeteries. The old High German and Portuguese Jewish graveyards – separated only by a small path – were brought into use around 1700. Halfway into the nineteenth century, new cemeteries were opened (in 1836 and 1869), and the old graveyards were slowly forgotten despite the fact that they were merely 100 metres down the road. Both cemeteries offer the visitor a fascinating view of changing Surinamese Jewish sepulchral culture. Horizontal bluestone tablets supported by small brick walls dominate the site. This was the predominant style of burial by the colonial elites in Suriname during the eighteenth and nineteenth centuries (Jews and non-Jews alike).

Gone are the rich engravings that are so typical of the Jodensavanne and Cassipora cemeteries, though some of the stones are adorned with modest engravings. The majority of the tablets are however rather sober epitaphs: the name of the deceased, dates of birth and death, sometimes accompanied by identifiable Jewish symbols, such as a *Magen David* [Star of David] or a *Menorah* [a seven-branched candelabrum]. Some epitaphs are written in Hebrew, the majority however are written in Dutch. Many of the tombstones found at the new Portuguese and High German cemeteries resemble the tombstones of 'De Oranjetuin' – a Christian elite cemetery where the governors, their families and the very rich were interred – and lack a clear Jewish signature. The tombstones and grave markers are still changing, adapting to new trends in burial practices. Striking is the appearance of tiled horizontal tombs (in white or pale blue) at both cemeteries. Nowadays, this type of tombstone is very popular among the (Afro-)Surinamese population and can be commonly found at cemeteries in Suriname, but is rather distinctive from traditional Jewish tombstones.

Surprisingly, the wooden creole grave markers with heart shaped heads reappear at both the new Portuguese and the new High German Jewish cemetery in Paramaribo. Criss-crossed between the tombs, vertical wooden stakes indicate the existence of many more graves; some have fallen over and lie down, hidden between the grass-covered soil. These wooden grave markers are identical to the grave markers found on the Creole cemetery. The stakes have the same form and height, and are headed with a heart symbol. Similar wooden grave markers also appear on (non-Jewish) graveyards like 'Oud Linah's Rust', a cemetery for the poor, and – to a lesser extent – the 'Oranjetuin'. There is one important aberration however: to underline the Jewish identity of the interred, many wooden grave makers have a large Star of David attached to the stake. Surrounded by traditional Jewish tombstones, their meaning alters and intensifies. The incorporation of Afro-Surinamese sepulchral culture in Jewish cemeteries is unique and presents a strong example of creolised Jewish grave culture. Perhaps the most eye-catching example

FIGURE 1
JODENSAVANNE CREOLE CEMETERY

of a creolised tomb can be found in the Portuguese cemetery: two graves with wooden grave markers and heart shaped heads at the top end of the tombs accompany two horizontal tiled tombs, while the Star of David is replaced by a heart symbol. These graves are unmistakably creole. Only their location in a Jewish cemetery provides these graves with a Jewish identity.

How should we interpret this use of creole grave markers at the Surinamese Jewish cemeteries? Are these grave markers an expression of a creolised Surinamese Jewish consciousness? Did relatives of the deceased place these grave markers, thereby creating a cultural boundary within the apparent homogenous space of the Jewish cemetery? Or is the appearance of creole grave markers at the Portuguese and High German Jewish cemeteries not so much the result of identity politics, but rather the outcome of economic and institutional constraints? Tombstones were placed a year after the burial had taken place. During the first year, graves were marked by a wooden stick alone. Surinamese Jews who could not afford a bluestone tomb for their deceased family members (or who simply had lost interest) may never have replaced the wooden grave marker after the first year of death. What remains then is the specific Afro-Surinamese form of the wooden grave markers: a style that appears on many nineteenth century cemeteries in Suriname. The curved wooden grave markers with round or heart shaped heads had become the dominant form of wooden grave marker in Suriname during the nineteenth century. Whatever their origin (West African symbols, a mimicry of Baroque curved headstones or some sort of mixture), the wooden grave markers present a strong example of creolisation in the Jewish cemeteries.

Here, the problems of a historical analysis of creolisation surface. Processes of creolisation suppose the existence of creolised culture. Yet phenomena of creolised culture reveal little to nothing on how these processes take place. As a consequence, enigmas will last and a good fare of speculation is inevitable. However, creolisation can be found in the archives as well. Although I did not find the story behind the creole grave markers in the archives, I came across various other cemetery stories that represent changing claims and contestations of Surinamese Jewish identity. The use of the cemetery as a boundary-making space in communal identity politics has been an ongoing story since the day of first settlement and provoked conflicts accordingly. Throughout the history of the Surinamese Jewish community, three 'border disputes' prevail: between so-called mulatto (coloured) Jews and white Jews, between Portuguese and High German Jews, and between Jews and non-Jews. Precisely these issues dominate in the cemetery stories. In the following section, I will focus on practices of inclusion and exclusion of coloured Jews, especially at the cemetery and in cemetery-related stories.

Burials and Boundaries: The Case of the Coloured Jews

The first coloured Jews (or mulattoes as they were called) were the offspring of colonial master–slave relationships. Although officially forbidden, sexual relationships between white men and slave women were widespread and commonly accepted in Suriname. Sometimes these sexual encounters led to more lasting relationships between Jewish men and African women. Although some of the

THE CREOLISATION OF THE SURINAMESE JEWISH COMMUNITY

FIGURE 2
HIGH GERMAN CEMETERY

resulting children will certainly have been left to their fate, there are stories of Jewish men who took some responsibility for their concubines and their illegitimate offspring. Some were given freedom; others received Jewish names and upbringings and found their way to the religious community of the Portuguese and the High German Jews. It is known that in the early colonial period some of the mulatto Jews were accepted as full members of the community and behaved accordingly. This changed halfway through the eighteenth century when the coloured Jews lost their rights as *Yachidim* and were listed as *Congregants* (it is important to note that the group of *Congregants* did not comprise a static category. At the late eighteenth century, white men who married coloured women or those marrying the 'other' community – High German or Portuguese – lost their status as *Yachid* and were listed as *Congregant* as well).[19]

The creation of inner-group boundaries in the mid-eighteenth centuries between white *Yachidim* and coloured *Congregants* went hand in hand with a continued admittance of coloured Jews to the community. During the closing decades of the eighteenth century a constant flow of requests reached the community elders to admit 'the free mulatto ...', or 'the slave bought for freedom ...' as *Congregants* to the community. Interestingly enough, all requests were agreed and the absence of a Jewish mother was never put forward as an obstacle to becoming part of the Jewish community in either case. The only requirement for admission was a basic tuition in Jewish law and customs. Slowly but surely the group of mulatto Jews grew up to about 100 admitted *Congregants*.[20] The

Mahamad of both the Portuguese Jewish and High German Jewish communities reacted to this 'colouring' of the community by sharpening the rules of community participation and erecting inner-group boundaries. The result was a remarkable combination of inclusion, exclusion and intermingling.

At the dawn of the eighteenth century the coloured Jews assumed an in-between position in the Surinamese Jewish community. The continued incorporation of the mulatto Jews in the Surinamese Jewish communities, albeit as *Congregants*, went hand in hand with the increased tendency to fence them out at the dawn of the eighteenth century. Little by little, the *Congregants* were driven to the margins of the community: in the synagogue they were denied all sorts of ritual rights and they had to sit on the benches for abelim [mourners]. Especially the instances of death and burial became decisive moments of exclusion: special rows were designated for their burial (the swampy and unwanted areas at the burial grounds) and they were only entitled to simple funerals, without the decorum reserved for the community elite. Coloured Jews were denied the right to burn wax candles during the funeral procession, nor were they entitled to an *ascaba* [soul-prayer].[21]

On 26 November 1775, the *Gabay* [treasurer] of the *Hebra Gesed* [the burial society] of the High German community turned to the *Mahamad*, uncertain how to act in the case of the death of a *Congregant* within the community 'amongst whom several mulattos and mulatresses'. Would he be obliged to bury them on the *Beth Haim*? The *Mahamad* responded quickly, and decided that: 'in the case of death, admitted *Congregants* are to be buried on a, for that purpose, designated area at the *Beth Haim*'. In the case of a burial request of non-admitted persons, the *Hebra* was ordered to consult the *Mahamad* before taking any further action.[22] The letter of the *Gabay* of the burial society concerning the separate burial plots for 'mulattos and mulatresses' indicates an ambiguous position of coloured Jews in the Suriname. The uncertain status of the mulatto Jews is fully displayed by a decree of the High German community of 5 November 1780, which states:

> It has been resolved that henceforth a Yachid, who requests for one or more of his children to be admitted as Congregants to the community, will have to verbally avow to the Mahamad that he is the father of those children. In addition [the petitioner] has to present letters of manumission (freedom) of the Court of Police of Suriname for the aspirant Congregant. ...
>
> Furthermore, it is has been resolved that in case of death, a Judeo Mulat or Mulatress belonging to one of our Yachidim and not being a Congregant, shall not be buried among the Congregants; a separate row will be laid on at the Beth Haim for that purpose. Neither will their funeral be accompanied by Lewaje [funeral procession] only the Sjamas [Sexton] of the Hebra will accompany the mourners to appoint a burial plot.[23]

And in a resolution of 6 April 1788:

> [At the cemetery] an area has been designated for the burial of Mulatto Congregants as well as other Jewish mulattoes. ... For that purpose, a list has been presented to the board of the Hebra with the names of admitted mulatto Congregants, and other Jewish mulatto belonging to our community.[24]

FIGURE 3
PORTUGUESE CEMETERY

Although a community law against a certain practice does not necessarily imply its frequent occurrence *per se*, the explicit reference to the inclusion of illegitimate mulatto children does indicate the social acceptance of the widespread practice of concubinage and its institutionalisation in the community laws. Further, the reference to 'a Judeo Mulat or Mulatress belonging to one of our Yachidim and not being a Congregant', in the resolutions of both 1780 and 1788, reveals another category in the Surinamese Jewish community. Apart from the white *Yachidim* and the free coloured *Congregants*, the High German community presumably included a (small) number of enslaved of mixed Afro-Jewish descent. Because of their slave status they could not become members of the religious congregation. That, nonetheless, these enslaved were considered to be part of a socially defined community is indicated by their burial at the community's *Beth Haim*. Whereas coloureds – apparently even enslaved – could participate in the social Jewish community, the religious community boundaries were far more rigid: only manumitted (freed) slaves could become members. However, during the nineteenth century, the expanding practice of manumission and a new manumission regulation brought about a number of cases in which slaves were actually admitted to the community. I will come back to this later.

It has been argued that coloured Jews were not accepted as full members because they lacked a Jewish mother.[25] In my opinion, this idea is flawed. As a matter of fact, I have not found any evidence that supports the idea that eventually *halakhic* law determined who could or could not become a member of the religious community – at least not until the second half of the nineteenth century. Up until then, all community laws and bylaws point at the colour of skin and a slave of free status as the boundary-making attributes. Thus, from the mid-eighteenth to midnineteenth century both the motivation and language of distinction between coloured and white Jews was racial rather than *halakhic*. This might be remarkable from a Jewish point of view, but makes perfect sense when following a Surinamese line of reasoning. After all, the entire Surinamese slave society was based on and legitimised by colour lines and characterised by all sort of complex social relationships. This prevalence of colour over halakhic law in the determination of community boundaries is a strong sign of the creolisation of the Surinamese Jewish community in this period.

The underlying tensions in the relation between the coloured Jews and the white Surinamese Jewish community (in this case represented by the *Mahamad* of the Portuguese Jewish community) are revealed to their full extent by the history of the *Darhe Jessarim* and the tumultuous burial of Joseph de David Cohen Nassy in April 1790.[26] The *Darhe Jessarim*, also referred to as 'Siva' (from *yeshiva*) was established in 1759 with the help and support of both the Portuguese and High German community. Various scholars have recounted the history of the *Darhe Jessarim*. These writings have contributed to the idea of a separate synagogue or prayer house for the coloured Jews located at the *Sivaplein* in Paramaribo that existed for several decades. Yet there is no evidence that the *Darhe Jessarim* ever functioned as a separate congregation or synagogue for coloured Jews. According to the archived documents pertaining to the *Darhe Jessarim*, the fraternity was not a separate congregation, but a *yeshiva* for both coloured Jews and *Blank Jooden* [white Jews] who choose to join them. Purpose of the fraternity was the *oogmerk tot stichten* [aim to edify] rather than worship.[27] At first, the meetings of the *Darhe Jessarim* were organised in the house of one of the members, later a small house was built on the ground belonging to one of the members of the fraternity.[28] The Portuguese regents not only accepted the existence of the *yeshiva*, but actively supported the fraternity as well.

In spring 1790 the relationship between the mulatto Jews and the Portuguese *Mahamad* grew tense. The mulatto Jews felt that their status and privileges in the religious community were increasingly restricted by the *Mahamad*, who in their turn were sensitive to any infringement of their authority. The conflict between the mulatto Jews and the *Mahamad* fully escalated after the burial of Joseph de David Cohen Nassy on 18 April 1790. Joseph de David Cohen Nassy was a coloured Jew. As a *Congregant* of the community it was beyond discussion that Nassy was entitled to a burial plot on the *Beth Haim*. However, what did cause a flaming row were the burial rituals and the exact location of Nassy's grave. In the eyes of the *Mahamad*, Joseph Nassy was a *Congregant* and as such entitled to a funeral appropriate for the status of *Congregant*. However, the Jewish mulattoes regarded him as a leading member of their society, and organised a funeral with all the rituals and decorum of a regent's funeral. The *Mahamad* was infuriated about such a display of disrespect to the community rules and the members of the *Mahamad*. The incident was viewed as a direct assault on their position as regents of the community. The mulatto Jews on the other hand, were enraged by the burial plot assigned to their leader by the overseer of the cemetery. The muddy and shallow slough on the edge of the cemetery in which Nassy was to be buried – 'a swamp and only one foot deep' – was clearly not a place for the grave of a deceased chairman of the fraternity![29]

In the course of events, the conflict over the funeral of Joseph de David Cohen Nassy turned out to be a dispute over authority, rule and community boundaries. After Nassy's controversial funeral, the *Mahamad* concluded that the coloured Jews were too self-willed and independent of the *Mahamad*'s rule. The Jewish mulattoes on their part conceived this position of the *Mahamad* as a blatant denial of their rights. It was only then that the coloured Jews, led by Robijn Mendes Meza and Ismael de Britto, addressed themselves to the *Mahamad* and requested to organise and run their fraternity, not as a *yeshiva*, but as a separate congregation under the protection of the Portuguese Jewish community. The latter was very important for the coloured Jews, since it implied that they would still be entitled to poor relief from the Portuguese community, burial at the *Beth Haim*, and other rights reserved to community members.

When the *Mahamad* refused to comply with this request to condone such an independent fraternity, the coloured Jews turned to the colonial administration to support their cause. They accused the *Mahamad* of discrimination and requested the Governor to acknowledge their fraternity. Not surprisingly, the *Mahamad* reacted fiercely. In a long and biting exposé, they stated that the 'agreement with the request of the mulatto Jews would jeopardize the colony's peace and result in a society wherein anyone could circumvent the law'. The law should be enforced, and as the authorized board of the Jewish community, the *Mahamad* was responsible for the observance of the law by the community members. While the argument of the *Mahamad* is based on a call for law enforcement at face value, the primary underlying motive was clearly to uphold the colonial ideas over colour and social status. In their memorandum to the Governor, the Portuguese regents referred to the burial of Joseph de David Cohen Nassy with deep concern with any implication that 'a manumitted Negro would be equal to a White'.[30] In the end, the Governor agreed with the arguments put forward by the *Mahamad* and the mulatto Jews were ordered to submit to the authority and rule of 'the Regents and Deputies of the Portuguese Jewish nation'. As such the *Darhe Jessarim* was officially disbanded in 1794.

Although the coloured Jews drew the short straw in the conflict over the *Darhe Jessarim*, the legitimacy of racial distinction had undeniably lost ground. The fact that these coloured Jews dared to challenge the white Portuguese Jewish elite indicates a changing status quo, not only in the Jewish community, but also abroad. At the turning point of the eighteenth to the nineteenth century, the Surinamese society was no longer that dichotomised society of the early colonial years. Instead Suriname's social realm had become highly creolised. Colour lines had blurred and mixing and mingling had become common practice in Suriname. Likewise, the Surinamese Jewish community was changing and would continue to change. The many mixed relationships (sometimes marriages) between Jewish men and Afro-Surinamese women and the increase in the number of requests by mulattoes to be admitted to the community changed the community from the inside.[31] Eventually the *Mahamad* realised that a continued practice of racial differentiation would only result in numerous new conflicts that would disrupt the community.

The first step towards removing the colour line in the Surinamese Jewish community and thus the full incorporation of the mulatto Jews in the religious community was – again – related to the cemetery. In 1802, the *Mahamad* of the Portuguese community decided to abolish all differences in burial rites between *Yachidim* and *Congregants*.[32] In August 1838, it was officially decided that *Congregants* were no longer to be buried in separate cemetery space at the *Beth Haim*.[33] This decree was reconfirmed in May 1841. Burial in separate places was no longer permitted, since the appointment of less honourable burial plots to community members who in one way or the other were not considered full members of 'real' Jews, would bring along this unwanted distinction between community members. This emancipation of *Congregants* in the cemetery was extended to the membership of the religious community at large. In the same month, the chairman of the High German community deliberated 'if it would not be more in accordance with the spirit of times of the present age, to dissolve this distinction [between Israelites not born from white parents and other members] and grant equal rights to the admitted *Congregants*'.[34] The Church Council agreed and a letter was sent to the Governor General to obtain his approval – which he granted on 17 May 1841.[35] With this resolution there comes an end to the documented history of the coloured Jews. After more than half a century of recurring conflicts over the coloured Jews, the archives suddenly fall silent.

Does this mean that colour ceased to be major issue in community affairs from the mid-nineteenth century onwards, or that anybody, black or white, could join the Surinamese Jewish community? Not exactly: when colour lost its function as a boundary-making practise, new boundaries were erected and other exclusionary practices became dominant. New rules were drawn regarding 'the admittance of persons who belong to the rank of slaves'. Slaves could be admitted as members of the community under the condition that they would receive freedom within a fixed period of six months and after the payment of a sum of 300 guilders to the community. The new regulations were first drawn by the Portuguese Jewish community on 11 March 1841, but applied to both communities.[36] Interestingly, in a letter to the Governor the High German community elders wrote: 'since the community does not have a separate cemetery for free persons and slaves, conflicts have arisen concerning the burial of slaves. To end these clashes the Church Council has decided to expedite the obtaining of manumission'.[37] These slave regulations were relatively short-lived. The end of slavery in Suriname in 1863 automatically ushered in the end of a religious community based on slave or free (rather than colour-based) status. Instead, *halakhic* law – especially the importance of a Jewish mother – would become more decisive in defining the religious community of the Surinamese Jews. Consequently, the cemetery space became a site for demarcating the differences between Jewishness and non-Jewishness from the late nineteenth century onwards.

Conclusion

From a historical point of view, the interests of the Jewish cemetery are manifold. The Jewish cemeteries of Suriname, and especially the site of Jodensavanne, have become the pillars of Surinamese Jewish historical memory, echoing the story of the wealthy (and white) Portuguese Jew. Yet there is more in Surinamese Jewish history and Surinamese Jewish cemeteries than this cramped narrative of colonial pride and lost glory. Apart from their function as *lieux de memoire*, places of sepulchral arts and sources for genealogical information; the Jewish cemeteries of Suriname can be used as a cultural doorway for understanding some of the underexposed aspects of Surinamese Jewish history. The transforming tombstones and wooden grave markers that dot the burial grounds of the High German and Portuguese Jewish communities in Paramaribo are a clear indication of a localising and creolising Surinamese Jewish community. Likewise, the diverse discussions and conflicts surrounding death and burial mirror a history of changing cultural identifications among the Surinamese Jews. Stories of cemetery conflicts show the importance of the cemetery as one of the spaces where ideas of bounded groupness are created and contested. Especially in the context of diaspora communities, the cemetery space offers an opportunity for drawing social boundaries and territorial demarcations against other groups. This places the Jewish cemeteries and cemetery related issues at the heart of a historical study of creolising and diasporic identifications among the Surinamese Jews.

NOTES

Research for this paper was supported by the Faculty of History and Arts of the Erasmus University Rotterdam and a travel grant by NWO (Netherlands Organisation for Scientific Research).

1. During the early years of settlement, the Portuguese Jewish community had been the sole Jewish representative in the colony. High German Jews who settled in Paramaribo were automatically incorporated into the Portuguese community. They attended the synagogue services in Jodensavanne or visited the house of prayer in Paramaribo, and were submitted to the will of the Portuguese Mahamad at Jodensavanne. However, with the number of High German Jews growing, the tension between both groups increased. In 1735, the separation between the two communities became a fact. Dutch National Archives (NA), 1.05.04.02:256, folios 50–65. The twentieth century saw a dramatic reduction of the number of Surinamese Jews, especially after the Second World War when many chose to migrate to the Netherlands, the United States or in some cases to Israel. In 1999, the Portuguese and High German community merged into the 'Israelitische Gemeente Suriname'. In an effort to preserve the community, the Surinamese Jews transformed from orthodox to liberal in 2004. Today the community counts 150 registered members, of whom only a few dozen visit the synagogue at a regular base.
2. Robert P. Swierenga, *The Forerunners: Dutch Jewry in the North American Diaspora* (Detroit: Wayne State University Press, 1994).
3. For an estimation of Suriname's white population see Maarten Schalkwijk, *Colonial State-Formation in Caribbean Plantation Societies. Structural Analysis and Changing Elite Networks in Suriname, 1650–1920* (Ithaca, NY: Desktop Publication, 1994), p.73.
4. Numbers based on the geographical maps of Suriname of 1737 and 1770 by Alexander de Laveaux.
5. I prefer the use of creolisation over the concept of assimilation, commonly used in Jewish Studies, for several reasons; first, because of the centrality of 'place' and 'migration' in the concept of creolisation. Second, in contrast to assimilation, creolisation does not imply a minority group that adjusts to a dominant group or culture. This is especially relevant in a Caribbean colonial context with its unequal power relations and the absence of a dominant culture. Third, assimilation (in a Jewish context) seems to imply a process of secularisation. The assimilated Jew is counterposed to the religious Jew.

Creolisation does not have this secular connotation. It is *not* about giving up a religious Jewish identity, but refers to dropping or moulding elements of it, and incorporating new ones.

6. I will use 'Creole', with the upper-case spelling, to refer to individual or group ethnic identification, while the term 'creole', with the lower-case spelling, refers to anything related to the process of creolisation (creole identities, creole grave markers, creole culture, etc.).
7. My understanding of creolisation as a process of localisation links up with the ideas of a growing group of scholars who argue that the concept of creolisation has limited analytical value when applied to general, global conditions. According to Karen Fog Olwig, the concept only takes on meaning when examined within a specific socio-cultural – hence local – context. Personal communication during 'Workshop on Globalisation and Creolization in World History' (Rotterdam, 2002).
8. See, for instance, the International Jewish Cemetery Project with its list of burial sites, and the Online Worldwide Burial Registry database: http://www.jewishgen.org/cemetery, 9 June 2004.
9. The Nassy family played an important role in the forging and development of the (Portuguese) Jewish community in Suriname. While colonist David Cohen Nassy initiated the establishment of a Jewish community with his organised group migration in the 1650s, his sons Samuel Cohen Nassy (who donated several acres of ground at Jodensavanne for the building of communal institutions) and Joseph Cohen Nassy were notorious for their expeditions against maroons. A century later, another David Cohen Nassy was a leading member of the community, and co-authored *Essai Historique sur la colonie de Surinam, sa foundation, ses révolutions, ses progress, depuis son origine jusqu'à nos jours; avec l'histoire de la nation juive portugaise et allemande y établie, leurs privilèges* (Paramaribo, 1788), which remained the standard work of Surinamese Jewish history for nearly two centuries. For the English translation, see Jacob R. Marcus and Stanley F. Chyet, eds., *Historical Essay on the Colony of Surinam, 1788* (Cincinnati, New York: KTAV Publishing House, 1974).
10. Strictly speaking, Jodensavanne does not include the Cassipora site. Both sites are, however, located in close proximity, only a few miles apart.
11. For a study of iconography of tombstones in the Surinamese Jewish cemeteries, see A. Ben-Ur, 'Still Life: Sephardi, Ashkenazi, and West African Art and Form in Suriname's Jewish cemeteries', *American Jewish History*, 92.1 (March 2004), 31–79. Also compare Lou A. Vega, *Het Beth Haim van Ouderkerk. Beelden van een Portugees-Joodse begraafplaats* [The Beth Haim of Ouderkerk aan de Amstel. Images of a Portuguese Jewish Cemetery in Holland] (Amsterdam: Van Gorcum, 1975); and Rochelle Weinstein, 'Sepulchral Monuments of the Jews in Amsterdam in the Seventeenth and Eighteenth Centuries' (Ph.D. thesis, New York University, 1979). For a study of sepulchral art in Jewish cemeteries, see Arnold Schwartzman, *Graven Images: Graphic Motifs of the Jewish Gravestone* (New York: Harry N. Abrams, Inc. 1993).
12. All epitaph readings and translations are derived from Aviva Ben-Ur and Rachel Frankel, *Remnant Stones: The Jewish Cemeteries of Suriname, South America. Reading Life through Death* (Cincinnati, OH: Hebrew Union College Press, 2005). Also http://people.umass.edu/juda390d/info/epitaphs.html, 29 April 2005.
13. David Nassy and M. P. de Leon, *Historical Essay on the Colony of Surinam 1788* [originally published as *Essai historique sur la clonie de Surinam, 1788* atc., ed. by Jacob R. Marcus and Stanley F. Chyet], pp. 65–9.
14. R. Frankel, 'A Fruitful Expedition to Jodensavanne', *Kulanu*, 6.1 (1999), p.3.
15. Neve Shalom Archives, Eskamoth 1734–1821, 5 November 1780.
16. The Creole cemetery poses some additional problems though. Take the simple fact that this cemetery is still recognizable as a burial place. Grave markers of slave graves – if marked at all – were made of wood. Normally, they would not have withstood the ravages of time especially considering Surinam's extreme tropical climate. The fact that this burial ground is still dotted with wooden grave markers makes an early colonial dating implausible.
17. R. Frankel, 'Antecedents and Remnants of Jodensavanne: The Synagogue and Cemeteries of the First Settlement of New Word Jews', in The Jews and the Expansion of Europe to the West, 1450–1800, ed. by Paolo Benardini and Norman Fiering (New York and Oxford: Berghahn Books, 2001), pp.394–436.
18. M. Ruth Little, *Sticks and Stones: Three Centuries of North Carolona Gravemarkers* (Chapel Hill and London: University of North Carolina Press, 1998), pp.32, 41–2. For an analysis of the creolisation process in Suriname, see Alex A. van Stipriaan, *Creolisering: vragen van een basketbalplein, antwoorden van een watergodin* [Creolization: Questions from a Basketball Court; Answers from a Watergoddess] (Rotterdam: Erasmus Universtiteit Rotterdam, 2000).
19. According to the 1754 Askamoth: 'experience has taught how prejudicial and improper it would be to admit Mulattoes as *Yachidim* [full members] as some of them have meddled with cases concerning the government of the community; therefore it is resolved that henceforth they will never be considered or admitted as *Yachidim* and will only be admitted as *Congregants*, as is the case in other *Kebiloth* [congregations]'. See NA, 1.05.11.18:106. In addition, a memorandum to the Governor of 1793 by a

group of coloured Jews, says that: '[T]hey [the coloured Jews] are familiar with the fact ... that in earlier years the persons of Gabriel del Mato, Joseph Rodrigues del Prado en Jacob Pelengrino [?] who were not mulattoes but in fact Carboegers [black slaves, not mixed], have enjoyed equal rights and privileges in the Jewish churches as the members [white Jews]'. See, 'Memorandum of the Couleurlingen to Governor Frederici', in NA, 1.05.10.01:527, 2 September 1793.

20. See Nassy and de Leon, *Historical Essay* (see note 13), pp.44, 142. The census of 1811 listed 79 Portuguese Jewish coloureds and 16 coloured belonging to the High German community, a total of 95 coloured Jews. The District register of 1845 listed about 60 coloured Jews. A fair amount of other coloureds whose family names and housemates suggest Jewish fathers, were not listed as Jews but as members of a Christian congregation. In this connection, the (non-Jewish) contemporary Adriaan F. Lammens remarked: '15 January, the children of a Jewish gentleman, the lawyer Presburg, were baptized by a protestant pastor, and thus incorporated in that church community, even though the father and the mother did not join that church. That the Jews were very indignant about this incident was to be expected, but does raise some surprise since all their children begotten by their housekeepers, and thus out of wedlock, are raised in one of the other church communities, that is outside Judaism. Apparently, this was not the case in the old days, since there are coloureds [in Suriname] who are dedicated to the Jewish religion'. Adriaan F. Lammens, *Bijdragen tot de kennis van de kolonie Suriname: dat gedeelte van Guiana het welk bij tractaat ten jare 1815 aan het Koningrijk Holland is verbleven, tijdvak 1816 tot 1822: eerste afdeling Geographie, statistica, zeden en gewoonten: vierde afdeling Voorname belangen der kolonie*, ed. by G.A. de Bruijne (Meppel: Geografisch en Planologisch Instituut, 1982), p.171.

21. 'Memorandum of the Couleurlingen, NA, 1.05.10.01: 527, 2 September 1753.
22. Neve Shalom Archives, Minutes 1772–1787: 26 November 1775; Escamoth 1734–1821: 26 November 1775.
23. Neve Shalom Archives, Eskamoth 1734–1821: 5 November 1780.
24. Neve Shalom Archives, Eskamoth 1734–1821: 6 April 1788.
25. For example, Frankel, 'A Fruitful Expedition' (see note 14), p.3.
26. The late Robin Cohen was the first to elaborate on this case. See Robin Cohen, *Jews in Another Environment: Surinam in the Second Half of the Eighteenth Century* (Leiden: E.J. Brill, 1991), pp.168–72. The conflict is extensively documented and archived. The original documents are to be found in the archive of the government secretary (NA, 1.05.10.01: 525–7).
27. See NA, 1.05.10.01: 525–7, in particular the documents dated 2 September 1793, and 7 March 1794.
28. 'Memorandum of the Couleurlingen', NA, 1.05.10.01:527, 2 September 1793.
29. Ibid.
30. Portuguese regents to Governor Frederici, NA, 1.05.10.01:527, 7 March 1794.
31. The prelude to this ending of an important episode in Surinamese Jewish history occurred in the 1830s and 1840s. During this time, the number of requests by mulattoes to be admitted as Congregants tripled. Now, whole families requested to be admitted as Congregants. Moreover, the number of slave requests for admittance increased considerably as well. Like, for instance, Lea Jacob Levy who successfully requested that her eight children and grandchildren were admitted as Congregants to the community. NSA, Repertorium 1838–1841: 24 February 1839. Between 1830 and 1840, I have counted 33 requests by coloureds or manumitted slaves for admittance as congregants in either the Portuguese or High German community.
32. NA, 1.05.11.18: 437, 13 April 1802.
33. Neve Shalom Archives, Repertorium 1838–1841: 16 August 1838.
34. Neve Shalom Archives, Minutes 1837–1841: 12 May 1841; Outgoing Letters 1838–1855: 17 May 1841.
35. Neve Shalom Archives, Minutes 1837–1841: 19 May 1841.
36. This regulation was closely related to the new Manumission Law of 1832. According to this law, one of the conditions for manumission was submitted evidence that the slave in question was admitted in a recognised church community, which also included the Jewish communities. In other words, 'heathens' could not be manumitted. This, of course, exerted pressure on the community elders to admit slaves to their communities.
37. See NA, 1.05.11.18:50; NA, 1.05.11.18:117; NSA, Outgoing Letters 1838-1855: 22 December 1842.

Memory, Place and Displacement in the Formation of Jewish Identity in Rangoon and Surabaya

JONATHAN GOLDSTEIN

This essay will examine the role of memory, source and location in the formation of Jewish identity in two of Southeast Asia's largest cities: Rangoon, Burma (today's Yangon in the Union of Myanmar), and Surabaya, also spelled Soerabaja and Surabaja, on the eastern end of the island of Java in the Dutch East Indies, today's Indonesia. In the nineteenth and first half of the twentieth century each of these cities had Jewish enclaves of approximately 2,000 individuals. The Jewish communities differed in terms of ethnic origin. The Rangoon enclave was originally composed mostly of Marathi- and Malayalam-speakers from the Bene Israel and Cochini communities of India. Arabic-speakers from Baghdad, Syria and Yemen and Central and Eastern Europeans augmented the mix. Surabaya Jewry consisted mainly of Baghdadis, Dutch, and Germans. Baghdadis nevertheless became the plurality and often the majority in both places. The cities also differed in terms of overall religious context: in Rangoon, Theravada Buddhism; in Surabaya, Sunni Islam. Lastly, each city had a different political context: in Burma, British colonialism which gave way to a Buddhist-oriented independent state; and in Surabaya, Dutch colonialism which gave way to an Islamic-oriented republic.

I have inspected the archives of these heretofore understudied Jewish communities in the University of Southampton's Hartley Library and Jerusalem's Central Zionist Archives. 'Memory' [*zachor*], 'source' [*makor*], and 'location' [*makom*] were key factors determining Jewish identity in both places.[1] Jews lived in alien contexts but tolerant surroundings. Immigrant Jews were civically included. Each city was a place of rest or tranquillity in which Jews could deepen their commitment to Rabbinic Judaism and/or Zion. On the other hand, precisely because Jews could organise freely, their internal arguments occasionally degenerated into divisiveness, belligerency, the abandoning of congregations and the formation of new ones. These characteristics are common to free Jewish communities worldwide. Even more seriously from the viewpoint of Jewish survival, these seductively sheltering environments enabled Jews to intermarry or convert, a process which began well before the Second World War. A brutal Japanese occupation of both cities plus post-war economic trauma and political upheaval obliterated the peaceful environments Jews had once known. By 1960 virtually all Burmese and Indonesians who remained Jews had moved on to new 'locations'.

Many found haven in the reborn State of Israel. A handful of stalwarts remained in both cities to tend their respective synagogues and cemeteries.

Rangoon

The original Jewish settler in Burma may have been Solomon Gabirol, a Bene Israel from the Bombay region of northern India. He served as a commissar in the army of King Alaungpaya, who ruled from 1752 to 1760.[2] According to an 1850 census, a Romanian Jewish merchant named Goldenberg made a fortune in the Burmese teakwood trade. In 1851 Salomon Rinmon, a Galician Jew, arrived in Rangoon as a supplier to the British military. He quickly established stores around the region. His *Masot Shelomoh* ['Solomon's Travels'], published in Vienna in 1884, contains a long chapter on Burma and is the first Hebrew account of the country and its towns.[3]

Rangoon was annexed to British India after the second Anglo-Burmese War of 1852–53. By 1885 Britain had annexed all of Burma. Under the protective umbrella of British rule more Bene Israel arrived from Bombay, creating an overwhelmingly oriental [*mizrachi*] community. Arabic-speaking Jews from Syria and Yemen and Malayalam-speaking Cochinis from Kerala in South India supplemented the original Bene Israel population. In 1896 the community built its major synagogue, Musmeah Yeshuah [Hebrew: *Mazmiach Yeshu'a*], followed shortly thereafter by a Jewish day school. A second synagogue, *Beth El*, opened in 1932.[4]

In the course of the late nineteenth and early twentieth centuries, approximately 2,000 additional Jews fled Ottoman and Iraqi persecution and found haven in Rangoon. Baghdadis became the plurality and often the majority of Rangoon's Jewish community. They maintained what ethnologist Chiara Betta termed 'overlapping identities'. After leaving the Ottoman empire, they became Anglicised but nevertheless retained strong links with their Judeo-Arabic heritage.[5] Their memories of suffering in Baghdad were reinforced by correspondence with hapless friends and relatives who remained behind. Memory served as the basis for the Baghdadis' appreciation of living under the twin umbrellas of benevolent British rule and Theravada Buddhist toleration.[6]

The rights and privileges which have already been described were a double-edged sword with respect to Jewish survival. When Israel Cohen, a London-based official of the World Zionist Organization, visited Rangoon in February 1921, he noted these mixed blessings. On the one hand, Cohen stayed in the palatial residence of A.J. Cohen, a Baghdadi who had extensive gardens and 36 Burmese servants. The main Baghdadi synagogue was maintained by rents from adjacent shops. Baghdadi Jews served as magistrates, municipal councillors, commissioners, and at least one as sheriff of Rangoon. Yehuda Ezekiel Street honours one of several Jews who served as mayor. Cohen received significant contributions for institutions in the Land of Israel. On the other hand, Cohen saw danger signals with respect to Jewish survival. Jews engaged in pitched legal battles with one another, including a much-publicised lawsuit between rival factions within one synagogue. He observed much intermarriage, including a Jewish merchant born in London who was married to a Burmese lady and another wed to a Japanese.[7]

The Japanese invasion of 1941 brought British rule to an abrupt halt and shattered the peaceful environment which Burmese Jews knew. Japanese rule caused most of Rangoon's 2,200 Jews to flee to the relative safety of India, along with most of the British colonial population. Fewer than 400 returned after the war.[8] The Burmese gained nominal independence under the Japanese-sponsored Burmese Independence Army, trained on Hainan island and led by Aung San, father of Burmese freedom fighter and Nobel laureate Aung San Suu Kyi.[9]

On 4 January 1948 Great Britain granted total independence to Burma. Nearly simultaneously, the British withdrew from their League of Nations-mandated territory of Palestine, paving the way for Israel's Declaration of Independence. The effect of both of these on Burmese Jews is made clear in a 20 April 1949 plea from Eliyahu Mordecai, a former Rangoon Jew who had been living in Ramat Gan, to Dr Nadad of Israel's Jewish Agency, the quasi-governmental authority involved in immigrant absorption. Mordecai requested

> the immediate granting of 150 visas to Burmese Jews and [the subvention of] their transportation to Israel. The Jews of Rangoon are living under war conditions – a neutral community in a country torn with strife between the Karens, Communists, and Burmans. Their existence is precarious in every respect. Their only fervent hope is to come to Israel.[10]

On 3 May 1949 Charles Manasseh wrote to the Jewish Agency from Rangoon about

> the chaotic conditions brought about by armed insurrection against the present government. Businesses have been stagnant owing to restrictive measures imposed by the government. Black marketeering is rampant and the cost of living has gone up by leaps and bounds. Law and order are things of the past. Armed robbery is the order of the day. What with communist threats from the north [China] and internal friction, I am inclined to think that the sooner people are evacuated to Israel the happier will be their lot.[11]

Manasseh described 45 destitute families who had left Burma during the Japanese invasion, returned to Burma after the war, and 'need immediate repatriation to Israel'.[12]

By 1953 most Burmese Jews had evacuated to Israel and other countries. In November of that year Israeli journalist Gershon Agron cabled *Keren Hayesod*, the Zionist charitable foundation, that the Rangoon Jewish community had 'dwindled almost [to a] vanishing point'.[13] In that same year, barely a handful remained to watch the government of Premier U Nu establish close relations with the Israel of Prime Minister David Ben Gurion and Foreign Minister Moshe Sharett. In November 1956, when Burma's Muslim minority rioted in the streets in the aftermath of the Sinai campaign, virtually all of the remaining Jewish stalwarts chose to leave the country.[14] Any sense of Burma as a nurturing haven for Jews had evaporated. At precisely the same time a New Jerusalem beckoned.

Surabaya

The Jews of eighteenth century Holland were extensively involved with the Dutch East India Company and its establishment of Batavia, today's Jakarta, as the colonial capital of the Dutch East Indies.[15] In 1861, when Jerusalem-based Ya'akov Saphir visited the Dutch East Indies as part of a larger fundraising trip to India and Australia, he met a Jewish merchant from Amsterdam who named 20 Jewish families of Dutch or German origin, including members of the Dutch colonial forces. He also noted that some settlers of Jewish origin were living in Surabaya. Few of them retained any links with Judaism. Most were intermarried and had even abandoned the custom of circumcision. He lamented that this happened

> in this place of freedom, under a government of grace and mercy such as the Kingdom of Holland that granted freedom to the Jews to keep the faith of the Torah of God, and here with all the riches of this land in their hands. From this place of plenty and joy they cast away all institutions of their faith and relieve themselves of the burden of the Kingdom of Heaven with no regret! Not so with our Baghdadi brothers in India who, wherever even ten of them gather, they first set up a synagogue and a slaughterer and a congregation for themselves, and do not kick away the commandments of God in disgust.

Saphir ended his profile of Dutch East Indian Jewry with an urgent plea to his colleagues in Jerusalem to petition the Amsterdam rabbinate to send out a ritual slaughterer [*shochet*], cantor [*hazan*], and circumciser [*mohel*]. He hoped such clergy would resuscitate Judaism in the Dutch East Indies. There is no evidence that Saphir's suggestions were ever acted upon.[16]

When Israel Cohen visited the Dutch East Indies in 1921, about 2,000 Jews lived there and still enjoyed great political and economic privileges. The resident governor of Surabaya, variously referred to as 'Coen' and 'Cohen', was a Jew. Several other Jews held governmental positions, and many engaged in commerce. Ritually observant Baghdadi and Adeni Jews had followed the European Jews and become a majority of the Jewish community of Surabaya as they had in Rangoon. They spoke Arabic and English at home, Dutch in school and in social circles, and Malay to their servants. Baghdadis such as the Bahars, Benjamins, Mizrahis, and Solomons retained close commercial ties to their brethren in Singapore, Calcutta, Hong Kong, and Shanghai.[17]

Baghdadi religious life in Surabaya resembled that in the aforementioned cities. *Makor*, the freedom Jews could enjoy in a particular place, plus *zachor*, their constant memory of persecution in Baghdad, provided the opportunity to deepen ethnic identity. Indeed, the Baghdadis were the only Jews in Surabaya to organise as a community. They had a central board of directors which purchased land for a cemetery and set up a burial society. They engaged local Chinese carpenters and masons to build a synagogue and an adjacent club. On the other hand, Israel Cohen reiterated Ya'akov Saphir's observation of some six decades earlier, that in this seductive environment many Jews 'concealed or denied their Jewish origin'. Mixed marriages were frequent. Cohen went so far as to say that, due to assimilation and intermarriage, it was 'impossible to form an [accurate] estimate' of the numbers of Jews in Surabaya.[18]

The community was ideologically divided over the question of Zionism, which had been introduced by European immigrants. Cohen described an Austrian Jew who 'proclaimed himself a skeptic on the advisability of bringing the Jews back to

Palestine and made no secret of his views that they should be absorbed among the nations'. The Austrian's mentality was typical of the bulk of the Jews in Java who, according to Cohen, chose to ignore persistent 'anti-Semitic pinpricks' in the local newspaper. Cohen complimented his Zionist colleagues for having 'bravely succeeded in maintaining their enthusiasm in this spiritually asphyxiating atmosphere'.[19]

In 1926 a handful of Surabaya's and Padang's European Jews took the additional step of organising the *Nederlands Indische Zionistenbond* [Dutch Indies Zionist Association]. The *Bond* affiliated with the World Zionist Organization, which had been founded by Theodor Herzl some 30 years earlier. On 9 September the *Bond* began publishing the monthly journal *Erets Israel (Het Joodsche Land)* [The Land of Israel] in Dutch, German, and English. S.J. van Creveld edited the journal until he left the Dutch East Indies in 1939. Surabaya became the Dutch East Indies' headquarters for *Keren Hayesod*. By 1928 *Keren Hayesod* also opened branch offices in Bandung (also spelled Bandoeng), Batavia, Malang, Medan, Padang, Semarang, and Yogyakarta (also spelled Jogjakarta).[20] The rise of Central and Eastern European fascism in the late 1920s and 1930s produced an influx of Jewish refugees to Surabaya and gave Zionism further momentum. By 1934 Zionist fundraiser Benzion Shein, from Jerusalem, received a warmer welcome and had much greater financial success in Surabaya and Medan than had Israel Cohen 13 years earlier. In July 1940 A. van Leer, the *Keren Hayesod* representative in Surabaya and editor of *Soerabjasch Handelsblad*, asked the *Hayesod* head office for data about and pictures of 'the Jewish army in Palestine' [*Haganah*] for inclusion in his newspaper.[21]

The Japanese invasion of March 1942 put a halt to Zionist and indeed all Judaic activity in Surabaya. At first the Japanese left the Jewish and Armenian civilians alone, classifying them as 'peoples without countries'. In the viewpoint of local Japanese officials, the Chrysanthemum Nation only saw itself at war with countries, not peoples. The Japanese treated Dutch Jews who were members of the regular armed forces as they treated ordinary Dutchmen, with no special consideration because of a soldier's Judaic origin. This included Jews like Nathan Gutwirth, a Dutch national who was a member of the Dutch East Indies Volunteer Army and who became a Japanese prisoner of war. In August 1943, Dr Helmut Wohltach, a German envoy from Tokyo, arrived in Surabaya. Shortly thereafter, at the urging of Wohltach and Eugene Ott, the German ambassador in Tokyo, the entire Dutch East Indies Jewish community – men, women, and children, irrespective of nationality – were taken to prison camps. Surabaya Jews then suffered the same hardships as virtually all Caucasians in Japanese-controlled areas of Southeast Asia who were not under the protection of neutral governments or of nations allied with Japan. Surabaya Jews suffered worse than most Rangoon Jews, who, as already noted, were able to flee into India for the duration of the war.[22]

When the Indian journalist Percy Gourgey visited Surabaya shortly after the war, he found that 'many [Jews], broken in health but not in spirit, emerged from the camps, and [then] went through another ordeal brought about by the Indonesian revolution'.[23] By this time there was a resuscitated but fragile Zionist leadership in Surabaya.[24] The post-war revival was stimulated by Jewish Chaplain and Captain

Bloch, of the British forces in Singapore, and E.J. (Vaandrig) Seeligmann, chaplain to the Jews among the Dutch forces who were trying to recapture the East Indies.[25] On 15 November 1947, Captain Joost Straus, one of Seeligmann's servicemen, advised the Zionist Executive in Jerusalem of the post-war economic hardships facing Surabaya's Baghdadi Jews. He wrote that

> this group expects that by clever maneuvering of competitors they will be completely cut off [of] their possibilities to earn a decent living. There are also those who fear aggression against their person. These people [who] have no ties with Europe or America and can not go back to Iraq have no other choice than Israel.[26]

Captain Straus was even more emphatic with respect to the European Jews remaining in the Dutch East Indies. He wrote that 'after what happened [Dutch collaboration with the Nazis during the Holocaust] the wish to go back to Holland is not so big, so many of them see the only way ... is *aliyah* [immigration to Israel]'.[27]

Because of the efforts of Bloch, Seeligmann, Straus, and others, most Surabaya Jews evacuated to Israel in 1948–50. After the last organised transport of Jewish immigrants from China reached Israel in 1950, the Surabaya-based Zionist Organization of Indonesia was the only fully fledged Zionist organisation in East or Southeast Asia. A trickle of immigration from Indonesia to Israel continued into the mid-1950s. In May 1955 F. Dias Santilhano, Chairman of both the Indonesian Jewish community [*Vereniging voor Joodse Belangen*] and its Zionist organisation requested that the Jewish National Fund in Jerusalem send some Israeli movies 'to maintain contacts with our small community here from which occasionally there are going some *olim* to our country [immigrants to Israel]'. Santilhano and his family themselves emigrated to Israel in October 1955.[28]

In Surabaya, as in Rangoon, a handful of stalwarts with close local ties remained to tend the cemetery and synagogue. While the Rangoon Baghdadis observed a flourishing relationship between an independent Burma and Israel, Surabaja Jewry witnessed the opposite. Indonesia achieved its independence under Sukarno (also spelled Soekarno) in 1949. It automatically became the world's largest Muslim nation and has remained so ever since. Sukarno brushed aside Israel's recognition of his regime and other friendly gestures and instead demonstrated unrelenting hostility toward the Jewish state.[29] Some of the more publicised episodes include the following. In November 1953 the Indonesian government refused to recognise a travel visa which its own Consul General in Bombay had issued to one of Israel's most distinguished journalists, *Jerusalem Post* founding editor Gershon Agron. The hapless consul was recalled and Agron had to make do with a meeting with the head of the Indonesian Jewish community at Raffles Hotel in Singapore.[30] On 3 May 1955 Haj-amin al-Husseini, the Mufti of Jerusalem and an outspoken and unrepentant Nazi collaborator, was accorded the honour of addressing the faithful in the great mosque of Yogyakarta. In a prequel to Al-Qaeda-linked Indonesian preachers of today, Husseini told his listeners that 'Jews begin with oppression of Arab people in Palestine. If we don't stop them, they will go still further and want to have in their power Medina and all Arab countries'.[31] In June 1956, Indonesia refused to issue visas to Israeli delegates to the World University Service annual meeting. The organisation chose to move its convention elsewhere rather than submit to Indonesian restrictions.[32] In August 1962 Indonesia banned Israeli athletes from participating in the Third Asian Games in Jakarta. The International Olympic Committee (IOC) lodged a formal protest, causing Sukarno in the following year to organise a counter-Olympics called GANEFO (Games of Newly Emerging States). The IOC retaliated by banning all Indonesian athletes and any GANEFO participants from the 1964 Tokyo Olympic Games.[33] In September 1971 *Jerusalem Post* Editor Ted R. Lurie, in Indonesia for the third annual assembly of the Press Foundation of Asia, was asked to withdraw from a group of delegates waiting to be received by President Sukarno's successor Suharto.[34]

Despite an official policy of *Pancasila*, or secularism, independent Indonesia also displayed hostility toward its own Jewish population. Indonesia recognised only five legitimate religions – Islam, Protestantism, Catholicism, Hinduism, and Buddhism. It demonstrated scant toleration of indigenous beliefs.[35] According to the American ethnologist Jeffrey Hadler, who made no secret of his Jewishness when he did research in Surabaya in 1994–95, 'foreign Jews encouraged one another to proclaim themselves "Buddhist" or better yet "Unitarian" rather than face the prejudicial and bureaucratic headaches that could come with being *Yahudi*'. Hadler notes that Surabaya's David Mussry had '*Hebrani*' on his national identity card until 1998, when he was shifted into the 'approved and uncontroversial "Hindu" category'. Shortly thereafter Mussry emigrated to the United States, as did the keeper of the synagogue. The sign on the building was removed, although a Star of David remains on the door.[36] The Jews of Surabaya, in a period of one century, with painful memories of Baghdad behind them, saw their place of refuge turn into an unpleasant if not unliveable environment. Some would rebuild their lives in America. Most Surabaya and Rangoon Jews would do so in a new 'location', the reborn State of Israel.

NOTES

Copyright Jonathan Goldstein 2006, used here with permission. This essay was prepared for a 3–5 January 2005 conference on 'Place and Displacement in Jewish History and Memory – *Zakor v'Makor*' at the Kaplan Centre for Jewish Studies and Research, University of Cape Town, South Africa. The author appreciates the research assistance of Jeffrey Hadler of the University of California; Anthony Reid and Didi Kwartanada of the National University of Singapore; Rochelle Rubinstein and the entire staff of Jerusalem's Central Zionist Archives; Jean Gelman Taylor of the University of New South Wales; C.M. Woolgar and the entire staff of the University of Southampton's Hartley Library; Moshe Yegar of the Truman Institute of the Hebrew University of Jerusalem; and Jan Zwartendyk (ret.) of The Pennsylvania State University. Final responsibility for the content is, of course, the author's alone.

1. Jews are commanded at least six times in the Torah 'to remember' [*zakor*], most prominently on the occasion of Passover, when the exodus from Egyptian bondage to freedom in the Land of Israel is encapsulated in the phrase 'we were once slaves in Egypt' ['*ovdim haeinu be-Mizraim*']. Overviews of the modern history of East and Southeast Asian Jewry include Isaac Schwarzbart, *The Rise and Decline of Jewish Communities in the Far East and Southeast Asia* (New York: World Jewish Congress, December 1957, mimeographed copy in Central Zionist Archives, Jerusalem [hereinafter referred to as CZA]); Reuven Kashani's *Kehillot Ha-Yehudim Be-Mizrah Ha-Rachok* [Hebrew: The Jewish Communities in the Far East] (Jerusalem: Sephardic Council, 1982); and my books *The Jews of China* (Armonk, NY and London: M.E. Sharpe, vol.1 1999, vol.2 2000) and *China and Israel, 1948–1998* (Westport, CT and London: Praeger, 1999).

2. Nathan Katz and Ellen Goldberg, 'The Last Jews in India and Burma', *Jerusalem Letter*, 101, 15 April 1988, p.6.
3. Salomon Rinman, *Masot Shelomoh Be-Erets Hodu, Birman Ve-Sinim* [Hebrew: Solomon's Travels in the Land of India, Burma, and the Chinese] (Vienna: Ba-defus shel G. Brag, 1884).
4. The Musmeah Yeshua synagogue is located at 85 26th Street in Yangon. Leo Paul Dana, 'The Iraqi Community of Burma', *Shalom Singapore*, 13 (April 2000), 17; David S. Sassoon, *A History of the Jews in Baghdad* (Letchworth, UK: Solomon D. Sassoon, 1949), p.211; George M. Kahin, *Governments and Politics in Southeast Asia* (Ithaca, NY and London: Cornell University Press, 1969), pp.77–8; Ida Cowen, *Jews in Remote Corners of the World* (Englewood Cliffs, NJ: Prentice Hall, 1971), pp.176–81; Warren Freedman, 'The Jews of South-East Asia', *Jewish Post*, 20 September 1979, pp.71–5; Moshe Yegar, 'A Rapid and Recent Rise and Fall', *Sephardi World* (Jerusalem), 3 (July–August 1984), 8; Sue Fishkoff, 'Burmese Jews Hang On', *Jerusalem Post*, 18 August 1993, p.7; [no author given]. *Asia-Pacific Survival Guide* (Melbourne: Asia Pacific Jewish Association, 1988), p.27; *Encyclopedia Judaica* (Jerusalem: Keter, 1971), Vol.4, pp.1526–28; Katz and Goldberg, 'The Last' (see note 2), p.6.
5. Chiara Betta, 'Foreword' to the special issue 'India, Singapore, Hong Kong, and Shanghai: Identities of Baghdadi Jews of the Diaspora'. *Sino-Judaica* (Menlo Park, CA), 4 (2003), ii.
6. Henry Kamm, 'Burma's Last Few Jews Living on Proud Memories', *The New York Times*, 10 August 1980, p.6; Cowen, *Jews* (see note 4), pp.179–80.
7. Israel Cohen, *Journal of a Jewish Traveller* (London: John Lane, 1925), pp.223–6; Joan Bieder, 'Jewish Identity in Singapore: Cohesion, Dispersion, Survival', Unpublished paper by a University of California journalism professor, p.19. The Bene Israel Jews, originally from Northern India, were barred from the 1926 and 1929 communal elections. In 1934, when they again asked to be included, they were struck from the list of voters. They sued in civil court. In April 1935, Chief Justice Leach ruled that Bene Israel could both vote and hold office, despite the claims of the synagogue that, because the Bene Israel ignored fine points of Jewish law on divorce and remarriage, they were non-Jews. The Israeli Rabbinate reaffirmed the ruling of Justice Leach in 1964, granting Bene Israel full citizenship as Jews in the State of Israel. Ruth Cernea, 'End of the Road', *Bnai Brith Jewish Monthly*, 102.10 (June–July 1988), 28–30; Cowen, *Jews* (see note 4), p.176.
8. Kamm, 'Burma's Last Few Jews' (see note 6), p.6.
9. Kahin, *Governments* (see note 4), pp.83–7.
10. Letter: Eliyahu Mordecai, Ramat Gan, to Dr. Nadad, Jewish Agency, Tel Aviv, 20 April 1949, File 520/546, CZA.
11. Letter: Charles Manasseh, Rangoon, to J. Vainstein, Jewish Agency, Jerusalem, 3 May 1949, File 56/6792, CZA.
12. Letter: Charles Manasseh, Rangoon, to Kurt B. Grossman, World Jewish Congress, New York, ca. 4 May 1949, CZA.
13. Cable: Gershon Agron, Singapore, to *Keren Hayesod*, Jerusalem, 18 November 1953, File KH4 13640, CZA.
14. On 7 December 1949 Burma recognised the State of Israel and was the first Asian country to do so. On 13 July 1952 Burma announced the exchange of diplomatic missions. High-level Burmese–Israeli contact began in December 1952 after Burmese Socialist Party Leader U Kyaw Nyein visited Israel. Israeli Foreign Minister Moshe Sharett attended a January 1953 Asian Socialist conference in Rangoon. At that time Burma and Israel were the only two countries in Asia in which Socialist Parties were in power. In July 1954 a Burmese delegation under Lt. Col. Bo Shein paid a visit to Israel which included the head office of the Keren Kayemeth in Jerusalem and Kiryat Anavim. Burmese Prime Minister U Nu spoke on behalf of Israel at Afro-Asian Summit Conferences in Bogor, Indonesia, in December 1954 and Bandung, Indonesia, in April 1955. After Bandung he planned to visit both Egypt and Israel. When Egypt asked him not to visit Israel he visited Israel for an entire week and cancelled his visit to Egypt. Burmese–Israeli trade agreements were followed by visits to Burma by Sharett in September 1956, Israeli Army Chief of Staff Moshe Dayan and Defence Ministry Director General Shimon Peres in January 1958. U Nu's successor General Ne Win visited Israel in June 1959. Israeli President Yitzhak Ben-Zvi paid a reciprocal visit to Burma in October 1959, followed by Israeli Prime Minister David Ben-Gurion in December 1961 and Foreign Minister Golda Meir in February 1962. Percy Gourgey, Rangoon, to Dr L. Lauterbach, Jerusalem, 18 January 1953, File 55/10.612, CZA; E. Marton, Jerusalem, to Lt. Col. Bo Shein, Tel Aviv, 13 July 1954, File KKL5/209.60, CZA; Moshe Sharett, *Mi-Shut Be-Asyah: Yoman Masa* [Hebrew: From Travelling in Asia: A Travel Diary] (Tel Aviv: Davar, 1957); David Hacohen, *Yoman Burmah* [Hebrew: Burma Diary] (Tel Aviv: Am Oved, 1963); David Hacohen, *'Et Le-Saper* (Tel Aviv: Am Oved, 1974), translated by Menachem Dagut as *Time to Tell* (New York: Cornwall, 1985); Chi-shad Liang, *Burma's Foreign Relations* (New York and Westport, CT: Praeger, 1990), pp.191–4; Yegar, 'A Rapid and Recent Rise' (see note 4), p.9; Freedman, 'The Jews of Southeast Asia' (see note 4), p.72. Burmese–Israeli military ties began with a 1954 Israeli shipment to Burma of 30 Supermarine Spitfire

fighters. The deal included machine gun ammunition, bombs, rockets, and spare engine parts. It was followed by military training and cooperation, including the shipment of Uzi 9 mm. submachine guns to Burma's State Law and Order Restoration Council. Andrew Selth, *Burma's Secret Military Partners* (Canberra: Research School of Pacific and Asian Studies, Australian National University, 2000), pp.46–60; Andrew Selth, *Transforming the Tatmadaw* (Canberra: Research School of Pacific and Asian Studies, Australian National University, 1996), p.53.

15. Ya'akov Saphir-Halevy, *Even Saphir* [Hebrew: The Sapphire Stone]; (Lusk, Russian Poland: *Hevrat Mekitzey Nirdamim*, 1866), pp.157 ff.; Thomas Forrest, *A Voyage from Calcutta to the Mergui Archipelago* (London: J. Robson, 1792), p.39; J.J. Benjamin, *Eight Years in Asia and Africa from 1846 to 1855* (Hanover, Germany: Published by the author, 1859), p.316; L.F. Brakel, 'Een Joodse bezoeker aan Batavia in de zestiger jaren van de vorige eeuw' [A Jewish Visitor in Batavia in the 1860s], *Studia Rosenthaliana*, 9.1 (January 1975), pp.63–89; Gilbert Hamonic, 'Milieux Marchands et Tentatives Commerciales: Note sur la communaute Juive de Surabaya' [French: Mercantile Environments and Commercial Ventures: A Note on the Jewish Community of Surabaya], *Archipel* (Paris), 36 (1988), 183. For a history of the Surabaya Jews based on a 1993 visit see Lindsey Shanson, 'Indonesian Jews: 5,000,000 to 1', *The Jerusalem Report*, 18 November 1983, reprinted in *Points East* (Menlo Park, CA), 9.1 (April 1994), pp.12–13.

16. Saphir-Halevy, *Even Saphir* (see note 15), pp.157 ff. Another edition of Saphir's travelogue was published in Mainz in 1874 by Buchdruckerei van J. Bril. For an English translation of parts of that edition that pertain to the Dutch East Indies, see Jeffrey Hadler, 'Translations of Antisemitism: Jews, the Chinese, and Violence in Colonial and Post-colonial Indonesia', *Indonesia and the Malay World* (London), 32.94 (November 2004), 295–99. That translation is excerpted here. See also Brakel, 'Een Joodse' (see note 15), pp.63–89.

17. P[ercy] S. Gourgey, 'My Visit to Jewish Communities of the Far East', *India and Israel* (Bombay), 20 April 1953, p.37; Eze Nathan, *History of the Jews in Singapore* (Singapore: Herbilu, 1986), pp.175–6; Cohen, *Journal* (see note 7), p.211. Hadler cites some commercial institutions in the nineteenth and early twentieth century Dutch East Indies which informally restricted or formally prohibited Jewish participation. This was true in just about every major city of the free world where Jews lived. Hadler's examples include the Netherlands Trading Company [*Nederlandse Handelmaatscappij*], which blocked Jewish membership on its board until 1936, and the Javanese Bank [*Javasche Bank*], the Dutch East Indies Commercial Bank [*Nederlandse Indische Handelsbank*], and the state shipping company [*scheepvaartmatschappijen*], all of which had no Jews in leadership positions until 1925. Hadler, 'Translations' (see note 16), p.299.

18. Cohen writes that he met a Romanian Jew in Surabaya who was married to a native of Madura and by whom he had children. 'There were five or six other Jews in the city who had native wives ... These mixed unions were one of the effects of the lack of an organized community'. Cohen, *Journal* (see note 7), pp.212, 215; Gourgey, 'My Visit' (see note 17), p.37; Israel Goldstein, 'In Search for My Brethren: The Jewish Remnant in Surabaja', *Jewish Frontier* (April 1972), p.21 Nathan, 'History' (see note 17), p.176; Hamonic, 'Milieux' (see note 15), p.183.

19. A middle aged Jewish merchant advised Cohen that there was 'no possibility of a solution of the Jewish question by the establishment of a Jewish commonwealth in Palestine ... the hatred of the Jew was too deeply rooted, and it was now more violent and widespread than it had ever been before the war. He considered the only solution lay in complete assimilation'. Cohen, *Journal* (see note 7), pp.211–16.

20. The first issue was entitled 'Een nieuw Joodsch blad *Erets Israel* [Het Joodsche Land] 9 September/1 Tischri 5687[1926]' [A New Jewish Newspaper, the *Land of Israel*]. S.J. van Creveld began to edit *Erets Israel* when he was an official of the Post and Telegraph Bureau (PTT) based in Padang. He continued until he left the Dutch East Indies in 1939. The journal ran until 1942, when it finally shut down during the Japanese occupation. See issue No.8 (May 1934); Letters: S.J. van Creveld, Bandung, to Leo Herrmann, Jerusalem, 31 August 1921, file KH4 13.371, CZA; Alexander Goldstein, Singapore, to 'friends', 5 December 1927, KH4B/1913 CZA; Hadler, 'Translations' (see note 16), pp.292, 299–300, 311; Hamonic, 'Milieux' (see note 15), p.186.

21. 'Dr. Benzion M. Shein M.D. Speciale Afgevaardigde de Zionistische Wereld Organisetie', *Erets Israel*, No. 8 (April 1934), p.2; Letters: Dr Benzion Shein, Medan, to Zionist Executive, Jerusalem, 10 August 1934, CZA; A. van Leer, Surabaya, to *Keren Hayesod* Head Office, Jerusalem, 29 July 1940, KH4 13.371, CZA.

22. Xaviera Hollander, *Child No More: A Memoir* (New York: Regan Books, 2002), p.50; F.C. Brasz, 'After the Second World War: From "Jewish Church" to Cultural Minority', in *The History of the Jews in the Netherlands*, ed. by J.C.H. Blom et al. (Oxford, UK and Portland, OR: Littman Library of Jewish Civilization, 2002), p.375; Email: Didi Kwatanada to the author, 25 September 2005; Gourgey, 'My Visit' (see note 17), p.37; Kahin, *Governments* (see note 4), p.197; Nathan, 'History' (see note 17), p.10; Hadler, 'Translations' (see note 16), p.303. On Gutwirth's and other Jews' escape from Eastern Europe

to East Asia with the assistance of Kaunas-based Dutch Consul General Jan Zwartendijk, see Jonathan Goldstein, 'Motivation in Holocaust Research: The Case of Jan Zwartendijk in Lithuania, 1940', in *Lessons and Legacies Volume VI: New Currents in Holocaust Research*, ed. by Jeffry M. Diefendorf (Evanston, IL: Northwestern University Press, 2004), pp.73 ff.
23. Gourgey, 'My Visit' (see note 17), p.37.
24. Letters: B.Ph. van Zuiden, Batavia, to Shabtai Rowson (at that time, a London-based Zionist official; he later Hebraises his name and becomes Israeli diplomat Shabtai Rosenne), London, 14 April 1947, CZA 55/12.170; J. Straus, Batavia, to Zionist Organization, Jerusalem, 1 January 1948, CZA 55/12.170.
25. In 1946 Bloch provided advice and support to approximately 1,000 Jews in the Dutch East Indies. About half of them were soldiers in the Dutch military. Letters: E.J. Seeligman, Jewish Chaplain, Netherlands East Indies (Batavia?), to Abe Berman, Jerusalem, 18 June 1947; Van Zuiden to Rowson, 14 April 1947; Straus to Zionist Organization, 1 January 1948, CZA; Brasz, 'After the Second World War' (see note 22), pp.374-6. Capt. Bloch was also responsible for the organisation of the Zionist youth movement 'Habonim' in Singapore in 1946. Ralph Sassoon, 'Habonim in Singapore', *Shalom Singapore*, 12 (April 1999), 3.
26. Letter: J. Straus, Batavia, to Zionist Organization, Jerusalem, 15 November 1949, CZA 55/12.170. Joost Straus Hebraised his name to *Yosef Tirosh* after immigrating first to Naharia and then to Rehovot, Israel.
27. Letter: Straus to Zionist Organization, 15 November 1949; Interviews with Yosef Tirosh (ne Joost Straus), Rehovot, Israel, 1968, 1970, 1977.
28. Letter: Dr. Lauterbach, Central Zionist Executive, Jerusalem, to M. van Beek, Jakarta, 15 November 1950, CZA 55/12.170. Santilhano additionally justified his request for films on the grounds that 'there are some groups of Indonesians who take a sympathetic interest in [the films] ... If, by means of the films goodwill could be strengthened another step towards improvement of relations between Israel and Indonesia would be taken'. Letters: Santilhano, Vereniging voor Joodse Belangen, Jakarta, to S. Leichter, Jewish National Fund, Jerusalem, 27 March and 24 July 1955, CZA KKL5/20960.
29. In December 1949 Israeli President Chaim Weizmann and Prime Minister Ben-Gurion sent telegrams to Indonesian President Sukarno and Vice President Muhammad Hatta congratulating them on their Treaty of Independence with the Netherlands. In January 1950 Israeli Foreign Minister Sharett sent Hatta a telegram granting Indonesia full diplomatic recognition. According to political scientists Greg Barton and Colin Rubenstein, 'Hatta responded to both Sharett and Ben Gurion with thanks, but did not offer reciprocal sentiments in regard to diplomatic recognition. Sensing Indonesia's evasiveness, Sharett wrote to Hatta suggesting that a goodwill mission be sent to Indonesia, to which Hatta responded courteously in May 1950, but suggested that such a mission be postponed to a later time'. Greg Barton and Colin Rubenstein, 'Indonesia and Israel: A Relationship in Waiting', *Jewish Political Studies Review* (Jerusalem and Baltimore, MD), 17.1-2 (Spring 2005), p.160. Indonesia's pro-Arab policy intensified thereafter. When Israeli Lt. Col. (ret.) Shaul Ramati visited on behalf of *Keren Hayesod* in 1951, he advised the handful of remaining Jews to cease expressing opinions and giving information about Israel, out of concern for their own personal safety. Limited fund-raising activity for Israel continued through 1953, when the Indonesian Jewish community advised the World Zionist Executive that 'owing to the fact that there are still no normal relations between Israel and Indonesia ... we may not expect that we will get the permission of the Exchange Control for transfer of money collected for the 1952 Israel campaign'. In November 1953 Indonesia ceased granting entrance visas to all Israelis. Letters: H. de Vries, Jakarta, to the Executive of the Zionist Organization, Jerusalem, 25 March 1952, CZA 55/11.744; to World Jewish Congress, 31 March 1953, MS 239/92/45, Hartley Library, University of Southampton; F. Dias Santilhano, Jakarta, to World Zionist Executive, Jerusalem, 25 April 1953, CZA 55/11.744; Ya'akov Shimoni, Director, Asian Division, Ministry of Foreign Affairs, Jerusalem, to B. van Tijn and M. van Beek, Zionist Organization of Indonesia, Jakarta, 15 April 1951, CZA 55/12.170.
30. Dr Mohammed Rasif, the Indonesian Consul General in Singapore, claimed that Agron was an 'undesireable person', revoked his visa, and advised all airlines on the Djakarta route not to issue tickets to him. The Indonesian government did expedite arrangements for Indonesian Jewish community chairman Santilhano to meet Agron in Singapore. Cables: Gershon Agron, Singapore, to *Keren Hayesod*, Jerusalem, 18 and 24 November 1953, CZA KH4 13640; *Daily Mirror* (Manila), 21 November 1953; *Evening Standard* (Manila), 21 November 1953; *Singapore Standard*, ca. 21 November 1953; *Jerusalem Post*, 21 January 1954; Barton and Rubenstein, 'Indonesia and Israel' (see note 29), p.161.
31. Translated from the Dutch-language daily *Java-Bode* (Djakarta), 3 May 1955.
32. Mimeographed leaflet: 'World Jewish Affairs Bulletin', American Jewish Congress, 28 June 1956, MS 2391 92/45, Hartley Library.
33. Ted R. Lurie, 'An Israeli in Indonesia', *Jerusalem Post*, 10 September 1971.
34. Ibid.

35. Barton and Rubenstein, 'Indonesia and Israel' (see note 29), p.160.
36. Hadler, 'Translations' (see note 16), pp.291, 302, 304, 309. As of 2008 Indonesia has yet to recognise the State of Israel. Nevertheless there were some improvements in Israeli–Indonesian relations during the Suharto (1966–98) and post-Suharto eras. On 25 October 1994 Abdurrahman Wahid, the leader of Indonesia's NU, the world's largest Islamic organisation, visited Jerusalem to witness the signing of the Israeli-Jordanian peace treaty. Wahid became Indonesia's first democratically elected president five years later. While he did not visit Israel during his presidency, he visited numerous times before and after. In March 1997 he joined the Board of Governors of the Shimon Peres Peace Center. There have also been some significant developments with respect to Israeli–Indonesia commercial ties. Up until 1979 that trade was negligible. Between September 1979 and July 1983 Israel was reported to have sold Indonesia via United States intermediaries approximately 30 surplus Skyhawk aircraft and 11 helicopters. In October 1993 Israeli Prime Minister Yitzhak Rabin met Suharto in Djakarta. His visit was followed the next year by that of a large delegation from the Israeli Chamber of Commerce. By fiscal year 1999 Indonesian–Israeli bilateral trade totalled US$20.5 million. It consisted of US$12.7 million in Indonesian shipments to Israel and US$7.8 million in exports from Israel to Indonesia. In May 2000 Aburizal Bakrie, President of the Indonesian Chamber of Commerce and Industry, lead a 34-member Indonesian business, trade, and investment mission to Israel. Victor Harel, Deputy Director General for Economic Affairs of the Israeli Ministry of Foreign Affairs, hosted a working luncheon for the delegation. Israeli–Indonesian trade caught the eye of Eugene Y.T. Chen, Director of the Economic Division of the Taiwan's Economic and Cultural Office in Tel Aviv. Mr. Chen served for six years as Taiwan's commercial attaché in Jakarta. In a 2004 interview he expressed the hope that Taiwan could play role of middleman in Israeli–Indonesian trade. He specifically mentioned the possibility of Taiwanese assistance in the establishment of Israeli-linked factories in Indonesia and in Israel's export of hi-tech electronics to Indonesia. Author's interview with Eugene Y.T. Chen, Tel Aviv, 5 June 2004; Speeches by Prime Minister Yitzhak Rabin to the Jewish Agency's Board of Governors, 25 October 1993, and to the Council of Jewish Federations, Montreal, 18 November 1993, in *Israel's Foreign Relations: Selected Documents 1992–1994*, ed. by Meron Medzini (Jerusalem: Ministry of Foreign Affairs, 1995), Vol.13, pp.164, 372–3, 426; 'Foreign Ministry Communique Regarding the Visit of an Economic Delegation from Indonesia, 16 May 2000', in *Israel's Foreign Relations: Selected Documents 1999–2001*, ed. by Meron Medzini (Jerusalem: Ministry of Foreign Affairs, 2002), Vol.18, p.224; Barton and Rubenstein, 'Indonesia and Israel' (see note 29), pp.163–7; C.G. Wilson, 'U.S. is Fronting Israeli Sale of Jets to Indonesia', *Washington Post*, 5 October 1979; Yossi Melman, 'Israel to Supply Skyhawk Planes to Indonesia', *Haaretz*, 1 July 1983 (Hebrew); Benjamin Beit-Hallahmi, *The Israeli Connection* (New York: Pantheon, 1987), pp.31–2.

Jews of Algiers

MOSHE TERDIMAN

The sea ports were usually cosmopolitan in character both socially and culturally. In this kind of environment it was very difficult, especially for a minority like the Jews, to develop an identity of their own. Were the Jews really able to form and build an identity of their own despite the cosmopolitan atmosphere prevailing in the seventeenth and eighteenth centuries in Algiers and their strong contact with Europe?

The relationship between the Livorno Jews on the one side and the native Jews on the other was an ambivalent one. On the one hand, the Livorno Jews were occupied mainly in trade through their contacts in Europe, whereas the native Jews were goldsmiths, tailors, peddlers and so on. On the other hand, the Livorno Jews served as *muqaddams* throughout the eighteenth century until the French occupation and did not try to separate the Jewish community of Algiers. On the contrary, together with the native Jews they benefited from community services and contributed to them. After saying all that, it must be remembered that the orientation of the Livorno Jews was outside Algiers. The Livorno Jews did not really develop an Algerian identity. They lived mainly in port cities, because of their engagement in international commerce, and were free to leave the country and enter it whenever they wished. They were not even subjects of the Algerian *deys*, whom they served. As long as the *dey* was popular the Livorno Jews enjoyed his support, but when his popularity decreased he used the Livorno Jews as scapegoats and sent them to exile, or the Jews themselves fled from Algiers when they sensed the possibility of trouble.

But the mutual dependence of the *deys* in the Livorno Jews and vice versa brought them to see themselves as a factor influencing the Algerian domestic and foreign policy. In this sense, they were Algerians.

Introduction

From time immemorial sea ports served as the entry gate for people and ideas to the mainland. The people who resided in the sea ports did so for various reasons: firstly, in a quest to find sources of livelihood and to better their lot; secondly, merchants and seamen used to come there and stay for long durations of time since the sea ports served as the main commercial centres; thirdly, sea ports had an important role as a haven for those refugees who chose the sea as their means of escape from hardships in their homeland. Sea ports were therefore usually cosmopolitan in character, both socially and culturally. Thus, it was very difficult to develop a distinctive identity especially for a minority like the Jews.

This paper will examine the case of the Jews of Algiers in the seventeenth and eighteenth centuries, focusing on Jewish identity against a background of strong contact with Europe.

Our knowledge about the Jews of Algiers in this period is derived mainly from Christians' accounts. There was a considerable wealth of material from a host of merchants, soldiers, sailors, ex-slaves, travellers, consular and diplomatic agents, and literary people who visited Algiers for one reason or another and left accounts of their experiences. It should be noted that most of these observers were hostile to Jews. This paper is based on diaries of European consuls in Algiers, mainly British and French, and some other secondary sources.[1]

Algiers under Ottoman Rule

Before dealing with the Jews, a few words about the situation in Algiers under Ottoman rule at this time are necessary.

The government of Algiers consisted of three major functional divisions: the palace organisation headed by the *dey* [from dayi in Turkish, which means 'maternal uncle'], who was in charge of the general administration of Algeria; the *ta'ifat al-ru'asa'* [association of ship captains (the corsairs)], headed by the *wakil al-kharaj* [the admiral], who patrolled the high seas in search of vessels possessing neither sufficient cannon nor 'passports' approved by Algiers; and, finally, the semi-independent governors of the *beyliks* [provinces], appointed by the *dey* and his *diwan* [council]. The *dey* was selected from among the *Janissaries* of the Turkish *ojak*, a body estimated at 6,000 men in 1800, whose ranks were replenished periodically by recruits from Turkish Asia Minor. The *dey*, in turn, paid a modest tribute to the sultan in Istanbul and received robes of investiture and gifts, and sometimes even war vessels.[2]

The *dey* appointed his *diwan* of high officials, which included the *khasanji* [the minister of finance and taxation]; the *agha* [head of the 6,000 *Janissaries*]; the *wakil al-kharaj* [minister of marine, head of the corsairs; lit., collector of the *kharaj* tribute]; the *bayt al-majli* [superintendent of the *dey*'s household]; the *khojat al-khayl* [administrator of the territories and their tribute]; and the *shaykh al-madinah* [charged with public order in Algiers]. The *dey* also maintained a *sirri defter* [first secretary], who helped manage the household but also assisted in foreign affairs.[3]

The territory of Algeria was divided into four *beyliks*: the *Dar al-Sultan* (the district around Algiers), controlled directly by the *dey* and administered by *kadis*, and three additional semi-independent governorates – Titeri, Oran and Constantine. Governors submitted annual taxes, but were expected to appear in person at the court of the *dey* once every three years. The *Janissaries* were charged with public order in every major city and the *kuloghlus* (the *Janissaries*' sons who could not inherit the post from their parents) and Moors were given supporting administrative posts. The tribes could be called upon to support the regular troops in times of major threats to the state. Among the politically significant classes in the cities were the *'ulama* [learned class], serving as judges, administrators, and teachers in the madrasas. There were also Jewish, Muslim and Christian merchants.

They usually enjoyed the protection of various European consular officials. Apart from the collection of taxes from the peasantry and the tribes, administered by the *beys* of the *beyliks* and the *amir bayt al-mal*, the *dey* could tap a vast array of revenue sources. In the towns, the artisans and merchants paid business taxes on products. There were also customs dues on all imports and exports. The Jews reportedly paid double fees, but Jewish partnerships with Christians or Muslims served to check this 'double taxation'.[4]

The main occupation in North Africa in the seventeenth and eighteenth centuries was piracy. In that period there existed two kinds of pirates. Firstly, the pirate was a freebooter, recognising no rule above his own will; and attacking indiscriminately the ships of any nation. His sole object was loot. Secondly, the corsair *reis*, who were privateers; making war only on the enemies of their prince or his god. Like the pirate's ship, the corsair's vessel actually was a private venture rather than a public charge. But the corsair carried a commission that legitimised his activities. He disposed of his prizes in a manner regulated by his prince.[5]

Algeria in the seventeenth century was the most important and the strongest state in North Africa. The Algerian corsairs scared the sailors and the European nations secured free navigation for their merchants in the Mediterranean by signing an agreement with the Algerian rulers. The prizes and the loot that the corsairs took made the inhabitants of the sea ports rich and encouraged commerce. However, in the eighteenth century Algeria suffered a severe economic recession that diminished its political prestige and importance. Epidemics and years of drought hastened this process. The number of ships sailing for piracy raids diminished and even the continental garrison shrank. The population decreased in greatly and with it the sources of livelihood. The export merchandise was sent to Marseilles and the imports came from Livorno and were in the hands of the Jews.[6]

The City of Algiers

Algiers in the seventeenth and eighteenth centuries was a cosmopolitan sea port. The population was composed of the *baldi* (native Moorish Algerians), the Turks (renegades and Levantines), the Tagarines and Andalusians (refugees from Spain), 'wild' Moors (Berbers) and Arabs from hinterland of the city, Christians, a few negro slaves, and Jews.[7]

In the city, the Turks were the ruling class, members of the army of occupation. These Turks along with the renegades who also became part of the *janissary* militia, were the rulers of the city. They alone could rise to positions of power in the military and political structure of the society. They stood outside the regular system of justice and punishment applied to the rest of the population.[8]

In addition to the recruits brought from the lands of the sultan, there were two other sources for the janissary militia: the renegades, who could become full members of the *janissary* corps and share equally with the Anatolyan, Syrian and Dalmatian recruits, and the *coulougli*, who were not allowed to hold high office either in the corps or in the government of the regency. The *coulougli* were the children of janissaries and Moorish women.[9]

The renegades played a more important role in the organisation of the militia and in the government of the regency. They were both a source of manpower and of skills lacking in the recruits from the East. Some were Christian children captured in raids and sold, often to a patron who brought them up in his own house. These youngsters found it easy to renounce the religion of their father for that of their patron, who in many cases made them his heir. There were adults who became renegades when they despaired of being ransomed and hoped to better their lot by denying their Christian faith. Among these were found several priests whose knowledge of Latin and ability to write enabled them to hold important positions in the government. Others were slaves who renounced their faith and joined the *janissary* corps.[10]

The other type of renegade was represented in the footloose Europeans who presented themselves in Algiers and renounced their religion for reasons of their own. Many of these men were hard-bitten characters who left their homelands for reasons of personal safety.[11]

The Berber or Moorish population of Algiers was made up first of the native *baldi*, the inhabitants of Algiers who were there when the Turks arrived; then of the refugees from Spain; and finally of tribesmen, mostly Kabilyes, and others who drifted in from the hinterland. The Moorish families made up a majority of the population. The Turks regarded them with mild contempt; they were peaceful, unsoldierly, unable to defend their own interests. While the refugee Tagarines and Andalusians were a minority in Algiers, they were nonetheless often very rich men who made their money by selling slaves back to their Christian families in Europe and investing the money in new corsair ships to capture more slaves. The Moorish population was made up of people of all social ranks. Some were rich merchants, owners of corsair ships or outfitters of those ships; some were artisans and petty merchants, some professional people, and some were very poor, carriers of burdens and workers in the fields. The Kabylie and other Berber peoples who migrated into Algiers were always a minority who played a very minor part in the native economy and even less in the corsair activity.[12]

The slaves of Algiers made up another large segment of the population. Although the majority was either Spanish or Italian, there were also slaves from every part of Europe. The vast majority were men, but landing raids and occasional capture of female passengers by the corsairs did bring in a few women. Their conditions varied greatly. Some worked the oars at sea, some laboured in quarries, on farms, at heavy road or construction operations; on the other hand, some were pampered servants, domestics who became part of the family, domestics clothed in fine costumes. Others operated wine shops, were artisans, even overseers and master craftsmen in the shipyards.[13]

Miriam Hoexter shows that the natives in Algiers were divided into two central groups: the permanent inhabitants of the city – the *khaddar*; and the migratory inhabitants – the *barania*, who came to Algiers to work in it for their livelihood. Their stay in the city was temporary. Most of Algiers' inhabitants were part of the *khaddar*. In Algiers there were Christians from different sects as well. Most of this group was composed of prisoners of the corsairs, who served as slaves in Algiers. The minority was composed of the representatives of the foreign nations with which

Algiers was at peace and of foreign merchants. From the jurisdictional point of view, that minority belonged to the *musta'mins* category, i.e., foreign subjects, not Moslems, who had a right to a permanent stay in an Islamic state by virtue of *aman* [auspices letter]. This minority lived in Algiers under the capitulation regime.[14]

Eizenbat found that in sixteenth century Algiers there were between 1,000 and 5,000 Jews out of a total population of 60,000 to 100,000. However, at the start of the seventeenth century there were 8,000–9,000 Jews and 10,000–12,000 Jews at the end. De Tassy claims that in 1725 there were 5,000 Jewish families, i.e., about 25,000 Jews. The total decrease of the population in the eighteenth century influenced the Jewish population too. At the end of the eighteenth century De Paradis estimated their numbers at about 7,000. In 1818 it had decreased to 5,000.[15]

De Brèves, who toured Tunisia and Algeria in 1604, found in Algiers Jews from Spain and Portugal, who spoke also Italian, Turkish and Arabic. They acted as the interpreters. D'Arvieux, who served as consul of France in Algeria (1674–75), noted especially David Zeyari, the representative of the Jewish nation, and Aharon Cohen, the Dey's confidant. He also claims that 10,000–12,000 Jews of varying sects lived in Algiers.[16]

The first sight of Algiers, when approaching from the sea, was rows of whitewashed houses, flat-roofed and set close together rising up the steep hillside to the Casbah fortress which dominated the city. On the landward side was the Bab Azoun, through which all traffic and travellers bound for the interior passed. On the west, the Bab el-Oued opened out onto a level expanse of ground normally used for the wares of wood and charcoal merchants, but sometimes cleared for the purpose of public burnings. The hillside beyond was dotted with pleasant country houses standing in the midst of gardens and orchards. The Marine Gate stood at the end of the great mole to link the city with the islet which the Spaniards had once fortified to keep the corsairs in check. A few hundred yards to the east was the Gate of the Fishermen leading to a strip of shore where the fishing boats were beached and warships built and repaired. Behind the ramparts, the lines of terraced roofs were broken by an occasional larger building – the Jenina, or dey's palace, the mosques, the public baths, the janissary barracks, the bagnios or slave prisons. The streets were exceedingly narrow. There was only one thoroughfare of any width which traversed the city from the Bab el-Oued to the Bab Azoun and served for some of its length as the *Bedestan*, or slave-market.[17]

Some Facts about the Native Jewish Community of Algiers

The Jews of Algiers were divided into one of two groups; *khaddar* and *barania*. The native Jews belonged to the *dhimmi* category – the non-Moslem subjects of the Islamic state, who were charged with all the obligations and who enjoyed all the rights of *'Ahl al-kitab*. The native Jews were subjected to limitations in different areas. They were obliged to wear dark coloured clothes, they could ride neither horses nor donkeys and mules within the city. They could not enter a mosque and when they passed in front of a mosque or the sovereign's palace, they were obliged to go barefoot. In addition, The Jews could leave Algiers only on Wednesdays and Saturdays without a permit.[18]

They were concentrated in two quarters located in the lower city of Algiers and not in the upper city, where all the Muslims lived – near Bab 'Azun and near Bab al-Wad. Most of them lived in Bab 'Azun quarter, on both sides of the big market street. In this area were located the Jewish *Khamam* (bathhouse) and slaughterhouse. Nearby was one of the *Janissaries* barracks, and the soldiers in it defended the Jews against the abuse of the local Muslims. The central synagogue, called La Hara, however, was located in Bab al-Wad quarter, on the other side of the city.[19]

It seems that the residence restriction was not kept strictly in all the periods. Fon Rahbinder states that whereas in the past the Jews had been restricted to special quarters in the city, this custom had been stopped gradually and in his time (the end of the eighteenth century), there were Jews all over Algiers. However, others claim that the Jews were restricted to one quarter only.[20]

Menahem Weinshtein suggests that the coming of the Jews expelled from Spain in 1391 to Algiers opened a new era in the history of the Jews of Algeria. This was a period of renaissance, including the presence of the then most prominent rabbi of Spain and Majorca, rabbi Itzhak Bar Sheshet and rabbi Shimon Bar Tsemach Duran and their descendants. These rabbis established a spiritual base in Algiers for the Jews of North Africa and the Mediterranean. However, the instability and the changes in the government of Algiers under Ottoman rule negatively influenced the status and the security of the Jews. This was especially the case in the sixteenth and seventeenth centuries, when Jews in Algiers were insecure.[21]

One of the Christian prisoners in Algiers in the sixteenth century, the Spaniard Diego de Haedo, described the humiliation of the Jews:

> Every Moslem who encountered a Jew in the street, be respectable as he will, could force him to take his hat and shoes off his head and feet in front of him. He could have also hit a Jew, if he wanted to, who would not dare run away or defend himself, and even the Christians took part in the humiliation of the Jews.[22]

Further evidence to the sufferings of the Jews in the sixteenth century is found in the manuscript Nafakh. In this manuscript there is a question and response that sheds light on the sufferings of the Jews. The Jews were accused of stirring riots in Algiers against the Turks and as such they were charged with hard labour every day, with humiliation; i.e., every Turk who encountered a Jew in the street could force him to take his load to his house, and Turkish soldiers could be lodged in Jewish houses. This last decree brought about a severe problem of prostitution and Islamisation amongst Jewish families.[23]

A book written by rabbi Avraham Gvishon, a doctor and a religious man, and among the second generation of Jews expelled from Spain, provides further evidence to this phenomenon. Avraham Gvishon settled in Tilmisan and declared that he could not settle in Algiers because of the problems and the rule of the Turks. According to Gvishon, communal life proceeded by regular customs, and the payment of taxes was made by the whole community, which collected from all Jewish persons their share according to the decision of the assessors, who were assigned by the community. Those appointed to collect the taxes for the ruling authority must have transmitted a detailed report to an authorised review committee acting within the Jewish community.[24]

According to Hirschberg it was only with the stabilisation of Ottoman rule that the descendants of the Jews expelled from Spain in 1492 and the marranos began to settle in Algiers. Diego de Haedo, whom we met earlier, narrated that the Jews of Algiers were divided into three groups: Spaniards, Balearics and Africans. They made their living mainly from trade, but some of them worked as goldsmiths, tailors and peddlers. Many Jews bought the spoils of the corsairs and sold it for large profits to Christian merchants. The Jews traded with Tunis, Jerba, Tripoli, Bonne, Constantine, Wahran, Tilmisan, Tetuan, Fez and even Istanbul. Most of the goldsmiths were Jewish. The Jews minted the gold, silver and copper coins, which was one of their obligations. The Jews taught their children Hebrew and to read and write Arabic in Hebrew letters. Haedo claims that the Jews stubbornly held on to their customs and beliefs. There were 150 Jewish families who lived in two quarters and in each quarter there was a synagogue. They had to pay the Pasha a tax, which amounted to 1,500 Dubles, i.e. 600 gold coins. They also had to pay special dues whenever the occasion arose. The dignitary who represented them before the Turkish authorities was called *Qasis*. The Jews lived in humiliation and even the children treated them with contempt. Spaniard Jews wore hats in Toledo style; the Jews of Provence, France and Italy wore another hat, the African Jews wore a kind of red hat called Shashia, that did not cover all the hair. The Jews from Istanbul wore a yellow turban. All the Jews, wherever they came from, wore black shoes. They lived in poverty, but employed numerous Christian prisoners and treated them well. Those Jews who chose to convert to Islam were called *Salami* and were socially inferior to the Maoris and Turks.[25]

In the eighteenth century Algeria suffered from years of drought, soaring prices, plagues, economic depression, a threat of Spanish invasions and internal conflicts. Because of that, the Jews were made scapegoats and were forced to pay large sums of money. At the beginning of the reign of Muhammad Baktash (1706–10), there were attempts to ruin the synagogue of Algiers in order to extract large sums of money from the Jews. The pasha abolished that decree after he received 80,000 grusus. Subsequently, rabbi Mordechai Narboni died after being charged with blaspheming Islam during a religious debate with his neighbour. Although he won the case, the kadi ruled that he be burned alive unless he converted to Islam. When he refused to do so he was burned at the stake in 1794.[26]

Notwithstanding these difficulties the Jews thought of themselves as a part of Algiers. For example, in 1775 there was a real threat to Algiers when the Spanish tried to attack it. The Spanish failed, and to celebrate that miracle a day of fasting was declared for the Jewish community a day after purim (tenth and eleventh of Tamuz) and the rabbis Nehorai Azuviv and Jacob Ben Naim and the Judges Aharon Cohen, Jonathan and Avraham Tovaina composed poems in the memory of the event.[27]

Until the eighteenth century the Jewish community of Algiers was regarded as one of the great Jewish communities in North Africa. However, in the course of the eighteenth century its status deteriorated. Its chief rabbi went to the Land of Israel and the Jewish community, which in the past used to guide all the Jewish communities in Northern Africa, was thereafter under the guidance of Jerusalem rabbis.[28] At that time Jews comprised 17–18 per cent of the whole population of

Algiers. There is no data as to the number of native Jews and of Livorno Jews within this estimate, but we know that 300 Jewish families were expelled from Algiers in 1805 and these were mainly Livornese Jews, suggesting that these Livornese Jews were, at least until the beginning of the nineteenth century, a large minority within the Jewish community.[29] They were part of what was called then the 'Christian Jews'. Who were these Christian Jews and what distinguished them from the local Jews?

The Christian Jews

In 1675, the British consul in Algiers wrote that in 1675 that there were about 13,000 Jews in Algiers: most of them were native Jews, whose forefathers had lived in Algiers for a long time. They were mostly artisans who lived in a ghetto, dressed inconspicuously in black, and were easily recognised as Jews. The others were 'Christian or European Jews' who came from Spain, Portugal, or Italy, dressed in 'European fashion', and merged into the European community. The latter were in contact with their co-religionists in Florence, Marseilles, Amsterdam, London and elsewhere. They had a poor reputation according to most of the Christian observers, probably because they were in economic competition with them.[30]

These 'Christian Jews' or 'Livorno Jews' belonged to the *Musta'min* category. As was the case for other foreigners in Algiers, these Jews operated under the capitulation regime. Because of their influence and their contacts with the European consuls, the Jewish merchants found refuge in times of trouble and persecution in the consuls' houses in Algiers. Since their country of origin did not maintain a diplomatic residency in the city, they were subject to the French consulate in Algiers. Thus they could leave and enter Algiers whenever they wished and live outside the Jewish quarter, including in the upper city. Moreover, they could wear whatever they wished. D'Arvieux noted the dress of those Jews from Livorno and Alexandria: they wore hats and clothes like those of the Italians or the Spaniards and adhered to their customs even in their homes.[31] They were known as 'the Christian Jews' because they grew up in Spain, Portugal and Italy, and looked like Spanish, Portuguese or Italians. As merchants they were much more capable than others.[32] They initially enjoyed freedom of movement and could leave the country whenever they wished, as long as they did not leave debts behind them. The Jewish subjects of the *dey*, however, could leave Algeria only after they had made a deposit that would guarantee their return. The European Jews enjoyed the right to live wherever they wished and not just in the *khara*, the native Jewish quarter. In addition they were exempt from carrying the marks of recognition on their clothes and hats, which was an obligation for the dhimmis. The Livorno Jews were also customs officers and tax collectors and were given the concession for oil exports. The *deys* chose some of them as diplomatic emissaries to the European states. Livorno itself served as an important diplomatic centre between Africa and Europe. English sources even claim that Livorno was the naval base for the ships of the Algerian navy. In some cases Algerian ships sailed from there for attacks on the Italian states.

Why was Livorno so important in the overall Mediterranean trade? The grand dukes of Tuscany sought to augment the maritime commerce of their realm by creating a major trade centre at Livorno. Livorno was located on the western side of Italy, directly across the Mediterranean from France and Spain. It was convenient for ships coming into the Mediterranean from the Atlantic ports of Spain, France, England, Holland, and from the Americas and Asia, to sail to Livorno. While these western traders were unlikely to settle in Livorno, there was another group of people, very active in Mediterranean trade but not officially allowed into Atlantic ports, who could potentially be attracted to Livorno, namely Jews and New Christians. Accordingly, Grand Duke Ferdinand issued a charter in 1591 which was reissued in definitive form in 1593. Known as 'La Livornina', it basically remained in effect until the end of the Grand Duchy of Livorno in 1860. The charter was intended primarily to attract Jews and New Christians. This famous edict accorded to Jews and Moors full rights to reside, trade, regulate debts, borrow money, and store goods in Tuscany and more specifically in Livorno. A Jew need only to reside in Livorno one day to be a protected subject of the Grand Duke of Tuscany under the right of ballotazione (petition). Livorno also became an important transfer point when direct international trade between countries was disrupted due to war or other restrictions. In time the port of Livorno came to be dominated by Jewish merchants who made the city a place of principal residence and their headquarters for various trade operations in addition a place of refuge in times of economic or political unrest elsewhere.[33]

The Livorno Jews and the Native Community

Eliezer Bashan claims that the eighteenth century was the golden era in the religious life of both Livorno and Algiers. Their respective rabbis maintained contacts. For example, rabbi Avraham Haim Rodrigues, a rabbi from Livorno (died in 1735), notes in his religious book the response of rabbi Avraham Ben Maimon Yafil, one of the rabbis of Algiers. Rabi Zemach Ben Shimon, one of the descendants of the Rashbats, who operated in Algiers, came to Livorno in 1742 as an envoy on behalf of a prisoners' group that had turned to the Jews of Algiers for assistance, to plead for the participation of the Jews of Livorno in their redemption.[34]

There is substantial information about the economic contacts between both communities from the eighteenth century, when Jews from Algiers came to Livorno and Jews from Livorno came to Algiers for business purposes. In the eighteenth century a few Jewish families from Livorno settled in Algiers. From there they managed their commercial business via agents not only with the Jews of Livorno but also with other central bases in Northern Africa, the Mediterranean lands and Europe.[35]

Those Jews of Livorno who settled in North Africa, maintained political, economic, social and cultural contacts with their place of origin. Those who came to Algiers were not the family heads, who chose to stay in Livorno and to manage the family business from there, but their younger brothers and relatives, who came there to manage the business branch. The links of the Livorno Jews who settled in the North African states with France and its consulates stemmed from the capitulations accords between France and the Ottoman Empire, by which all the subjects of European states that did not have representatives of their own in the Empire were put under French auspices. Therefore all the 'Christian Jews' were under French protection.[36]

It must be noted that in Algiers there was an important community of Spanish Jews – among them descendants of the Jews expelled from Spain in 1391 and 1492. They retained a distinct character. As long as the Livorno Jews arrived in Algiers in small numbers, they did not stand out because they were not distinct in almost anything from the previous Spanish waves; they merged socially and culturally, but did not mingle with the native Jews. They married within their own community; did not intermarry with the native Jews, indeed scarcely associated with them. They even sent their children abroad to study.[37] But they never established a separate community. This continued to be the case when their numbers and influence in Algiers grew. The Jews of Algiers were never divided into two separate communities as was the case in Tunis. They enjoyed joint communal services – such as synagogues, kosher slaughter, rabbinical judgement and so on – and participated in financing these services. The Jews, apparently, spoke Hebrew among themselves and used the lingua franca in speaking to others. This lingua franca was nearly universal; it was a mixture of Spanish, Portuguese, Italian, and French, with Spanish as the predominant component. The Livorno Jews served in the role of heads of the Jewish community throughout most of the eighteenth century.[38]

As in many Jewish communities, the leadership of the Jewish community of Algiers was divided into religious and lay leadership. The rabbis served as religious judges and as the religious leaders of the community, whereas its lay leadership was given to the *muqaddam*, who is called nagid in the Jewish sources. The Jewish *muqaddam* was appointed by the authorities. His main role was to maintain contact between the Jewish community and the authorities. He was perceived by the authorities as the only leader responsible for the Jewish community. This *muqaddam* was always appointed from amongst the people of the community, which he served as its head. There is no evidence for the involvement of the Jewish community in the election process. The sources stress that bribery was involved in the buying of the job. Cahen notes that the job of *muqaddam* was always bought with money or was given as a reward for personal services for the *dey* or the Turkish administration.[39]

In the early eighteenth century, the Spanish-Jewish families of the Jakets, the Boucharas, the Busnachs, and the Bacris had become the leading families in Algeria, although they were in fact considered to be Livorno Jews. Their position in Algiers had been enhanced by the late eighteenth century when their family members and agents had broken the monopoly of the Marseilles merchants during the turmoil following the French revolution. Thus the powerful Jewish families of Algeria maintained close connections, and sometimes outright bases for trade and banking and the accompanying political influence in Algeria, Livorno, and France. They also maintained good trade connections in Spain and Gibraltar.[40]

The official title of the head of the Jewish millet in Algiers was *muqaddam*. His responsibility was to manage the Jewish courts, oversee tax collection, and maintain the Jewish schools. The aristocratic families often vied with each other to obtain this powerful and prestigious post. The personal authority of the *muqaddam* applied just to the native Jews. The foreign subjects among the Jews were entitled to a consular discretion. Although they had the right to turn to the *dey* to arbitrate for them.[41]

Clearly it was the wealthy Jews who received the post since only they could afford it. From 1735 to 1800 two of the Bushara Livornese family served in this post, each for 30 years. But from 1800 until the French occupation in 1830 the post switched eight times under the Bacri family. Native Jews served in this post for just a little more than a year. It needs to be noted that in this period there was no case of a rabbi serving as a *muqaddam*.[42]

The *muqaddam* also served as the consul of Ragusa and the commercial agent of the *dey*. These latter posts were financially lucrative; hence they were a source of competition between the wealthiest Jewish merchants in Algiers. In this competition the Jewish community was not involved. The *muqaddam*, who was elected by the authorities and who enjoyed their support, managed the community by dictating, arbitrating, extorting and pressurising in an effort to gain more sources of income.[43]

The Jewish community was unable to oppose the policy. When a delegation of the Jewish community, led by the rabbi of Algiers, dared complain about blackmailing on the part of the *muqaddam*, it resulted in the rabbi and six of the community's dignitaries being executed by the authorities in 1815. These actions resulted in unrest, leading to the exile of the *muqaddam* from the city.[44]

From Traders to Pirates

Although small groups of Spanish Jews found refuge in Algiers from the thirteenth century, the largest wave of Jewish immigration took place after the great expulsion of 1492. They brought with them a tradition of large scale maritime trade which contributed to the prosperity of Algiers. The early Spanish Jews introduced ostrich plumes, coral products, wool, wine, hides, dates, raisins, tobacco, sponges, olives and olive oils and, occasionally, grain. From the eighteenth century, the important Jewish trading houses had begun making large commissions from the ransoming of captives and the sale of contraband that had been picked up by the Algerian corsairs. Among the important Jewish commercial houses were Alvarenga Y Luzada, Jacob Machoro Y Itzhak Baruch, Aharon Molcho, Benjamin Zakut. Jewish trading companies increasingly grew stronger and, in cooperation with the deys, discouraged direct Algerian trade with French merchants, preferring to manage both ends of the transactions through their correspondents in Livorno and later in Marseilles itself. Their increasing personal influence over the *deys* of Algiers made such a growing monopoly possible.[45]

The strength of the leading Jewish families in Algiers derived from the extent of their international commercial relations. Ayoun and Cohen suggest that with the coming of the Turks to Algeria in the sixteenth century, the traditional Muslim status of *dhimmi*, enjoyed earlier in Muslim lands by the Jews, lost its special significance and had become merely a financial obligation. In addition to taxes levied on each profession, the community as a whole was expected to pay the special levy of 14,000 francs each year. Moreover, the government, in their opinion, generally made less of an effort than previously to protect Jews from the sporadic abuse of Muslim townsmen.[46]

However, with the broad international commercial relations developed by the Livorno Jews in the eighteenth century, the *deys* became sufficiently dependent on this trade to treat the elite Jewish merchants with great respect and even favour. As examples of this trade, one could mention Jewish involvement in ransoming European captives, and the *dey*'s granting them monopolies including the trade in grain, wax, leather, and ostrich feathers. The monopolies were later expanded to include financial transactions, loans, and trade in precious metals and luxury goods. These privileges appear to have become especially important as the income of the *deys* from corsair activity diminished greatly in the late eighteenth century. Not only had the recruitment of corsairs declined, but also the navies of European powers began rapidly to outclass the naval strength of the amirates. With the decline of recruitment of Turkish troops from Anatolya, it also became much more difficult to collect the taxes from the Algerian countryside.[47]

Why did the *dey* allow almost the entire international trade of the regency to fall into the hands of European or Jewish merchants? Part of the answer can be found in the increasingly important role of the Jews in the government of Algiers. As the *dey*'s regime became more bureaucratised, Jewish financiers assumed a larger role. The Turks regarded themselves as soldiers and rulers, not as financiers. Thus Jewish merchant houses with contacts all over Europe became more and more important for the ongoing business of the regency. With influence came power and greater importance in the commercial society. The *dey*'s government was the principal agent for most of the commodities that Algiers sold to Europe: wool, hides, horses, wheat, and other such primary goods were the virtual monopoly of the *deylik*. But the *dey* could not market these good himself: he had to depend upon the foreign merchants – mostly Frenchmen – and the Jews to manage his business. Why did the *reis* not step in and participate in the profitable business? The answer is simple when we look at rules and regulations that Christian powers and Christian harbours placed on Moslem commerce. There were dozen of rules, tariffs, and regulations all aimed at keeping Moslem traders out of the European market. And *reis* who happened also to be renegades had the added hazard that their lives would be in danger if they landed in a Christian port.[48]

So, if we look into the relationship between the Algerian *deys* and the commercial house of Bacri-Busnach as an example of the role played by a leading merchant house in an Islamic society, we see that, in fact, most of the time there appears to have been a convergence of interests between the highest government officials and the firm of Bacri-Busnach. They shared in legitimate investments, shipping, international trade, foreign loans, but also in piracy and the ransoming of captives. They also cooperated in the processes of tax collecting and in the operations of the customhouses. There is no doubt that the *askeri* class possessed a near monopoly of force which could be used against offending groups. Given their distaste for commerce, the Janissaries and similar military organisations throughout the Middle East were generally content to leave the supply side of their military functions – the provisioning of the army and the cities and the providing of cloth, uniforms and firearms – to Muslims and non-Muslims of lower classes. This became the case particularly in Algiers where the military elite assured to themselves a share in the commercial profits. To the minority groups, in particular, the *askeri* class left the dual advantages of grossing large financial profits from various enterprises, while not having to serve in the frequent wars to defend Muslim territory.[49]

How much were the Jews involved in the corsairing system, which was very widespread in Algiers? Already at the end of the sixteenth century there is evidence of Jews involved in piracy in Algiers. In the list of captains of the 35 ships of Algiers in 1588 one Jew is mentioned.[50]

D'Arvieux stressed the part of Jews and non-Jews in buying the spoils of the corsairs, which they transferred to Genoa and Livorno with a nice profit. The Jews profited from the corsair activity. First, some of the money needed to outfit the corsair ships came from Jewish merchants. Second, some of the merchandise brought into Algiers by the corsairs was sold to Jewish entrepreneurs, who then re-exported it to Italy, France and even as far away as the islands in the Atlantic Ocean. Finally, these Jewish merchants were deeply involved in the business of transferring ransom money from Europe to Algiers for the release of slaves. The Duke of Tuscany was personally involved in this business, since he supplied prisons to protect the Christian slaves until the ransom money was actually transferred.[51] For example, Salomon Saquete, a Livorno Jew, owned a corsair ship and leased a wax concession. He used to inform the Algerian authorities regarding the Christian lands; only through him could prisoners be ransomed.[52]

Eliezer Bashan claims that it is a mistake to suggest that all the Jews in the Maghrib were engaged in commerce. The publicity that was given to the great Jewish merchant families in Algiers put them in focus and they served as a window reflecting all the Jews. But it must be remembered that they were a minority among the Jews of Algiers. Most Jews in Algiers belonged to the middle and lower classes and were engaged in peddling. Some of them were artisans. Rosenshtock claims that most of the Jews in Algiers between 1790 and 1848 were small merchants and petty artisans, living in poverty.[53]

Conclusion

The relationship between the Livorno Jews on the one side and the native Jews on the other side was an ambivalent one. On the one hand, the Livorno Jews were occupied mainly in trade through their contacts in Europe, whereas the native Jews were goldsmiths, tailors, peddlers and so on. On the other hand, the Livorno Jews served as *muqaddams* throughout the eighteenth century until the French occupation and did not try to separate themselves from the Jewish community of Algiers. On the contrary, they worked with the native Jews on communal matters and took part in the maintenance of the community.

Nonetheless, it must be noted that the orientation of the Livorno Jews was always outside Algiers. This depended on the Algerian *deys* for support and in gaining wealth. And since they managed the finances of the *deys*, they were blamed for every financial problem between the *deys* and external powers. Put simply, the Livorno Jews were perceived by external forces as those who managed Algiers and this was apparently the cause of the French occupation.

In essence, however, the French military intervention had its origins in the era of the Directory (1796), when the two influential Jewish merchants, Bakri and Busnach, supplied France with wheat, most of which belonged to the *deylik* rather than to the merchants. The Directory did not pay, but in 1801 Napoleon, as consul, recognised the debt and authorised payment. The money, however, was not forthcoming. Nothing was done to mollify the *dey*'s irritation until after the restoration of the Bourbons. In 1818 a treaty was drawn up and signed, placing the debt at seven million livres. Two years later the chamber passed a bill authorising the payment. At this point a group of French merchants brought a suit for the collection of debts amounting to some five million livres that Bacri and Busnach owed them. The two merchants abruptly left Algiers for fear of their lives after the French consul explained to the *dey* that his money could not be recovered until the debts were settled and that he would receive only what was left after that settlement.[54]

In retrospect the Livorno Jews never developed an Algerian identity. They lived mainly in port cities because of their engagement in international commerce and were free to leave the country and enter it whenever they wished. They were not even subjects of the Algerian *deys* whom they served. As long as the *dey* was popular, the Livorno Jews enjoyed support. When his popularity decreased, the Livorno Jews were used as scapegoats and sent into exile. Alternatively the Jews themselves fled Algiers when they sensed possible trouble. But, the mutual dependence of the *deys* and the Livorno Jews allowed them to see themselves as a factor influencing the Algerian domestic and foreign policy. In this sense, they were Algerians.

NOTES

1. H.Z. Hirschberg, *A History of the Jews in North Africa from Antiquity to Our Time*: Volume Two (Jerusalem: Bialik Institute, 1965), p.43; John B. Wolf, *The Barbary Coast: Algiers Under The Turks 1500 to 1830* (New York: W.W. Norton and Company, 1979), pp.104–6.
2. C. Max Kortepeter, 'Jew and Turk in Algiers in 1800', in *The Jews of The Ottoman Empire*, ed. by Avigdor Levy (Princeton, NJ: The Darwin Press, Inc., 1994), p.329; Hirschberg, *A History of The Jews* (see note 1), p.40.
3. Kortepeter, 'Jew and Turk' (see note 2), p.329; Hirschberg, *A History of the Jews* (see note 1), p.41.
4. Kortepeter, 'Jew and Turk' (see note 2), pp.330–31.
5. C.R. Pennell, *Piracy and Diplomacy in Seventeenth-Century North Africa: The Journal of Thomas Baker, English Consul in Tripoli, 1677–1685* (London: Associated University Presses, 1989), pp.45–6.
6. Stepphen Clissold, *The Barbary Slaves* (London: Elek Books Limited, 1977), pp.149–50; Hirschberg, *A History of the Jews* (see note 1), p.42.
7. Wolf, *The Barbary Coast* (see note 1), pp.97–8.
8. Ibid., pp.100–101.
9. Ibid., pp.101–2.
10. Ibid., p.102.
11. Ibid., pp.102–3.
12. Ibid., pp.103–4.
13. Ibid., p.107.
14. Miriam Hoexter, 'The Jewish Community in Algiers and Its Place in The Turkish Rule System', *Sefunot: Mehkarim veMekorot leToldot Israel baMizrah*, 17 (1983), 134.
15. Hirschberg, *A History of the Jews* (see note 1), p.43.
16. Ibid., pp.48–9.
17. Clissold, *The Barbary Slaves* (see note 6), pp.38–40.
18. Hoexter, 'The Jewish Community' (see note 14), pp.134–6.
19. Ibid., p.136.
20. Ibid., pp.136–7.
21. Menahem Weinstein, 'Algiers' Community and Its Scholars in the Sixteenth and Seventeenth Centuries', *Bar Ilan*, 14–15 (1977), 139–41.

22. Ibid., p.141; Diego de Haedo, *Topographia e Historia General de Archel* (Valladolid, 1612), chapter 28.
23. Weinstein, 'Algiers' Community' (see note 21), pp.141–2.
24. Hirschberg, *A History of the Jews* (see note 1), pp.46–7.
25. Ibid., p.48.
26. Ibid., pp.52–3.
27. Ibid., p.53.
28. Hoexter, 'The Jewish Community' (see note 14), p.141.
29. Ibid., p.139.
30. Hirschberg, *A History of the Jews* (see note 1), p.49.
31. Hoexter, 'The Jewish Community' (see note 14), pp.135, 137.
32. Hirschberg, *A History of the Jews* (see note 1), p.49.
33. Benjamin Ravid, 'A Tale of Three Cities and their Raison d'Etat: Ancona, Venice, Livorno, and the Competition for Jewish Merchants in the Sixteenth Century', in *Jews, Christians, and Muslims in the Mediterranean World After 1492*, ed. by Alisa Meyuhas Ginio (London: Frank Cass and Company, 1992), pp.155–7; Yitzhak Avrahami, *Pinkas Hakehila Hayehudit Haportugezit Betunis 1944–1710* (Lod: Orot Yahadut Hamagreb, 1997), p.43; Kortepeter, 'Jew and Turk' (see note 2), pp.335–6.
34. Eliezer Bashan, *Sefer Mimizrah Shemesh 'Ad Mevoo Prakim Betoldot Yehudei Hamizrah ve Hamagreb: Hevra veKalkala* (Lod: Orot Yahadut Hamagreb, 1996), pp.74–5.
35. Ibid., p.75.
36. Hirschberg, *A History of the Jews* (see note 1), p.54.
37. Hoexter, 'The Jewish Community' (see note 14), p.137.
38. Avrahami, *Pinkas* (see note 33), pp.45–6.
39. Hoexter, 'The Jewish Community' (see note 14), pp.141–2.
40. Kortepeter, 'Jew and Turk' (see note 2), pp.333–4.
41. Hoexter, 'The Jewish Community' (see note 14), p.141.
42. Ibid., p.142.
43. Ibid., pp.142–3.
44. Ibid., p.143.
45. Kortepeter, 'Jew and Turk' (see note 2), p.333.
46. Ibid., p.334.
47. Ibid., p.334.
48. Wolf, *The Barbary Coast* (see note 1), pp.294–5.
49. Kortepeter, 'Jew and Turk' (see note 2), pp.348–9.
50. Stanley Lane-Poole, *The Barbary Corsairs* (London: T. Fisher Unwin, 1890), pp.200-201.
51. Wolf, *The Barbary Coast* (see note 1), p.156.
52. Hirschberg, *A History of the Jews* (see note 1), p.58.
53. Bashan, *Sefer Mimizrah Shemesh* (see note 34), p.177.
54. Wolf, *The Barbary Coast* (see note 1), pp.333-4.

Jewish Identity in Two Remote Areas of the Cape Province: A Double Case Study

JOHN SIMON

This paper deals with two communities hundreds of miles away from each other, but each representing important 'milestone' communities. They were established by those Jewish pioneers who, having landed in Cape Town as their entrepôt into South Africa (principally from Eastern Europe between c.1880 and c.1900 or later in the 1920s from the successor states of the former tsarist Empire) chose not to remain in the Metropolis, but set out to establish themselves in distant and largely unknown areas.[1] One would expect those who chose this route for whatever reason to be of a more adventurous character and so indeed they were. Various reasons prompted the early Jewish pioneers to follow the routes and reach the destinations that will be described. In many cases the process known to demographers as chain migration was at work; a brother or brother-in-law, an uncle or cousin or even a *landsleit* would send a report that he had found a place where hard work and the willingness to forgo urban comforts could provide a living and a future. In each case examined, there was also, as will be seen, a particular commercial niche which could be occupied by enterprising newcomers. And so they set forth.

There were two routes and destinations out of Cape Town. The one travelled north along the west coast of what was then known as the Cape Province and, traversing such towns as Malmesbury, Morreesburg, Vredenberg, Piketberg and Garies, reached the area at the extreme north of the Province known as Namaqualand. The other route, travelling east from Cape Town broadly along the southern coast, passed or skirted Stellenbosch, Somerset West, Caledon, Swellendam, Riversdale, Albertinia, Mossel Bay and George before turning somewhat north-west over the mountains to Oudtshoorn. Although the paper will examine the two terminus points, Namaqualand and Oudtshoorn, the little towns in between are mentioned because in every one of these little towns sufficient Jews would settle to establish congregations with synagogues, halls and *Talmudei Torah*. They would all constitute so-called three digit communities and would all have more or less thriving and Jewishly active congregations until the forces of demography took over and the communities dwindled as the Jews moved to the cities, mainly in search of better educational opportunities for their children.[2] Namaqualand and Oudtshoorn deserve and will receive special mention and examination in this paper for a number of reasons: each was located in an identifiable area with a distinctive climate and historical and demographic circumstances; each acquired an active vibrant and picturesque

Jewish community with its own internal activities, but with its members participating prominently in local public life; each was the centre of a unique commercial, mining and agricultural world which provided opportunities for and in turn benefited from the Jewish element; each contributed outstanding individual Jews who made their mark locally and further afield; and each engendered a unique community spirit which characterised its Jews even long after their departure to far-flung areas. This is not to derogate from the work and character of other communities but I hope to show that the Jews of Namaqualand and Oudtshoorn merit particular mention.

The name Namaqualand is said to originate from the Khoi-san word meaning Land of Wearers of Skins. The area known as Namaqualand covers a fairly large area some 335 miles north-west of Cape Town, bounded on the west by the Atlantic Ocean, north by the Orange River, east by the area known to early settlers as Bushmanland and south approximately by the Buffels River. It is not a friendly area. It is semi-desert, hilly, sandy and waterless. Only for a few weeks in springtime, if some rain has fallen just at the right time, does this desert area become a wonderland of brightly coloured wild flowers spreading as far as the eye can see across the veld, transforming it into a sea of orange, blue, purple, white and yellow. But the wild flowers of Namaqualand are a pleasure for today's tourists that did not make anything easier for the early settlers. The area had been travelled by Simon van der Stel, one of the early Cape Governors, but it was really opened up by *trekboers*[3] and missionaries in the early years of the nineteenth century and was officially included in the Cape Colony in 1847. Some traces of copper had been found as early as the Dutch occupation, but it was in the 1850s that copper was found in quantities which would lead to an important mining industry with its offshoot in the fields of transport, shopkeeping and farming.

The earliest known Jewish residents of Namaqualand were Aaron De Pass and his wife Esther. The firm of De Pass Brothers was a very prominent Cape Jewish family[4] who were inter alia engaged in shipping and trading up the west coast as far as Port Nolloth. In that little port they are known to have celebrated *Yom Kippur* alone in their home in 1856.[5]

But as has been noted, it was the last two decades of the nineteenth century, the period of the great Jewish migrations from Eastern Europe, which saw the first appearance of Jews in any numbers in these areas. By the end of the nineteenth century, or within a decade thereafter, there were Jews in almost every one of the little towns mentioned earlier in this paper and certainly in the picturesquely named dorps of Namaqualand: Garies, Bitterfontein, Vanrhynsdorp, Bowesdorp, Nababeep, O'Okiep, Port Nolloth and what became the principal Jewish community in Namaqualand, Springbok.[6]

It is extremely unlikely that there were ever more than 200 Jews in Namaqualand.[7] At first glance this may prompt the thought that the whole community is hardly worth a mention on its own. It is suggested however that the very fact that so small a number produced the various results which will be outlined in this paper provides its own reason for it being recorded; and the comparisons and contrasts which will be drawn with the Oudtshoorn community certainly provide a study worth noting.

The early arrivals of course were almost solely Yiddish-speaking. Somehow they got by although many never lost their accents which sometimes became an embarrassment to their locally born children. But there was a certain affinity between Yiddish and High Dutch (the precursor of modern day Afrikaans) and so the new migrants were able to understand and be understood by those with whom they came into contact. This contact usually arose from the fact that the occupation most frequently pursued by the Jewish newcomers was that of itinerant peddler or *smous*.

The *smous*, also known as a *tocher* or a *shmoyzer*, was a frequently encountered figure in the story of outlying Jewish communities in South Africa and had his counterpart also in other pioneer communities.[8] On commencing his trade, he perhaps carried his goods on his back and by stages acquired first a donkey and then a horse and cart until he was eventually able to open his own shop. Indigenous South African literature contains many references to their activities and they were particularly well-known in the Oudtshoorn area and Namaqualand, and are still affectionately remembered by the descendants of the farmers with whom they traded. On 18 September 1989 a plaque was erected outside the Eastern Cape town of Graaff Reinet at the side of the main street with an inscription reading as follows:

> In honour of the pioneer Jewish pedlars known as *smouse*, who traded in outlying and remote country districts. They supplied their customers with many of the necessities of life. In the course of their trading they made a contribution to the economic development of this country.

By 1918 there were sufficient Jews in Namaqualand to take formal steps to establish a Hebrew Congregation centred in Springbok. Negotiations were entered into with the local Dutch Reformed Church whose 'Ou Kerkie' (Little Old Church) was no longer required. This was acquired by the congregation as the first synagogue but only two years were to pass before the need arose to build a larger synagogue.

These transactions with the Dutch Reformed Church were symptomatic of what was at least in the early days largely (but by no means entirely) a harmonious relationship between the Namaqualand Jews and their non-Jewish neighbours, a number of whom have recorded their appreciation of the quality of their Jewish neighbours. One man whose family has been in the area since the late 1800s included in his unpublished memoirs the following passage (translated from Afrikaans): 'Together with [the speculators who had come from various European countries in the wake of the copper rush of the 1850s] came the Jewish people. But they did not come to mine or to get rich quickly, they came to stay, to survive, because they were dirt poor. They came to do a little business, to buy and sell and to make a small profit.'[9]

There were two important mineral finds in the Namaqualand area, namely copper in the 1850s and diamonds in the 1920s. Jewish newcomers to Namaqualand during these periods were not by and large prospectors, miners or speculators but they were well situated to take advantage of the trading opportunities which came in the wake of these two 'mini-booms'. It was no longer necessary for the *smous* to pack his cart and travel to outlying farms. It was possible to open a small general dealer's store, first in one and then in another of the little towns which expanded in the wake of the mineral finds. There arose a need for hotels, sometimes just a grandiose term for lodging houses, but larger commercial hotels developed in time. These enterprises required bookkeepers and soon the population needed a pharmacist, a doctor, a lawyer.[10] All these activities brought Jews into direct contact with non-Jews and such contact was increasingly conducted in the Afrikaans language. The first generation who came, as has been mentioned, grafted their Yiddishisms onto Dutch and later Afrikaans. The next generation, who were educated in the local schools, grew up with Afrikaans, if not as their first language certainly as a close second. There were times when the occupations pursued by the Jews enabled them to be of assistance to their neighbours. The doctor, the lawyer, the pharmacist would often have to wait for his fee, particularly during the depression years of the 1930s when the South African economy was in desperate straits. Even more so, the shopkeeper saw his debtors' list mount ever higher as his customers were unable to pay him for the necessities of life which he stocked and they needed. A letter from a hard-pressed Jewish shopkeeper to his merchant creditors is worth quoting for its quaintness and even more for the humanity which shines through it.

> Dear Sirs, you asked me for money to pay my account. But do you know that we have a drought? Do you know that there is no harvest? Do you know that the sheep are dying? Do you know that the farmers are going bankrupt? Do you know that we must still help the farmers? Well I know that you don't know or you would not ask me for money which I haven't got. Anyhow I don't blame you for trying but don't worry if I don't pay you then God will pay you. Goodbye and good luck. Yours truly, Sores Klass.[11]

Jowell and Folb make this comment: 'It is not surprising therefore that there was a rapport between the Jews and the Afrikaners in Namaqualand. First the *smous* and later the shopkeepers and hoteliers provided an economic service to the local inhabitants and together they struggled through and survived the hard times.' As so often, of course, this rapport frequently did not extend to the good times. The depression left a residuum of bitterness which was exacerbated by the perceived upward mobility of the Jew who prospered in his trade or profession. This would have its resonance in the political development of South Africa.[12]

Did the close interaction with the general community serve to dilute the Jewish commitment of the Namaqualand Jews? The reverse seems to have been the case. Reference has already been made to the early creation of the congregation and the erection of the synagogues. Small Zionist societies existed. Every effort was made to hold services on Sabbath and Holy Days. Commercial travellers who visited the Namaqualand shopkeepers canvassing orders for their respective firms were sure of a warm Sabbath welcome and were expected to turn up at services. Up to a very late stage when the community had dwindled to a handful of Jews, it is heartwarming to read the records of the Cape Town Jewish Institutions who received a guinea or two after the High Holy Days from the Namaqualand Hebrew Congregation being the proceeds of '*shenoddering*'.[13]

It is noteworthy that of all the Jewish families whose names appear and reappear in the Namaqualand records, most remained for only one or two, or at most three generations. The lure of the cities was very strong, particularly because of the increased commercial opportunities for able businessmen and most importantly the educational facilities for their children. During these comparatively few years Namaqualand Jews created 'diep spore' [deep traces].

The Anglo-Boer War (1899–1902) brought strife to the area as in so many other locations and Jews were to be found engaged on both sides.[14]

We are fortunate that the Jews of Namaqualand were enthusiastic amateur photographers and not infrequently recorded their lives and activities. Picnics, family outings, sporting occasions and celebrations of all types on public and private occasions have been recorded for us in a host of snapshots, many of which have been gathered and reproduced in such works as Jowell and Folb's *Into Kokerboom Country*.[15]

There was nothing of the hick about Namaqualand Jews. They were well turned out, indeed elegant, and took a prominent part in all sports, entertainment and other general community activities. Many of them or their children would go on to achieve distinguished careers in the major cities of South Africa. But one man amongst them, Joe Jowell of Namaqaland, stands out for the success of his public and commercial career, and his life has been well recorded by his daughter-in-law.[16] Jowell came to Namaqualand in 1929. He had to give up his chosen legal career because of poor eyesight and he acquired the local Chevrolet sub-agency. This was the commencement of a career which made him one of the most distinguished entrepreneurs of the transport industry in South Africa, culminating in the Stock Exchange listing of the company which became known as Trencor. He was an example of a Jew whose sense of public service led him to be one of the principal leaders of the Jewish community and the community at large. There have been a few South African Jews whose stature have enabled them, if not to overcome, certainly to override local anti-semitic prejudice. In public life, as elsewhere, nothing succeeds like success. Joe Jowell was Mayor of Springbok for some 30 years. On the occasion of his 1967 Mayoral Sunday celebration involving a synagogue service followed by a tea party, there was an attempt by the local Dutch Reformed Church to urge their members not to attend either function and their circular recording the resolution of the Church Council is still extant. It had minimal impact. There were 150 people at the Mayoral service and 175 at the tea party.[17] It should be noted that according to a Board of Deputies investigation three years earlier there were about 29 Jewish souls in Namaqualand at this time.[18]

Namaqualand was always on the itinerary of Ministries who paid pastoral visits to country areas, not least because they were contributors to national Jewish causes above the national average. The Cape Town Board of Deputies wrote to the Johannesburg Board on 9 August 1960: 'We are trying very hard to obtain an officiant for the High Festivals in Springbok. It is imperative that we find someone for them as they are admirable supporters of the Board and the UCF.'[19]

But the exodus which had started in earnest after the Second World War continued and it was impossible to maintain a communal structure. In 1970 the constitution was revised recording that there were only 12 members, of whom seven lived in Namaqualand, four in Cape Town and one in Johannesburg. On 12 October 1979 it was resolved to donate the *shul* to the Springbok Municipality for use as a museum, subject to the following conditions: (a) the property was only to be used as a museum; (b) the foundation stone and front façade were not to be altered; (c) the Jewish cemetery at O'Okiep was to be maintained; (d) Joe Jowell's name was to be incorporated in the museum; (e) any local Jews had to be consulted regarding exhibits in the museum.[20]

It is a matter of record that these conditions were complied with and the museum is regularly visited by Jews and non-Jews. The final gift of the Namaqualand Hebrew Congregation which has been recorded is the gift of two *Sifrei Torah* to the Sephardic Congregation of Cape Town.[21]

The story of the Oudtshoorn Jewish community has many similarities with that of Namaqualand but two principal differences, namely that the community attained considerably greater numbers and were far more concentrated in and associated with one particular industry, the ostrich industry with whose fortunes those of the community rose and fell. The town of Oudtshoorn lies about 300 km east of Cape Town and is the largest town of the area known as the Little Karoo (the word is said to mean arid, hard and sparsely covered). It lies in the shelter of the Swartberg mountains to the north and receives its water supply from the mountain ranges on both sides flowing eventually into the Olifants River. Its vegetation is not lush but it has sufficient water to be less of a desert area than Namaqualand and the warm, dry Karoo climate ensures a healthy environment and sufficient vegetation to support a modest farming community. Also, the railway line has (at least since 1902) reached Oudtshoorn and beyond, unlike the position in Namaqualand where until comparatively recently and long after any significant Jewish settlement, the line ended at Bitterfontein. The town of Oudtshoorn was officially named and proclaimed in 1847[22] and the first Jews began to arrive, if only in a trickle, within a few years. The first *minyan* was held in 1884 in a private home with 30 Jews present; the first split occurred in 1886! Mention has been made of how the Jews of the district prospered with the Ostrich feather industry. It was in the 1880s that the industry became firmly established in the Cape Colony just at the time that the first large immigration of Jews arrived from Eastern Europe. Those whose inclination or family connections or just a hunch took them eastwards along what is today called the Garden Route, began to settle in the Little Karoo and they came and stayed in such numbers that Oudtshoorn would become known as the Jerusalem of South Africa, but not for its numbers alone. As it happened most of the Jews who settled in Oudtshoorn came from Shavel or Kelm. By 1904 the total population of Oudtshoorn and district was 8,849 of whom 4,145 were whites (Europeans as they were then termed) and 797 were Jews. Jews thus numbered 15 per cent of the white population at that time. By 1918 there were 1,073 Jews, possibly the largest number ever attained, and in the wake of the decline and collapse of the ostrich feather industry the number had fallen to below 1,000 in 1926 and fewer than 600 in 1936. The fact of the matter is that the Jews as pioneers of the ostrich feather industry played a vitally important part, totally disproportionate to their numbers, in bringing the industry to its high peak both as traders and farmers. When the industry failed largely as a result of world conditions including fashion changes they suffered proportionately.

The story of the Jewish community of Oudtshoorn cannot be properly understood without reference to the ostrich feather industry. After an uncertain beginning the ostrich feather trade began to rise dramatically in the first decade of the twentieth century. By 1911 records show some 750,000 birds under control. At its peak the industry was valued at some £19 million and represented the fourth largest South African export. Naturalisation figures in the 1880s when the industry was in its infancy show how Jews predominated as feather dealers. Between 1883 and 1887, 17 out of 17 Jews who were naturalised gave their occupation as feather buyer or feather sorter. The following year, out of seven successful applicants, there were three feather buyers, three shopkeepers and one merchant. There were only two Jews naturalised in 1888/89, both feather buyers. The following year there were 35 feather buyers, one merchant, one tailor, one shopkeeper, one clerk, one schoolmaster and one Rabbi. These figures are quoted because they contrast with other centres (see Namaqualand above) where there was always a wide spread of occupations pursued by Jews.

As has been said, Jewish feather dealers became involved in the trade from the 1880s and they would walk from farm to farm buying the feathers which they brought back to the town by Friday; the feather dealers' street came to be known as the Jewish Street. Of the trade, Jews represented barely 10 per cent of the farmers but some 90 per cent of the dealers. We must remember that a feather buyer, unlike the early diamond buyers in Kimberley, did not sit in his shop waiting for hopeful sellers to visit him. He went with his horse and cart from farm to farm to ply his trade. There were indeed attempts made to keep them out of the trade by changing the licensing laws relating to feather dealers. the *S A Jewish Chronicle* of 17 May 1907 reported the formation of the Oudtshoorn Jewish Vigilance Committee to counter a resolution passed at the Central Association Farmers' Congress held at Oudtshoorn on 13 March 1907 seeking the discontinuance of 'the indiscriminate issue of licences for the purchase of ostrich feathers through the Post Office on payment of £5 and requiring licence applications to be considered by the local Divisional Council'. The Vigilance Committee included in their argument (which is fully reported in the issue of the *S A Jewish Chronicle* of 17 May 1907) the following points:

1. There are a large number of small and struggling dealers engaged in the trade who manage to eke out a bare existence and were this trade to be deprived them, they would be thrown on the public charge and becom paupers;

2. The ostrich feather industry had been developed and brought to present flourishing and profitable condition solely through the competition engendered by the large number of dealers;

When the industry collapsed shortly before the First World War many of the Jewish dealers were virtually wiped out with it but there always remained a tiny remnant who would in due course prosper again when the industry recovered, although it would never attain its original importance.

As in Namaqualand, however, Oudtshoorn Jews became actively involved in other trades and occupations which were either offshoots of the ostrich industry or necessary accompaniments to the general growth of the area. Thus here again we find Jewish hoteliers, general dealers, pharmacists and shopkeepers in all departments. They were as involved with granting credit and other assistance to local farmers and other victims of the depression as were the Jews of Namaqualand.

As to their congregational activity, the soubriquet Jerusalem of South Africa did not only arise from numbers but from the early growth and growing intensity of Jewish congregational and religious life. By 1884 regular services were being held and the Oudtshoorn Jews formally constituted themselves into a congregation. In 1885 the first Jewish wedding was performed. The report of the ceremony and the reception in the local press[24] referred to a reference made in his speech by Rev. Ornstein of the Cape Town congregation who had come from Cape Town to Oudtshoorn to officiate at the ceremony. The Reverend gentleman pointed out that the congregation was now sufficiently well established and had enough members to set about the erection of a permanent synagogue. The congregation acted on the hint, although there is reason to believe that they had already been discussing the matter. The foundation stone was laid in 1888 and the *shul* became known as the Queen Street *Shul* after its location. By this time there were some 250 Jews in the area. At about the time of the opening of the Queen Street *Shul*, Rabbi Myer Wolfson was appointed Minister and served for over 50 years.

The laying of the foundation stone of the *shul* was fully reported in the local newspaper, the *Oudtshoorn Courant* of 1 February 1888. It was estimated that the cost of erection was £1,000. A unique feature of the building committee established for the purpose was that its honorary secretary was a non-Jew, one Charles B. Black. As far as can be ascertained this is the only occasion in South African Jewish history where a Christian served as the Secretary of a Hebrew congregation. Warm tribute was paid to him by Rev. Ornstein in his address; after referring to many sources from which assistance had been received, he said:

> Above all I find the most valuable, nay incalculable assistance has been given by a Christian, the honorary secretary, Mr. Charles B. Black, without whose indefatigable labours the committee could not have arrived at so happy a consummation and whose heart and soul have been in the work.[25]

It is convenient at this point to refer to a factor in the development of the South African Jewish community, as in certain other immigrant communities, namely the interaction between Jews of Anglo-Jewish background on the one hand and those who came from Eastern Europe on the other.[26]

Although many of the pioneers who built and established the Queen Street *Shul* hailed originally from '*Der heim*' their affairs were conducted principally along the lines of Anglo-Jewry under the guidance of the Minister of the Cape Town Hebrew Congregation and through him the Chief Rabbinate of the British Empire. It became known as the *Anglisher Shul* and in 1892 there was a breakaway by members, most of whom came from Keln, who opened another *shul* in 1896 which became known as the *Greuner Shul*. It has always been generally accepted that the reason for the breakaway was the dissatisfaction of the *Greuners* with the 'English customs' of the Queen Street *Shul* under Rabbi Wolfson. There is an indication however that in any event by this time the Queen Street *Shul* was, or would soon become, too small and so it would become inevitable that another *shul* had to be built.

The piety and learning of the Oudtshoorn Jews must not be under-estimated. At its height Oudtshoorn had two *Batei Midrash* [study centres] a *Mikva* ([ritual bath], situated on the farm of one Lipshitz, said to be the richest Jew in the area)[27] a Rabbi, a Reverend, three *Shochtim* [ritual slaughterers], Hebrew teachers, a *Talmud Torah* [afternoon Hebrew school], a *Chevra Kadisha* [burial society], a *Chevra Shas* [society for study of the *Talmud*], a *Chevra Tehilim* [society for study of the Psalms] and interest-free loan society, Women's and Zionist Societies.[28]

Because Oudtshoorn is much nearer to the Cape than Namaqualand, those Jews of the district who were engaged in action in the Boer War were on the British side and were reported to have done good work in the local town militia. Oudtshoorn was also home to a large number of Jewish war refugees from the Transvaal.

A snapshot of the community as it was at the beginning of the century can be gleaned from the following report submitted by an Oudtshoorn Jew to the *London Jewish Chronicle*.

> [The ostrich feather trade] is almost entirely in the hands of Jews. The feather buyers are in nearly every instance Russian Jews who have arrived in this country poor men but who by dint of industry and frugality combined with keen business faculties have become rich and respected men in a community of Jews and Christians. Some of the largest businesses are owned by Jews. They form part of committees and boards on almost every occasion when anything is brought forward for the good of the community at large. They hold offices in Masonic gatherings, in music they have a colonial reputation ... in amateur entertainment they outshine their gentile townsmen, in fact hardly an entertainment is ever arranged here without Jewish assistance in a large share. Their social gatherings are often the envy of their Christian townfolk ... their communal institutions are not lost sight of. They have two synagogues ...; a philanthropic society doing much good, a Chevra Kadisha, social societies and the hundred and one other little things common to every Jewish community which help to make Jewish life liveable.[29]

Making due allowance for the enthusiasm of the local residents it is not unfair to say that this description could fairly be applied to the Oudtshoorn Jewish community up to comparatively recent times.

Another snapshot view of Oudtshoorn Jewish life is a description of a typical Jewish general dealer's shop given by the South African novelist Pauline Smith in her novel, *The Beadle*.[30] Pauline Smith was the daughter of a doctor in Oudtshoorn and often accompanied her father on his rounds in the district. This is the impressionistic, but largely accurate account which she gives of the store owned by the fictitious Esther Shokolowsky at Harmonie, said to be a little settlement near the town of Platkopsdorp (clearly based on Oudtshoorn).

> Here they sold prints and calicos, bags of coffee beans, rice, sugar, salt, spades and buckets, cooking pots, kettles, gridirons, combs and mouth organs; sweets, snuff and many patent medicines. Money was but little used in the valley and in payment for their goods, the Jew woman and her grandson took from the bywoners and their wives such produce as they brought them from their land – mielies, pumpkins, dried fruit, porridge and tobacco, pigs and poultry. These in turn the young man took to Platkopsdorp exchanging them there at the market or at the stores for such goods as were needed to replenish his stock at

Harmonie ... At the end of the previous month young Shokolofsky had bought part of the bankrupt stock of a Platklops storekeeper and the little shop at Harmonie was now overflowing with such an assortment of goods as had never before been seen in the valley. With these the young man expected to do much trade at the coming sacrement (nagmaal) ... roundabout Harmonie the talk for some weeks had been of the colourful prints, the ribbons and laces, the cheap gay jewellery and the little mirrors rimmed with pink and white shells to be seen at the Jew woman's store.

The *SA Jewish Chronicle* of 10 July 1903 reported that the Oudtshoorn Jewish community had decided to start a Jewish school and this duly took place. This was the first Jewish school of its kind to be established in South Africa at a time when the Jewish population numbered 400 families or more. Hebrew was a recognised part of the curriculum and a number of well-known Hebrew teachers taught at the school at various times. Most remarkably this was not a private school run by the community as later Jewish day schools would be, but was a government-subsidised state school and the most distinguished and long-serving principal was an Afrikaner, Johan Smit who served as Headmaster for some 20 years until his retirement at the end of 1956.[31] The Jewish Boy Scout Troop also had a non-Jewish Scout Master, A. Jonker.[32]

If the most notable Namaqualand Jew in terms of national commercial achievements was Joe Jowell, the equivalent status in Oudtshoorn must go to Max Rose. He came to South Africa in 1890 from Shavel and went straight to Oudtshoorn where he had an uncle who sponsored his arrival. He immediately set up as a feather buyer and shortly afterwards as an ostrich breeder. He became a national authority on the industry, called on by government to serve on various boards and committees of enquiry. Indeed he was regarded as the greatest living world authority on ostriches and had the undisputed title of 'Ostrich King' of South Africa. He justifiably at the height of his career claimed to own one-fifth of the total number of ostriches in South Africa. His career is worth mention and examination because it represents yet another instance of an immigrant Jew becoming absorbed in, and in turn making his mark upon the local situation.[33]

The Zionist ideal was grasped at an early stage by the Oudtshoorn community, the first Zionist association having been established in 1899 and the Ladies' Zionist Society the following year. Interaction with non-Jews varied. In the very early days when the recent arrivals made more strenuous efforts than perhaps their successors to maintain strict dietary laws, there were several colourful stories told in the district. For example stories circulated amongst the Afrikaner farmers in the district about 'ash-cookies-Jews' namely those Jews who during their stay amongst the farmers would not even eat their hosts' bread because of the fear of non-kosher fat having been used in its preparation, so they themselves baked cookies on the hot ashes of the fires. It was also said that during Pesach some Jews would not even drink water at the farmhouses for fear of *chometz*, but drank rather from the pools and streams. This is a touching picture and there is no doubt that the Oudtshoorn Jews maintained to a fairly late stage a standard of observance probably considerably above the national average if such a thing could be measured. It must be borne in mind however that the Jews who left Eastern Europe to seek their fortune overseas did not do so because they were prevented from practising their religion at home. They did so in search of economic opportunities and a brighter future for their children than they could hope for in tsarist Russia. The vital thing which motivated them therefore was to make a living and hopefully from this to advance to security, thence to comfort, thence hopefully to wealth. To be accepted, to 'be somebody', to see their children launched in life, these were the things that mattered and if this meant that the laws of *Shabbat* or *Kashrut* had to be in abeyance, this had to be endured.[34]

Unfortunately we do not have for Oudtshoorn books of the quality and nature of those which we have for Namaqualand. Certain chapters in published books and published articles help to draw the picture. We are also much indebted to the descendants of Leibl Feldman, a Johannesburg industrialist and also a Yiddishist and writer of some competence. In 1940 he wrote a somewhat impressionist and idiosyncratic but most illuminating book on the Jews of Oudtshoorn entitled *Yerusheloyim b'drom Afrika*. In 1989, under the sponsorship of his family, this book was deftly translated by Lilian Dubb and Sheila Barkusky of Cape Town and published in an elegant limited edition, edited and with a comprehensive introduction by Joseph Sherman. Unfortunately only 150 copies were printed for private circulation, but if a copy can be obtained it is well worth perusal. This book is mentioned not only for its own sake but as an opportunity to note the important part which Yiddish played amongst the Jews of Oudtshoorn. In 1904 a Yiddish theatre group visiting South Africa thought it worthwhile to include Oudtshoorn in their tour. In 1922 the famous Yiddish writer, Peretz Hirshbein, visited Oudtshoorn and addressed a crowded City Hall about modern developments in Yiddish literature and of Yiddish life outside of Palestine. In his book *Völker un Lender* [People and Lands],[35] Hirshbein had the following to say about his visit to Oudtshoorn which is quoted also as a commencement to a discussion on Jew–non-Jew relationships in Oudtshoorn:

> As was customary the conversation opened in broken English in an Afrikaans accent. When Jews meet here this is the normal way they engage in conversation; it is not thought proper to start a conversation in Yiddish. Only one middle-aged gentleman who met me at the station and with whom I travelled in the car immediately began to talk with me in Yiddish. His language and pronunciation were fluent, idiomatic and interspersed with Hebrew expressions. This gentleman however was not a Jew. He was a full-blooded Christian, the Mayor of the most Yiddish speaking of all towns in South Africa. He had travelled out to meet the Yiddish writer and to pay his respects to him. Yankele – this was how the Jews called him. He was theirs. He had grown up among them and with them. They had helped him to be elected Mayor of Oudtshoorn.

This Yiddish-speaking Mayor was a local Afrikaner dignitary, Jannie de Jager, said to have been one of a great number of Afrikaners who worked or came into daily contact with Jews who could speak Yiddish. He appears frequently in reports of functions, meetings and celebrations of communal occasions, but of course Jewish children spoke Afrikaans more than Afrikaners spoke Yiddish.

Another important local figure whose interaction with the Jews played an important part in defining the relationship was C.J. Langenhoven, one of the most distinguished figures in Afrikaans culture and literature. Although as a passionate proponent of the national identity of the Afrikaner people (he wrote the words of 'Die Stem van Suid Afrika', the former South African national anthem) and although he was conscious and somewhat resentful of what he saw as the general alignment of the Jewish people towards the English section, he had many close and important Jewish friends and connections and nowhere in his work can there be found a trace of anti-Jewish feeling. His long-serving secretary and literary executrix was Sarah Goldblatt, the daughter of David Goldblatt, a pioneer of the South African Yiddish press. After Langenhoven's death she devoted herself to his memory. Max Rose was a particularly close friend and confidante of Langenhoven and a portrait of him with Langenhoven's widow still hangs in Arbeidsgenot, the Langenhoven home in Oudtshoorn which has become a national shrine.

Despite these warm recollections, the rise of militant anti-semitism in South Africa before and during the Second World War did not pass Oudtshoorn by. Aggressive attitudes by a growing number of young and not-so-young Afrikaners towards the Jews of the district ranged from school-ground scuffles and sports-field brawls to serious and widespread outbreaks of arson and other property damage in the 1940s.[36] It is also necessary to add that S.P. Le Roux who represented Oudtshoorn in Parliament from 1923 to 1958 and served as Minister of Agriculture and Forestry in the Nationalist Government, was a virulent and vocal anti-semite.[37]

To round off this description of the multi-faceted Oudtshoorn community within the context of the theme of this conference, it is necessary to say that Oudtshoorn always regarded itself and was regarded as an important link in the general South African community. As early as 1903 we find Rabbi Wolfson collecting for the Kishinev Fund[38] and when Morris Alexander was busy working to establish the Cape Jewish Board of Deputies he received a message of encouragement and promises of support from the Oudtshoorn Hebrew Congregation.[39] Perhaps the last important task which Oudtshoorn performed for the South African Jewish community as a whole was to provide hospitality and comforts for Jewish trainees who served their period of military service at the important military base at Oudtshoorn.

An investigation by the South African Jewish Board of Deputies in 1964 showed that there were approximately 350 Jewish souls living in Oudtshoorn of whom 60 were children below *Barmitzvah* age. The assets included the synagogue, the *Talmud Torah*, the hall, 12 *Sifrei Torah* [scrolls of the Law] a *mikvah* and various properties. There were some 3,000 Jewish graves in the cemetery which was well kept and in good condition.[40]

The Oudtshoorn Jewish Museum forms part of the Municipal Museum and contains a vivid recreation of Jewish life and the activities of the community. In 1988 the centenary of the building of the Queen Street synagogue was commemorated by a series of functions attended by representatives of central and local government and many former members of the community who travelled to Oudtshoorn for the occasion. It is a feature of the community which falls squarely within the topic covered by the conference that former Oudtshoorn Jews *and their descendants* maintain a close affinity with their origins. In 2004, the 120th anniversary of the holding of the first Minyan in Oudtshoorn, not only did over 300 people attend the celebrations in Oudtshoorn, but further celebrations were held as far afield as London, Sydney and Israel. It seems that the Oudtshoon memory is a potent force.[41]

These two frontier communities which have been briefly sketched illustrate in a minor key many of the characteristics which marked larger communities in more important centres. Other writers have shown, for example, that Jews who were drawn to Kimberley by diamonds and to Johannesburg by gold arrived at the very beginning of the respective flourishing of those two cities. They came because of the perceived fortune-making potential of the new Eldorado. But as the minor centres became little towns and later big cities, the Jews brought their trading skills into all the offshoots which followed the first big find. How those trading skills were born or developed in the *shtetlach* of Eastern Europe is beyond the scope of this paper. With all respect to those who have written on the subject I am not convinced that they have yet explained this phenomenon.[42] However, the point I am concerned to make is that the Jews of Namaqualand were involved in all the necessary direct and indirect outflows of the copper and later the diamond discoveries. The Jews of Oudtshoorn were an essential part of the growth of the ostrich feather industry in fulfilling all the roles from the farmer to the ultimate consumer. In both these cases they moved out from the core industry into its offshoots. Entirely different considerations applied to those Jews who came to other big cities such as Cape Town or Durban where there was no originating principal product or activity; there they were distributed from the beginning amongst the wide variety of trade and occupations.[43]

So too in the smaller towns, wherever there was a trading opportunity or an opening for a new venture, a Jewish arrival who had just come at the behest of his local relative would fill the gap.

Just as the towns which have been examined presented a particular aspect as far as occupations are concerned, so the relationship between the Jew and his neighbours merit examination. Space considerations permit only a most cursory examination of the relationship between the South African Jew and his neighbours – black, English, Afrikaans. In country communities like Oudtshoorn and Namaqualand most of the dealings were with white Afrikaners. These as we have seen could be warm and hospitable,[44] but particularly from the early 1930s they became largely harsh and confrontational.[45] In the cities confrontation with English-speaking whites produced different issues. Shain has shown how anti-semitism was social and subtle[46] but it often had a resonance beyond the cities. Either way, whether dealing with the aggressive Afrikaner or smooth Englishman, the Jew was regarded (and indeed regarded himself) as 'the other'. There was never a melting pot syndrome in South Africa. This indeed was one of the reasons why by and large the rate of assimilation amongst South African Jews was always very low; there was just nowhere to go, and it was an insignificant minority of Jews who became '*boerejode*' or who sought acceptance in social clubs and sports clubs which were closed to Jews.

It is a sad fact of history that during the years which have been examined and for many years to come the Jew had no meaningful relationship with his black neighbour other than as between boss and servant and as between trader with a (not very highly regarded) customer. But the Afrikaner that he dealt with in

Namaqualand or Oudtshoorn differed hugely from the Englishman he dealt with in Cape Town and Durban. By and large, of course, the evidence is largely anecdotal and many stories go both ways.

We can expect alas to hear little more of Oudtshoorn Jewry and still less of Namaqualand, but the issues which forged them and the mindset which drove them is still at work elsewhere. In physical and material terms, South Africa is no longer a frontier society and South African Jewry is no longer a frontier community. But there are mental, psychological and even spiritual frontiers too. There the encounters continue between black and white, English and Afrikaans; and the Jew remains a somewhat enigmatic figure in between. These encounters continue because the main protagonists are too close to disengage and the Jew for better or worse is right there.

NOTES

1. For an overview of the early history of the South African Jewish Community, see Louis Herrman, *A History of the Jews in South Africa* (Johannesburg and Cape Town: SA Jewish Board of Deputies, 1935); G. Saron and L. Hotz, eds., *The Jews in South Africa, A History* (Oxford: Oxford University Press, 1955).
2. By 2002 the Country Communities Research Project of the SA Friends of Beth Hatefutsoth had identified 324 such communities in South Africa.
3. M. Wilson and L. Thompson, eds., *The Oxford History of South Africa*. Vol. 1 *South Africa to 1870* (Oxford: Clarendon Press, 1969).
4. See L. Hermann, *A History of the Jews* (see note 1), chapters IX, X and XI for an account of this interesting family.
5. This house is still (2005) in Jewish ownership. See Introductory note to Phyllis Jowell and Adrienne Folb, *Into Kokerboom Country: Namaqualand's Jewish Pioneers* (Cape Town: Fernwood Press, 2004).
6. The latest and most authoritative book on the Jews of Namaqualand is Jowell and Folb, *Into Kokerboom Country* (ibid.).
7. The official census figures for 1918 (N.G. 19/20 Namaqualand) reflected 135 Jews. By 1921, the figure had dropped to 113.
8. See note 18 s.v. 'Tokhers, Shmoyzers or Travelling Pedlars', in Leibl Feldman, *Oudtshoorn, Jerusalem of South Africa*, ed. by Joseph Sherman, trans. by Lilian Dubb and Sheila Barkusky, Historical notes and commentary by John Simon (Johannesburg: Friends of the University of the Witwatersrand Library, 1989) (hereafter 'Feldman'). See also Milton Shain '"Vant to puy a Vaatch?" The Smous and Pioneer Trader in South Africa Jewish Historiography', *Jewish Affairs* (September 1987, p.111 ff.
9. Theunis Uys, 'Die Jodemense van Namakwaland: Hulle Invloed op Kulturele, Maatskaplike en Ekonomiese Gebied' [The Jews of Namaqualand: Their Influence on the Cultural, Civic and Economic Community], unpublished manuscript, 2003.
10. Jowell and Folb, *Into Kokerboom Country* (see note 5) have identified the following occupation amongst the Jews of Namaqualand; tailors, bookkeepers, jewellers, lawyers, mineral prospectors, farmers, engineers, pharmacists, doctors, dentists, garage owners, transport operators. Obvious omissions from this list are general dealers and hoteliers. Compare the Oudtshoorn situation (below).
11. Abe Schapera, *Golden Days in Namaqualand* (Springbok: Namaqualand Tourist Development Co., 2001).
12. Milton Shain, *The Roots of Antisemitism in South Africa* (Charlottesville and London: University Press of Virginia, 1994).
13. University of Cape Town, Manuscript and Archives Department, BC 792, Box 51. 'Shenoddering' [he who has given] describes a gift to a charity promised by one who receives an honour in a synagogue on a sabbath or holy day.
14. Or if not, were neutral between the combatants wherever they lived without criticism. 'Neutrality was a perfectly acceptable course of action and one the majority of recently arrived Jews quite sensibly chose. ... Their abstention drew little comment for there was no obvious civic reason that they should risk their lives for either side.' Richard Mendelsohn, 'The Boer War, the Great War and the Shaping of the South African Jewish Loyalties', in *Memories, Realities and Dreams. Aspects of the South African*

Jewish Experience, ed. by Milton Shain and Richard Mendelsohn (Johannesburg and Cape Town: Jonathan Ball Publishers, 2000).
15. Jowell and Folb, *Into Kokerboom Country* (see note 5).
16. Phyllis Jowell, *Joe Jowell of Namaqualand* (Cape Town: Fernwood Press, 1994).
17. UCT Manuscripts and Archives Department BC 792 Box 44.
18. Ibid. It was also reported that the community still had the synagogue and the communal hall, and the Jewish cemetery at O'Okiep was well kept and there were no graves without tombstones.
19. UCF stands for United Communal Fund through which the South African Jewish Community raised funds for its local educational and other communal needs.
20. Namaqualand Hebrew Congregation Minute Book. CT Manuscripts and Archives Dept BC 792, Box 51.
21. Ibid.
22. Feldman, *Oudtshoorn* (see note 8), Notes 4 and 8.
23. *Oudtshoorn Courant*, 1 February 1888.
24. *Oudtshoorn Courant*, 12 March 1885.
25. *Oudtshoorn Courant*, 1 February 1888.
26. See my unpublished paper *English Jews and Russian Jews: The South African Experience* delivered at the 11th World Congress of Jewish Studies, Jerusalem, June 1993.
27. *SA Zionist Record*, 14 January 1949.
28. Joseph Sherman, Introduction to Feldman, *Oudtshoorn* (see note 8).
29. *London Jewish Chronicle*, 15 November 1901.
30. Cape Town: Jonathan Cape Publishers, First published 1924. Republished 1979.
31. *SA Zionist Record*, 4 January 1957.
32. *SA Jewish Chronicle*, 20 February 1948.
33. *SA Jewish Times*, 12 March 1948.
34. John Simon, 'A Study of the Nature and Development of Orthodox Judaism in South Africa to c 1935', unpublished MA Dissertation, University of Cape Town, 1996.
35. Peretz Hirshbein, *Felker un Lender* [People and Lands] (Kletzkin: Vilna, 1929).
36. For a thorough and insightful survey of the Oudtshoorn community and its integration see also Daniël Coetzee, 'Immigrants to Citizens: Civil Integration and Acculturation of Jews into Oudtshoorn Society 1874 to 1999', unpublished MA dissertation, University of Cape Town, 2000. See also the same writer's article 'Fires and Feathers: Acculturation, Arson and the Jewish Community in Oudtshoorn SA 1914–48', *Jewish History*, 19.2 (2005), 143–87.
37. For a useful summary of the rise of anti-semitism in South Africa in the wake of 'the rise of an illiberal antimodernist and exclusivist Afrikaner Nationalism' before, during and immediately after the Second World War, see Milton Shain, '"If it was so good, why was it so bad?" The Memories and Realities of Anti-Semitism in South Africa Past and Present', in *Memories, Realities and Dreams*, ed by Shain and Mendelsohn. This article also serves to place in context the somewhat roseate recollections of many former Oudtshoorn Jews who were interviewed by Daniel Coetzee and who reported somewhat nostalgically on their relationship with non-Jews (see note 36).
38. *SA Jewish Chronicle*, 3 July 1903.
39. *SA Jewish Chronicle*, 9 October 1903.
40. UCT Manuscripts and Archives Dept BC 792 Box 44.
41. This observation is particularly interesting as bearing upon the themes of the conference for which this paper was prepared. Daniel Coetzee's article in *Jewish History* (see note 36) has pointed out that second and third generation Oudtshoorn Jews attained a high level of acculturation by the 1930s. They knew little Hebrew or Yiddish but almost all were equally fluent in English and Afrikaans. Despite this dilution of the Jewish content of their lives however, displacement maintained and even strengthened their Jewish commitment.
42. See for example G. Saron, 'Jewish Immigration 1880–1913', in *The Jews in South Africa*, ed. by Saron and Hotz; Antony Arkin 'Economic Activities', in *South African Jewry a Contemporary Survey*, ed. by M. Arkin (Cape Town: Oxford University Press, 1984); M. Kaplan, *Jewish Roots in the South African Economy* (Cape Town: Struik Publishers, 1986).
43. UCT Manuscripts and Archives Dept BC 792 Alexander papers.
44. See for example Uys, 'Die Jodemense van Namakwaland' (see note 9).
45. Shain, *The Roots of Antisemitism* (note 12 above).
46. Ibid.

PART III:
PLACE, MIGRATION AND MEMORY WORKS

Migration, Location and Memory: Jewish History through a Comparative Lens

NANCY FONER

That place or location matters in understanding the immigrant experience is obvious. What is not so obvious, however, is just how it matters. The basic premise of this article is that a comparative perspective – that looks at migrants across nations as well as, within nations, across cities – can help to better understand the role of place in the lives of those who moved as well as in the lives of their descendants.[1]

The concern here is the massive, and monumental, Eastern European Jewish migration of a century ago which led to the emergence of large Jewish settlements in cities all over the globe. As background to the discussion, I begin with a few general comments about the benefits of a comparative analysis for understanding the immigration experience. Next, I explore – through a comparative lens – how the context or place where Eastern European Jews moved 100 years ago shaped their lives in their new homes at the time of initial settlement. And finally, I consider some issues concerned with memory. One is how the historical experience of migration in specific locations influenced memories of it. Another is a topic that stems from my work on contemporary immigration in the United States – how the memory of Jewish migration 100 years ago has affected the reaction to and interpretation of current-day migrations.

Throughout the analysis, the main focus, or starting point, is New York – the city which has come to epitomise the Jewish experience in America and which received the overwhelming majority of Jewish migrants in the great exodus of Jews from Eastern Europe a century ago. It also happens to be the city where I was born and grew up, where I live now, where I have done much of my research on migration – and where my own grandparents came from Russia at the turn of the twentieth century.[2] But New York-centric as this paper may, at times, seem, it is not just about New York, and I will bring out factors that need to be considered when comparing Jews in different locations and, along the way, make comparisons with Jewish migration in other areas of settlement.

The Benefits of a Comparative Approach

First, a few words about a comparative approach in migration studies. Why, after all, bother to compare? Why not just look at migrants – in the present case, Jewish migrants – in one place and leave it at that? Is it not enough to simply try to uncover the complexities of how Jewish communities in one location formed and changed over time?

Obviously, in-depth studies of particular places are critical. Indeed, without them comparative analysis would be impossible. Yet I think it is important, as well, to look beyond one place – especially if the goal is to better appreciate how location affects the options available to migrants and their descendants. By location, I mean not only the peculiarities of the migrant flows there – but also the particular social, economic, and political institutions and structures found in the destination.

One of the many benefits of a comparative approach that looks at migrants in different destinations is that it can bring fresh perspectives to old problems. It has the quality of calling attention to – or bringing into sharper focus – dynamics that might be missed or minimised if only focusing on one case. Or as the sociologist Reinhard Bendix put it in another context, comparative studies 'increase the "visibility" of one structure by contrasting it with another'.[3]

A comparative approach, as the historian George Fredrickson reminds us, can undermine two contrary but equally damaging presuppositions: the illusion of total regularity and the illusion of absolute uniqueness.[4] Or, to put it another way, it enables us to see what is unique to a specific situation and what is more general to the migration experience – or, in our case, the Jewish migration experience. Of course, to some degree it is a matter of emphasis. Or of finding what you are looking for. If you look for similarities across places, you find them, if you look for differences across places, you also find them.

In my view, though, what is especially useful about comparisons is that they bring out *both* the similarities and the differences between migrations to different places. Comparisons also force us to try to account for these similarities and differences – a process which is useful in 'in enlarging our theoretical understanding of the kinds of institutions and processes being compared'.[5] Comparing migrants in one group in different destinations or locations – what Nancy Green has called a divergent comparison – broadens our understanding of the migrant experience in each place and sheds light on both the structural constraints and cultural choices framing the migration experience.[6]

Jewish Migrants in Different Locations

These are general comments, but how they do they apply to the case of Jewish migration in different locations? There are of course many parallels in the Jewish migrant experience in cities around the world where Eastern European Jews settled in significant numbers a century ago. The Jews brought with them a common culture from Eastern Europe, a common religion and language, and a history of exclusion and experience with anti-semitism. In major cities where they settled in North America, Latin America, and Western Europe, they formed social, religious, and political organisations that often resembled each other; there were tailors everywhere and many worked as peddlers. Even today, when Jews in New York meet Jews in London, Paris, Buenos Aires, or Cape Town there is often a strong sense of kinship based on these shared institutions, their shared historical experience as Jews, and their past (and in some cases present) exclusion.

At the same time, of course, being Jewish in London or Paris, for example, is not the same as being Jewish in New York – today or 100 years ago. Any thorough comparative study of Jews in different locations needs to consider how geographic and historical factors affected the characteristics of the migrants who moved there. Along with the occupational/class and gender composition of the migration to particular places, there is the area of origin in Eastern Europe. In her article on the South African Yiddish theatre, Veronica Belling suggests that the origins of most Eastern European Jews who went to Johannesburg in the late nineteenth and early twentieth century in a cluster of small towns and villages in Lithuania and White Russia may have something to do with the less hospitable setting for the development of Yiddish theatre than in places like New York, where more of the immigrants came from areas sympathetic to and nurturing of Yiddish and Yiddish culture.[7] Comparative analyses need, as well, to take into account the history of the migration itself, including the timing of arrival and how long the movement lasted. And there is the sheer size of the Jewish migrant population – which is a critical feature in the context of each location. Here we are talking not just about absolute numbers of Jewish migrants but also their proportion of the total population in places where they settled.

Demography is not destiny – but numbers make a real difference. In this regard, New York stands out as the behemoth of Jewish communities, not just in the United States but in the world. In 1907, 600,000 Jews lived there, by 1927 the figure was 1,765,000 – or more than a quarter of the city's population. In the United States, Chicago, the second most popular city did not come close – home to 100,000 Jews in 1907 and 325,000 in 1927, or, in that year, about 10 per cent of Chicago's population. Outside of the United States, the numbers – and proportions – were much smaller. The inner boroughs of London were home to an estimated 184,000 Jews in 1921 or 4 per cent of the total; some 35,000 settled in Paris between 1880 and 1914, by which time it was a city of well over two million people; and by the First World War Buenos Aires was home to some 50,000 Jews out of a total population of about 1.5 million.[8]

How do these numbers matter? We know that wherever they went, Jewish immigrants clustered together in neighbourhoods and occupations and created community institutions that bound them together. Yet the much greater numbers in New York – and in particular areas of New York like the Lower East Side (a neighbourhood of over half a million Jews in 1910) and Brownsville and Williamsburg in Brooklyn – provided the base for a dazzling array of congregations, organisations, and institutions. In New York, the recent arrivals – and their children – had the ability to be Jewish by virtue of just living in Jewish neighbourhoods where it was possible to live out their lives in a completely Jewish – and Yiddish – world. As Lee-Shai Weissbach notes, in small-town America, by contrast, where Jews were few in number, there was no possibility of the kind of anonymity that was afforded by the large New York City Jewish community or of being able to take one's Jewishness for granted the way this could happen in New York's dense ethnic enclaves.[9]

Everywhere they settled, Jews from Eastern Europe preferred to marry other Jews. Yet, as sociologists have shown, group size has an impact on the rate of intermarriage – affecting the likelihood, to put it in demographers' terms, of satisfying preferences for a mate of the same or similar ethnic background within the group. Whether and how this demographic principle applies to Jews, both past and present and in different locations, is clearly a topic that requires study. One of the fascinating things about the Jewish diaspora is how, even in communities where Eastern European Jews were few in number, high rates of in-group marriage were often maintained in the pre-Second World War era.[10]

In the early days of settlement in the United States, in communities where it was hard to find Jewish spouses locally, a common practice was to send back to the old country – or other migrant communities – for Jewish wives.[11] Prior to 1965, endogamy rates were extraordinarily high for Jews everywhere in the United States – over 90 per cent. Research shows that in the contemporary period, when intermarriage rates have soared in the US, there is a correlation between numbers and density of Jewish settlement and the rates of intermarriage; the mixed marriage rate for males in the New York metropolitan area – an area that is home to an estimated two million Jews – in the late 1980s was about half that found elsewhere in the United States. According to 1990s data, a much higher percentage of Jewish New Yorkers said that most of their close friends were Jewish than those in the nation as a whole.[12]

Demography has other effects. The fact that a huge number of Eastern European Jews came and remained in New York meant that the city possessed a larger reservoir of jobs in the ethnic enclave and a bigger consumer market than other cities with far fewer Jews. And numbers – and residential concentration – gave Jews power at the ballot box.

Because Jews were such a large proportion of New York's population at the beginning of the twentieth century – and had large numbers of voters in concentrated areas – they were able to win political influence and office not long after arrival. As early as 1900 a Jew from the Lower East Side won a seat in Congress; in 1913 the Lower East Side's Aaron Jefferson Levy became the Democrats' majority leader in the New York State Assembly; and in 1914 the Lower East Side elected Meyer London as the first Socialist Congressman from New York. Over the years, as the second, third, and fourth generations came of age, Jewish influence in politics increased – in the past 30 years, New York has had three Jewish mayors, from Abe Beame in the 1970s to Ed Koch in the 1980s to present-day Michael Bloomberg.[13]

Writing in 1963, Nathan Glazer and Daniel Moynihan noted in *Beyond the Melting Pot* that one-third of the Congressmen from New York City and rather more of the judges, state senators and assemblymen were Jewish.[14] Certainly, Jews gained political office in communities where they were few in number and a small proportion of the total population – as the numerous Jewish mayors of Cape Town, for example, and many small American towns indicates.[15] Taken as a whole, however, Jews have had nothing like the kind of political influence or impact in other major areas of settlement that they have had in New York – and numbers are one part of the story. (Glazer and Moynihan also mention class factors – Jews' financial contributions to electoral campaigns and the large number of lawyers among them – and high rates of voting participation.)[16]

Demography matters in another way. In a recent book on assimilation in America, *Remaking the American Mainstream*, Richard Alba and Victor Nee argue that a group's contribution to the public culture is most salient in regions where the group is concentrated.[17] Clearly one can say that Jews have contributed to the public culture of New York – from theatre and food to Jewish humour. Certain Jewish holidays eventually became New York City holidays – at least in the city's public schools and City University of New York. The 'Jewishness of New York' – and in particular the huge numbers of Jewish public school teachers and principals (by 1940, more than half of the public school teachers in New York were Jewish) – led the New York City Board of Education in the post-Second World War era to close the schools on Yom Kippur and Rosh Hashanah for all children, Jewish and non-Jewish alike. Even though the ethnic makeup of the teachers is changing (and Jews are now only a very small proportion of the public school student body), Yom Kippur and Rosh Hashanah remain part of the pantheon of holidays when the public schools close – alongside federal holidays like George Washington's birthday.

Quite apart from numbers, many other features of the receiving context must be considered in comparing Jews in different locations. Let me mention just a few. One is the culture, or one might say the cultural ethos or dominant set of values, of the receiving area – or, if we are looking cross-nationally, the receiving country.

The role of culture comes out in Andrew Godley's analysis of why Jewish immigrants in New York progressed up the socioeconomic ladder at a considerably faster rate than their cousins in London at the turn of the twentieth century. The answer according to Godley is the much higher levels of entrepreneurship in New York. And the reason for this, Godley argues, is that American and British cultures placed a different value on entrepreneurship. In America, Jews assimilated the cultural preference for entrepreneurship; in London's working class culture, high status was accorded to highly-skilled craft workers.[18]

Other contextual factors no doubt also played a role in explaining why upward mobility came sooner to Eastern European Jews in New York than in London. Selma Berrol – who has devoted a great deal of her career to studying education among Jewish immigrants, especially in New York – emphasises the opportunities provided by New York's educational system.[19] After 1900, when major school reforms were instituted, the New York public schools provided greater opportunity for upward mobility through education than schools in London. And by 1930, post-secondary education was more extensive in New York owing to the city's municipal colleges which were larger and grew faster than was the case with the only comparable institution available in London, the University of London.[20]

Berrol also argues that additional contextual features in New York provided opportunities to Jewish immigrants that were not available – or were less available – to their cousins in London. A larger host community of German Jews in New York gave the newcomers more support than the smaller Sephardic and German community was able to in London. Again there is the size of the New York Jewish community – much bigger than in London, with a bigger consumer market. And Berrol suggests, as well, that the more rigid class structure in English society was a greater obstacle in London.

If the comparison between London and New York brings out the role of culture and the structure of the educational and class systems, other features of the urban context also need to be factored in to any comparison of Jews in different locations. One is occupational opportunities available. Bookbinding was a Jewish trade in

London, for example, but the province of native-born workers in New York. As Nancy Green points out, there were many Jewish cigarette makers in London and cigar makers in New York, but virtually none in Paris, where tobacco was a state monopoly.[21] In small-town America in the early twentieth century, without an industrial base, Jews clustered in retail trade as merchants or as salespeople, clerks, and bookkeepers in mercantile establishments, leading Wessbach to refer to them as merchant communities.[22]

Green also notes the difference in political cultures in the different places where Jews settled as well as different forms of political organisation. In New York, Jews built the International Ladies Garment Workers Union in their image, and the first meeting reports and constitution were drawn up in Yiddish. In Britain and France, where national unions already existed, Jewish bootmakers and garment workers could organise separately, but generally did so within the context of the national labour movement.[23]

Still other contextual features need to be put into the mix, among them the structure of the city's (and indeed the nation's) political system and civic institutions. The character of ethno-racial relations in the city is also important. In New York City, at the time of initial settlement, before the mass migration of blacks from the South, blacks were a tiny proportion of the population – a little under two per cent in 1910 – and the newly-arrived Eastern European Jews, along with southern Italians, were the main focus of racial hostility and fears of native whites.[24] This is clearly different, for example, from the dynamics of early twentieth century white supremacy in South African cities in the context of large black African and Coloured populations or cities and towns in the segregation-era American South with significant numbers of African Americans. In Glasgow, to mention yet another pattern, it has been argued that there was relatively little anti-semitism in the 1920s partly because there was so much hostility to Catholics.[25]

Also, there is the impact of the Holocaust – which though it did not occur at the time of initial settlement that I am speaking of here in the late nineteenth and early twentieth centuries, affected the lives of immigrants with full force in the 1930s and 1940s. It goes without saying that the Holocaust was a major event for Jews everywhere, destroying their home communities in Eastern Europe and the people in them. Yet, the experience of the Holocaust was obviously much different for Jewish migrants in the United States than in German-occupied European cities – or in cities where government leaders and major figures were aligned with the Nazi cause.

Memory and Location

And this brings us to the role of memory. First there is the question of how the historical experience of Jews in particular locations has shaped the memories of their origins. For Jewish communities that endured the Holocaust at first-hand – such as in Paris – memories of the Holocaust experience often eclipse those of the migration at the turn of the century. (Paris, in addition, saw a huge in-migration of Eastern European Jews in the inter-war years – greater in number, in fact, than the 1880–1914 inflow.)[26]

In the United States – as Hasia Diner has highlighted in her book, *Lower East Side Memories* – New York, and particularly the Lower East Side, has, in her words, been 'canonized into mythic status as the focal point of American Jewish remembrance'.[27] Indeed, she argues that no Jewish neighbourhood elsewhere in the Diaspora has resonated as widely in Jewish popular consciousness as New York's Lower East Side.[28]

What is particularly intriguing is why Jews in America outside of New York – as well as those who live there – have turned to the Lower East Side as the place of memory to explain, as Diner writes, who they were, where they came from and how they got there. Diner goes so far as to call the Lower East Side a 'sacred space' in American Jewish consciousness – achieving iconic status in the 1960s as a place that all American Jews could recognise as a symbol of their communal origins, and remembered as a place that smelled and sounded Jewish and that pulsated with Jewish life. The pushcarts, tenements, sweatshops, and synagogues of the Lower East Side have become synonymous with the American Jewish experience.[29]

So why did the Lower East Side become the emblem of American Jewish history? Demography again is one factor. New York attracted more Jews than any American city – by 1927, 44 per cent of American Jews lived there – and they were a huge proportion of immigrant New Yorkers in the early twentieth century. Still, other American cities had significant numbers of Jewish residents. Chicago, in 1927, was home to 350,000 Jews; Philadelphia had 270,000; Boston 90,000, Cleveland 85,000, Detroit 75,000.[30]

Population size is only part of the answer, as Diner makes clear. Other factors are involved, too. New York, for one thing, was the centre of Jewish culture production – of the Yiddish press and theatre and a range of organisations – as well as the centre of the entire US publishing industry and the Progressive Reform movement, which focused heavily on the plight of Lower East Side Jews. Moreover, after the Second World War, the Holocaust destroyed older communal sites in Europe at the same time as Jews were becoming more American – moving to the suburbs and into the middle class – and as the barriers to the professions, housing, and higher education were crumbling. In this context, Jews turned to the Lower East Side as a yardstick of authenticity – which became, in Diner's revealing phrase, their collective 'shtetl'.[31]

Indeed, I would suggest that one reason American Jews may focus so much on – and have such nostalgia for – the past is precisely because the barriers to inclusion have fallen. In countries where anti-semitism continues to be a significant issue, there may be more focus on the problems of the present – and less nostalgia for the early days of settlement.

American Jews' memory of the Lower East Side reflects a search for identity – and also reinforces this identity. At the same time there is another way that memories of the earlier Jewish migration operate today – and thus I conclude with some thoughts on this topic, since it is one that has been a taking off point in my own work on contemporary immigration.[32]

The fact is that memories of the earlier Jewish migration in New York have influenced the way current-day arrivals from Asia, Latin America, and the Caribbean are seen – and New York is a city that is, once again, an immigrant city, with three million immigrants or more than a third of the population.

When scholars, politicians, and journalists look back to immigrant New York in the last great wave of immigration – and this is something they frequently do – it is the Jewish experience that is salient, particularly since so many of the commentators in the popular media as well as academics are themselves Jewish and because so many New Yorkers are Jewish. Many look back with nostalgia to their 'roots' in the Lower East Side and to the trials of the earlier immigrants in overcoming adversity to make it in America. A process akin to what historians have called the invention of tradition has taken place – a kind of invention of immigration. Many difficulties of the early years have long been forgotten in a haze of history, replaced by images that glorify the past. For many New Yorkers, their Jewish immigrant forebears have become folk heroes and heroines of a sort – and represent a baseline against which current arrivals are compared.

The problem is that it is hard to measure up to the myths. They set up unrealistic expectations for the newest New Yorkers. Against an image of immigrant giants of the past who made America great – who strove to become assimilated, who pulled themselves up by their own Herculean efforts, who were 'the people of the book' and had strong family values and colourful roots – present-day arrivals often seem like a pale imitation. A common popular fear is that the newcomers will have trouble – indeed, often resist – fitting in; that they have come for government handouts rather than to work; and that their origin in non-Western cultures is poor preparation for American life.

So while memories of the past help today's Jewish New Yorkers to understand who they are and where they have been, these very same memories may place a burden on the newcomers who are arriving today. I have heard it over and over, in informal conversations and in responses when I have given talks about my book *From Ellis Island to JFK*. The basic message is why cannot today's immigrants be more like our ancestors who came 100 years ago – and what too often gets lost is the many parallels between then and now. 'My grandparents learned English right away' – this is a not uncommon remark, but it often was not true. 'My grandparents a hundred years ago took school seriously and that was why they got ahead' – yet large numbers then were school dropouts without the passion for education that is so often celebrated in memory. And early on it was business, not education, which was the stepping stone to success for so many of the second generation.[33]

And this brings me to the conclusion. I started out with the historical experience of Jews in different locations and have ended up discussing immigration to New York today. I have sketched out some of the factors that ought to be considered in comparisons of different locations where Jews settled in the past and raised some questions about memory, but obviously there is much more to do on both these topics. In looking at comparisons across locations, I focused on the period of initial settlement, but we also need to explore the parallels and contrasts in the Jewish experience in different places in the mid and late twentieth century and now the twenty-first in terms of different urban and national contexts and changing immigration flows. New York, for example, has witnessed a massive inflow of Russian Jewish immigrants in recent decades, so that, according to one estimate, there are now about 300,000 immigrants from the former Soviet Union and their children living in the broad metropolitan area.³⁴ Alternatively, some cities have seen a substantial Jewish exodus in recent years, Cape Town and Johannesburg being prime examples. Whether gaining or losing Jewish residents – and whether in the past or the present – what is clear is that location matters in significant ways, and a comparative perspective that goes beyond one destination to make contrasts among them has much to offer to the analysis and understanding of the Jewish migrant experience.

NOTES

1. I have long been an advocate of a comparative perspective in migration studies. See Nancy Foner, *In a New Land: A Comparative View of Immigration* (New York: New York University Press, 2005) and *From Ellis Island to JFK: New York's Two Great Waves of Immigration* (New Haven, CT: Yale University Press, 2000).
2. Foner, *From Ellis Island to JFK* and *In a New Land* (see note 1). I have edited several books on immigration to New York, including *New Immigrants in New York* (New York: Columbia University Press, 2001) and *Islands in the City: West Indian Migration to New York* (Berkeley: University of California Press, 2001).
3. Reinhard Bendix, *Nation-Building and Citizenship* (New York: John Wiley, 1964), p.17.
4. George Fredrickson, *The Comparative Imagination: On the History of Racism, Nationalism, and Social Movements* (Berkeley: University of California Press, 1997), p.65. For a recent work on comparative history, with a focus on Europe, see Deborah Cohen and Maura O'Connnor, eds., *Comparison and History: Europe in Cross-National Perspective* (New York: Routledge, 2004).
5. Fredrickson, *The Comparative Imagination* (see note 4), p.23.
6. Nancy Green, 'The Comparative Method and Poststructural Structuralism – New Perspectives for Migration Studies', *Journal of American Ethnic History*, 13 (Summer 1994), 3–22.
7. Veronica Belling, 'A Slice of Eastern Europe in Johannesburg', paper presented at International Conference on Place and Displacement in Jewish History and Memory, Kaplan Center, University of Cape Town, 5 January 2005 and her contribution to this volume. Ideologically, Belling argues, many of the Jews who came to South Africa between 1890 and 1914 were committed to the revival of the Hebrew language. In contrast, few Polish Jews and 'thus very few of the Bundist intelligentsia, the General Jewish Workers' Union in Lithuania, Poland, and Russia, who were ideologically committed to Yiddish, came to South Africa' in these formative years of the Jewish community. Belling also suggests that other factors were at work and may have been more important, including the lack of a large Yiddish-speaking proletariat in Johannesburg as compared to New York, the Zionist orientation of mainstream Johannesburg Jewish culture, and, later on, in the South African racial and political context, an antipathy to leftist politics among established South African Jewry.
8. Gerald Sorin, *A Time for Building: The Third Migration, 1880–1920* (Baltimore, MD: Johns Hopkins University Press, 1992), p.137; Nancy Green, 'Introduction', in *Jewish Workers in the Modern Diaspora*, ed. by Nancy Green (Berkeley: University of California Press, 1998), pp.6–9.
9. Lee-Shai Weissbach, 'Place and Jewish Identity in Small-Town America: The Distinctive Experience of Smaller Jewish Communities in the United States, 1880–1950', paper presented at conference on Place and Displacement in Jewish History and Memory, Kaplan Center, University of Cape Town, 4 January 2005.
10. See, for example, Lee-Shai Weissbach, *Jewish Life in Small-Town America* (New Haven, CT: Yale University Press, 2005).
11. See ibid. for a discussion of the strategies used to ensure in-group marriage in small-town America.
12. Samuel C. Heilman, *Portrait of American Jews: The Last Half of the 20th Century* (Seattle: University of Washington Press, 1995), pp.127, 129.
13. Glazer and Moynihan argue that given the number and proportion of Jews in New York City, in combination with their relatively high naturalisation rates and high rates of voting participation, they could have dominated the Democratic Party – and presumably elected Jewish mayors – even earlier had not so many devoted their energy to the Socialist Party and other left-wing political groups. See Nathan Glazer and Daniel Moynihan, *Beyond the Melting Pot* (Cambridge, MA: MIT Press, 1963), pp.169–70.
14. Ibid., p.170.
15. Between 1903 and 1963, Cape Town had six Jewish mayors. On small-town America, see Weissbach, *Jewish Life in Small-Town America* (see note 10).
16. Glazer and Moynihan, *Beyond the Melting Pot* (see note 13), p.170. Jews, throughout the 1980s and 1990s, continued to represent a very significant proportion of New York City's voters. In 1989 and

1993, Jews in the outer boroughs alone (outside of Manhattan) were the second largest bloc of voters in the mayoral elections just behind white Catholics, and ahead of both blacks and Latinos. John Mollenkopf, *A Phoenix in the Ashes: The Rise and Fall of the Koch Coalition in New York City Politics* (Princeton, NJ: Princeton University Press, 1994).
17. Richard Alba and Victor Nee, *Remaking the American Mainstream: Assimilation and Contemporary Immigration* (Cambridge, MA: Harvard University Press, 2003), p.83.
18. Andrew Godley, *Jewish Immigrant Entrepreneurship in New York and London, 1880–1914* (London: Palgrave, 2001).
19. The discussion of Berrol's argument draws on her analysis in Selma Berrol, *East Side/East End: Eastern European Jews in London and New York, 1870–1920* (Westport, CT: Praeger, 1994).
20. The availability of excellent free college education at the City University of New York is one of the factors mentioned by David Cesarani in his analysis of why cultural historians write about New York but not London Jewish intellectuals. 'London and New York Jews Remember', paper presented at conference on Place and Displacement in Jewish History and Memory, Kaplan Center, University of Cape Town, 5 January 2005 and his contribution to this volume.
21. Nancy Green, 'Conclusion', in *Jewish Workers in the Modern Diaspora*, ed. by Green, p.236.
22. Weissbach, 'Place and Jewish Identity in Small-Town America' (see note 9).
23. Green, Conclusion' (see note 21). P.235.
24. The distancing from blacks that is often mentioned as a factor involved in the process of racialisation, in which Jews, once disparaged as racial outsiders, eventually became part of a white racial majority, did not occur until after the First World War and the massive influx of blacks from the South into New York. See Foner, *From Ellis Island to JFK* and *In a New Land* (see note 1).
25. Senay Boztas, 'Why Scotland Has Never Hated Jews ... We Were Too Busy Hating Each Other', *Glasgow Herald*, 17 October 2004. See also William Kennefick, 'Comparing the Jewish and Irish Communities in Twentieth Century Scotland', paper presented at conference on Place and Displacement in Jewish History and Memory, Kaplan Center, University of Cape Town, 5 January 2005 and his contribution to this volume.
26. Green, 'Introduction' (see note 8), p.7.
27. Hasia Diner, *Lower East Side Memories* (Princeton, NJ: Princeton University Press, 2000), p.7.
28. In his account of Jewish small-town life in America, Weissbach notes that after the Second World War, and the demise of what he calls the classic era of small-town Jewry, there was an idealisation or romanticisation of Jewish small town life among the descendants of the original settlers who had left for greener pastures; Jewish small-town life, or an idealised version of that life, became, as he puts it, the stuff of nostalgia. Weissbach, 'Place and Jewish Identity in Small-Town America' (see note 9).
29. Diner, *Lower East Side Memories* (see note 27), pp.8, 19–20, 145.
30. Sorin, *A Time for Building* (see note 8), p.137.
31. Diner, *Lower East Side Memories* (see note 27), p.170. See chapter 3 for Diner's analysis of the reasons for what she calls the 'sacralisation' of the Lower East Side.
32. Foner, *From Ellis Island to JFK* (see note 1).
33. See ibid. on the realities of Jewish education and mobility patterns in New York in the past.
34. See Aviva Zeltzer-Zubida, 'Affinities and Affiliations: The Many Ways of Being a Russian Jewish American', in *Becoming New Yorkers*, ed. by Philip Kasinitz, John Mollenkopf and Mary Waters (New York: Russell Sage Foundation, 2004); and Annelise Orleck, 'Soviet Jews: The City's Newest Immigrants Transform New York Jewish Life', in *New Immigrants in New York*, ed. by Nancy Foner, rev. edn (New York: Columbia University Press, 2001).

Putting London Jewish Intellectuals in their Place

DAVID CESARANI

The 'sense of place' and the relationship between a location and the feeling of belonging somewhere have long interested urban sociologists and social geographers. Robert Park and Louis Wirth, members of the Chicago School of the 1920s, were among the first to explore the ways in which urban settings contributed to individual and group identities. However, their approach took the built environment as a given, with identity emerging from localities that were characterised geographically and morphologically. This position was challenged in the 1960s by a new urban sociology that took its inspiration partly from behavioural analysis and partly from Erving Goffman's work on the formation of 'self'. New research inverted the assumption that location determined the self-perception of discrete urban populations. For example, Kevin Lynch demonstrated how people formed an image of the city that reflected their own sense of who they were and that, in turn, coloured how they perceived their locality – a process he dubbed 'cognitive mapping'. T.R. Lee elaborated methods for assessing how denizens of particular areas drew up 'mental maps' according to their interaction with their surroundings as well as other denizens. 'Cognitive mapping' and 'mental maps' showed that a sense of place emerges over time from paths repeatedly or occasionally taken through the cityscape, social interactions at particular points, and the landmarks that mark districts or the edges that surround them.[1]

In contradistinction to the 'ecological' approach of the Chicago School, by the 1970s it became accepted that place was socially constructed. In the words of Edward Relph:

> Places are fusions of human and natural order and are significant centres of our immediate experiences of the world. They are defined less by unique locations, landscapes and communities than by focussing experiences and intentions onto particular settings. Places are not abstractions of concepts, but are directly experienced phenomena of the lived world and hence are full of meanings, with real objects, and with ongoing activities. They are important sources of individual and communal identity and are often profound centres of human existence to which people have deep emotional and physical ties.[2]

To humanist geographers, inspired by Yi-Fu Tuan, place existed in an experiential dimension. Yi-Fu Tuan maintained that place 'has more substance than the word location suggests: it is a unique entity, a "special ensemble"; it has history and meaning. Place incarnates the experiences and aspirations of a people. Place is not only a fact to be explained in the broader frame of space, but it is also a reality to be clarified and understood from the perspectives of the people who have given it meaning'.[3] Place is an amalgam of bounded spaces, physical structures and affective sentiment generated by constant interaction between individuals and sites, and between people engaged in routine activities centred on particular locations. These interactions give meaning to place and the accretion of such meanings over time give symbolic potency to location.

According to another pioneering humanist geographer David Ley: 'At the heart of the life-world is a web of familiarity, predictable places and people, and some differentiation of detail — the summation of varied experiences over time. ... The social reality of the city is not simply given. It is also constructed and maintained inter-subjectively in a semi closed world of communication and shared symbolization.' The city space is experienced variously as regions of security or stress, stimulus or ennui, status or stigma.[4] Ley and others increasingly recognised on the basis of empirical investigation that ethnicity played a role in the social construction of space and place by over-determining both behaviour and image formation. It had long been recognised anecdotally that the ethnic character of a population conferred status or stigma on a zone, inspiring or repelling settlement. Research also showed that ethnicity had an impact on the frequency, nature and distribution of interactions skewing a person's mental map of a city. The sense of safety of an ethnic minority person began in the home, extended through the neighbourhood where their ethnic group had a significant presence and ended at its edges where the zone of insecurity began.[5]

If place and the sense of place is constituted in the present by the intersection of ethnic identity with location, place is no less important in the past as an individual or social memory. As the geographer Karen Till puts it: 'Place is the cultural and spatial context within which we construct and locate our individual and collective memories ... It is through and within places that we frame our social memories.'[6] Just as we are who we are through interaction with places, our memories or our past lives, how we became who we are, remain attached to locations. For people with an ethnic identity, formed in a certain place, the memory of that location becomes a key marker of ethnicity.

When assessing this relationship between ethnicity and 'sense of place' it has been common practice for sociologists and geographers to use literary sources as material alongside metric studies. In this context ethnicity has long registered as an element in the formation of the image a place has and in mediating the human interactions that contribute to the feeling of belonging in a locality.[7] Literary historians have also noted the importance of landscape, but have paid less attention to the dynamic of relations between place and ethnicity — least of all in an urban setting.[8] Relatively little attention has been paid to writing by Jews that provides powerful evidence of the reciprocal shaping effect of environment and ethnicity.[9]

This lacuna is surprising because the connection has been made repeatedly. During the 1980s several studies exploring the phenomenon of the New York Jewish intellectuals were published, all of which drew attention to their common ethnic-faith and geographical origins.[10] Not only did these intellectuals often evoke place in their writings, especially memoirs and autobiographical essays, they frequently made location and identity a subject of research or reflection.[11]

According to Alexander Bloom in his 1986 study *Prodigal Sons. The New York Jewish Intellectuals and their World*, place was crucial to the formation of the cohort that emerged in the inter-war and immediate post-war years:

> They had assembled on the edge of American society. Coming from the immigrant ghettos in which their parents had settled upon arrival in America, they moved towards the center of American intellectual life by a circuitous route through left politics and the avant-garde cultural life of the 1930s. They exchanged the peripheral world of the immigrants for the marginal world of radical intellectuals. But even here, among those who all conceived themselves cosmopolitan and universalistic, they felt different.[12]

Bloom identifies remarkable continuities of experience in the life history of the American Jewish intellectuals who emerged in the 1920s, 1930s, and 1940s. Despite poverty and a daily struggle to exist, Jewish neighbourhoods offered young Jews a familiar, protective environment in which they were encouraged to learn. Jewish youngsters grew up within tight-knit communities that were, at the same time, highly diverse religiously, culturally and politically. In synagogues, cultural associations, youth groups, and on the streets they were exposed to every current of Jewish life from *der beym* – a polyphonic expression of recent Jewish history relocated to the new world.[13]

Place and space had multiple significances. The Jewish immigrant neighbourhoods of the Lower East Side, Brooklyn and the Bronx were not only safe homes: they were portals, a liminal space between one world and another. The parents of most of these intellectuals had come from Eastern Europe. Yiddish was frequently the language of the home and the locality: of newspapers, theatre, political meetings, and street signs. Whether orthodox in religion or radical in politics, parents represented another world, another set of allegiances. Yet these very same parents encouraged their offspring to embrace America, its language, culture, and constitution. As a result, the children grew up in a schizoid environment. Bloom remarks that 'Maturing in a half-English, half-Yiddish environment, they always carried with them some of that divided world'.[14]

Bloom's analysis has been criticised for its reductive emphasis on New York and ethnicity. However, even his detractors accept that the life and career patterns of New York Jewish intellectuals owed something to their starting point, the city's Jewish neighbourhoods. Terry Cooney sees the proximity between America's cultural dynamo, Manhattan, and its largest concentration of immigrants as a key to understanding the shaping of modern American culture.[15] Hugh Wilford has emphasised the connection between the ethnic origins and politics of the New York intellectuals, arguing that their shared experience of social and economic marginality found expression in the adoption of an independent, vanguard position.[16]

If it is the case that the formation of the New York Jewish intellectuals as individuals and as a collectivity has such a strong ethnic and spatial dimension, is there no equivalent in London? Over the same time span, from the 1920s to the

1950s, London witnessed the emergence of a stunning concentration of Jewish intellectuals. Many emerged from London's East End, which in this respect seemed to perform a similar function to New York's Jewish immigrant districts. Like their New York counterparts many of these London Jewish cultural figures knew each other and collaborated on common projects. Yet cultural historians have not delineated a prototypical London Jew or London Jewish intellectual. Indeed, remarkable as it may seem, aside from some literary and artistic histories there is *no* cultural history of Jewish intellectuals in London or Britain. Little progress has been made towards a sociological analysis, let alone one investigating the relationship between place and ethnicity in the emergence of a distinctive intellectual cadre.[17]

Almost the only comprehensive attempt at such an approach is Efraim Sicher's *Beyond Marginality. Anglo-Jewish Literature after the Holocaust.* Sicher commences with a similar cultural geography to that used by the literary and critical historians of New York, a spatial approach signposted by the *double entendre* in the title. Sicher maintains that the majority of post-1945 Anglo-Jewish writers were shaped by their early years in marginal, immigrant neighbourhoods, notably London's East End, and the subsequent process of suburbanisation. For this reason he organises the chapters and, rather less promisingly, the subjects of his study according to a geographical progression from the East End to the suburbs – another peripheral location.[18]

Sicher suggests that the work of the 'East End Writers' – Emanuel Litvinoff, Wolf Mankowitz and Bernard Kops – is determined by their roots and relocation to the suburbs.

> The radicalism natural to the group's immigrant experience disappeared with bourgeois prosperity. The demographic move from the poor quarters of East London incited a general protest that looked back at the East End which was no more and which contrasted to the hypocrisy and philistinism of their parents. The loss of community in the East End and the loss of six million because they were Jews do much to explain the ethnicity of modern Anglo-Jewish writers.[19]

Setting aside the notion that the Nazi mass murder of Europe's Jews had consequences in any way commensurate with the results of moving ten miles from Bethnal Green to Golders Green, it is surely necessary to question the validity of Sicher's claim that Anglo-Jewish writers lapsed into nostalgia and simply used the East End as a template for an authentic way of life and a site of lost values.

In Sicher's own words: 'The dissolution of the East End was to be a point of departure and a point of no return for the East End Jewish writers as they overcame their marginality and tried to find a way back to roots.'[20] Thus the loss of one way of being Jewish, linked to a specific locus, provoked the search for other forms and sites of Jewishness – itself an expression of being a Jew. Indeed, I would suggest that a closer examination of Jewish intellectuals in London reveals that place was critical to the formation of ethnicity and outlook, be it the East End or the suburbs. This distinctive sensibility was carried with them in a series of journeys. Nor did these odysseys end with nostalgia or self-effacement. On the contrary, London Jewish intellectuals punched their weight as Jews. If they were marginalised it was precisely because they asserted their Jewishness.

In the rest of this essay I will look at the life and work of six London Jewish intellectuals born in the East End whose work exemplifies the connections between place and ethnicity. Emanuel Litvinoff, born in 1915, went on to become a poet and novelist. His younger brother, Barnett, born in 1918, became a journalist, writer and historian. Bernard Kops, born in 1926, became a leading playwright of the 1960s. Arnold Wesker, born in 1932, was often bracketed – like Kops – with the 'Angry Young Men' who transformed the English theatre in that decade. John Gross, born in 1935, became a literary critic and edited the *Times Literary Supplement* for over 20 years. Steven Berkoff, born in 1938, is a film and theatre actor and writer with a string of award winning plays to his credit.

In their autobiographical writing, all these men describe in remarkably similar terms how a sense of being Jewish was inscribed in their consciousness by the workings of domestic space and the distinctive, ethnically coloured locations in which they grew and matured. Of course, retrospect may not offer an accurate reconstruction of how things really were. We should not read these memoirs simplistically as an accurate evocation of passed youth and a lost world. Some of the writers strive for verisimilitude while others are highly stylised. The point to bear in mind is that in later life these Jewish intellectuals fixed on certain topographical features as key reference points for their sense of self. They came to define themselves in relation to past places. They may have essentialised, romanticised, or even distorted the people they grew up amongst and the places they knew, but in this context the reality is less important than what they imagined it to be. Indeed, each came to believe that their imagination, like their self-image, was inextricably linked to these settings.

All adults trace the formation of character to the crucible of home and family but for the London Jewish intellectuals home and family differentiated them from the majority and created bonds with a specific ethnic-faith group in a certain locality. Home and parents did not act to socialise and acculturate them: on the contrary, family worked to set them apart. Their parents or grandparents were immigrants, speaking a foreign language and observing a faith different from the majority population. The boundary of family overlapped with the boundary of their ethnic-faith group. The sense of being 'other' was constituted out of a complex of familial behaviour, language, food, and rituals all acted out within tightly bounded and discreet spaces. Otherness was fortified by a sense of family and home being safe locations.

Emanuel Litvinoff opens his reminiscences with a chapter entitled 'Growing up with mother'. This is perfectly natural place to begin a life story, except that his mother was a single parent as the result of ethnically specific events – the forced repatriation of Litvinoff's Russian Jewish father to his 'homeland' in 1917–18.[21] More conventionally Bernard Kops opens his memoir under the heading 'Child in the Family' and describes his doughty mother as its hub and unifying force. But as he soon informs the reader she is not just a parent: she is a conduit of ethnicity.[22]

The home was not a neutral domestic space. The use of Yiddish or yiddishisms, the celebration of the Sabbath and Jewish festivals, and the cuisine reproduced difference. Emanuel Litvinoff recalled sentimentally that: 'The tenement was a village in miniature, a place of ingathered exiles who supplemented their Jewish speech with phrases in Russian, Polish or Lithuanian. We sang songs of the ghettos and folk tunes of the old Russian Empire and ate the traditional dishes of its countryside.'[23] Although his mother was English and Anglicised, John Gross was taught Hebrew by his father, who had been a rabbinical student in Russia and London. Gross was fascinated by the Hebrew alphabet: it was 'idiosyncratically un-English'.[24] Berkoff's father was English-born but his occupation, a tailor, and his interest in gambling and boxing, placed him firmly in the East End Jewish fraternity.[25]

If private space was ethnically and religiously charged, so was the public space beyond. Locality contributed to the construction of a sense of self and a sense of difference. Berkoff fixes his father's shop in Leman Street, which was a throughway for immigrants arriving from the London Docks. He also recalls that later on he lived with his parents in lodgings with 'two rooms and an outside loo in Anthony Street (off Commercial Road, E1)'.[26] The use of the postal code recurs in many of the retrospective accounts by ex-East Enders and is a highly significant marker on their 'mental map'. It was an evocative signifier of 'alien London' and possessed remarkable metonymic qualities. The author's biographical note for the memoir by John Gross notes that 'He lives in London SW2 – several miles from E3'.

Place has mnenomic functions and ethno-cultural as well as class valences when these authors recall their childhood. Buildings, streets and districts help to identify people but they also descry a specifically place- and time-bound socio-cultural formation. The concatenations of names and places that are so characteristic of these memoirs verbalise 'cognitive maps', geographies of ethnicity and genealogies of migration. For example, one of Wesker's first memories was of 'my paternal grandfather tapping his way with a white stick from Rothschild Buildings in Flower and Dean Street to Fashion Street, the parallel street to where we lived in Stepney, London, E1'.[27]

Places of memory denoted family and ethnicity. As a child Wesker played in Fashion Street, where he could call up to his mother in the overlooking flat or in the vast courtyard of the nearby Charlotte de Rothschild Buildings, 'a safe area enclosed by family and friends'. In the 'tight, close streets' of Whitechapel, 'nowhere was far away'.[28] Even after the family home was relocated to Weald Square, Upper Clapton Road, in 1942, 'We were surrounded by family, no one too far away'. He follows this remark with a list of family members, each with their address.[29] The local was infused with intimacy, closeness and safety. According to Kops, 'It was a self imposed ghetto, but a happy world. And there was a spirit of community as in a village'. The neighbourhood 'meant security and happiness'.[30]

Place was constituted sensually and reconstituted from memory in the language of the senses. A 'sense of place' was literally assembled out of sights, sounds, smells, and feel. The adult self recovers the childhood self as a receptor of inputs that are embodied and carried through life. Emanuel Litvinoff recalled his journey from the Jewish Board of Guardians to a job as an apprentice furrier in terms of smells and sounds.

Even blindfolded, I'd have known where we were by the smell of the different streets – reek of rotten fruits: Spitalfields; scent of tobacco warehouses:

Commercial Street; the suffocating airless stench of the Cambridge Picture Palace; Hanbury Street and the pungency of beer from Charrington's brewery. Then Brick Lane with half the women from our street jostling among the market stalls.[31]

Bernard Kops remembered the 'strange mixture of Yiddish and Cockney' heard in the streets of Whitechapel and Mile End. He identified a superficially unremarkable but in fact deeply significant feature of the district; 'Men stood everywhere'.[32] The streets were trading areas, employment exchanges, political meeting places, and recreational zones. Such was the overcrowding in the tenement buildings and the fitful nature of employment that people treated the pavements and street corners as an extension of the home. This kind of 'exotic' street life was common to few parts of London. It is not by chance that pondering where to begin his reminiscences, Wesker wonders, 'So many possible beginnings – streets, smells, family life, family history, social background'.[33]

But the converse of proximity and boundedness inscribed on 'cognitive maps' was the awareness of other locations, distant and dangerous, populated by those who were unlike. Barnett Litvinoff captured the duality well: 'Sixty years ago this enclosure in a corner of Bethnal Green constituted the whole of my world, bounded by Victoria Park to the north, the London and North Eastern Railway in the west, Whitechapel Road in the south, and unknown terrors leading to the enemy territory of Shoreditch further east.'[34] For Kops, 'It was my world, and Aldgate East was the outside frontier of that world, a world that consisted mainly of Jewish people.'[35] When Leah Wesker was offered new accommodation in Hackney Marshes she refused because is was 'not a Jewish area'.[36]

Even John Gross, who left the East End at the age of four and returned as an adolescent, reflected the antimony of the ethnically familiar locality surrounded by other places. '"Our" East End, that of my family and friends, was certainly Stepney; Bethnal Green seemed rough and menacing in comparison.'[37] Steven Berkoff and his family moved to Stamford Hill in the late 1940s, where he found ethnic territorial divisions no less stark than in the East End itself. Local youth clustered around the crossroads at which the Hackney Road, the main conduit south to the East End, terminated, staking out their patch. The Jews congregated in the E&A Milk Bar, known as the '*shtipp* house' because of the pinball machines that were *shtipped* or pushed when played.[38] The local criminals gathered at another place where, once, the notorious Kray twins put in an appearance. They 'were East Enders from the other side. The other side meant, of course, the Gentiles'. To underline the concatenation of parents, domesticity, religion and ethnicity he continues: 'They weren't softened by too much mother love, or gentle Friday night rituals of chicken soup, fish cakes and soft sabbath candles.'[39]

Paradoxically, neighbours could provoke the feeling of difference. Emanuel Litvinoff dreaded passage down the nearby but appropriately named Bacon Street where only a few, wretchedly poor Jews lived. The non-Jews living there seemed to be drunk a lot of the time and hurled abuse at passing Jews.[40] Wesker's attitude towards the English working class was poisoned by his interaction with non-Jewish neighbours in Weald Square who were 'uneducated, intolerant, bloodless, shiftily unreliable'.[41] When John Gross was moved to Egham during the blitz, he found 'my sense of the singularity of being Jewish was heightened by the fact that our Jewishness found very little expression at the time outside the house'.[42]

But what was Jewishness? Gross observes that 'Anyone who wanted to give an adequate idea of what being Jewish meant in the London of fifty years ago (or at any time since) would have to take into account the most varied phenomena, some of them quite mundane' and lists, inter alia, shops, schools, restaurants, Petticoat Lane.[43] Wesker's mnemonic map includes as well as Petticoat Lane, Toynbee Hall, which offered evening courses to immigrants and their children, the Whitechapel Library, days out in Victoria Park and shopping at Wickams, the local department store. Wesker and Berkoff fondly recall the local public baths. Wesker patronised the establishment in Goulston Street while Berkoff remembered that 'Friday night was bath night and at Betts Street baths, just off Cable Street, you would take your sixpence and wallow in the luxury of a huge tub'.[44]

Both recalled the local passion for boxing, and Wesker in particular summoned up the image of Curley's Café, a haunt for the predominantly Jewish fighters and promoters.[45] They also benefited from the profusion of clubs for Jewish youth in the East End and North London, 'since benevolent philanthropists and wise heads of community had decreed that there should be a boys and girls club on nearly every street corner of the East End, so that our youth would not be prone to the evil temptations of slum life and fall into bad ways'.[46]

Jewish abstinence from alcohol was a crucial demarcating factor in the affective net cast over districts of London and their inhabitants. Berkoff enthused that 'we were of the café society and didn't go to pubs – in fact none of us ever went to a pub, for our heritage was rather more Continental and it was talk, talk and more talk that governed our lives'. Echoing Wesker's ethnic ambivalence that cut across class, Berkoff commented that 'the boozer was the sanctuary for the English working man'.[47]

Recreation was also ethnic creation because Jews and non-Jews followed different leisure pursuits in separate locations and when they commingled the Jews conducted themselves warily.[48] The recreational-geographical divide ran along the axis from the West End to the East End. The West End was not only the opposite pole of London: it was the antithesis of the East End in many other ways. It was the location of mainstream popular culture, unlike the Yiddish theatres and concerts of the East End patronised by the older generation. The West End was home to Lyons Corner House, the chic alternative to *haimish* food in local kosher restaurants. Along with the dance halls there were art galleries and bookshops. All offered a glimpse of sex and the promise of forbidden liaisons conducted beyond the gaze of watchful elders. It was, to Kops, 'Eldorado'. The prospect of 'Going Up West' acted like a magnet on Gross: 'From early on, I was fascinated by the idea of the West End.' Its potency was so memorable to Berkoff that he composed a set of plays titled 'East' and 'West' that explored the phenomenon.[49]

The dyad of East/West exemplifies the duality of life experienced by the London Jewish intellectuals. The sense of boundaries, of self and other, that was fostered in the domestic environment and the locality eventuated in a feeling of doubleness sometimes characterised as alienation. This schizophrenic position was aggravated because they were subjected to forces of acculturation that both laid down lines and obliged them to cross over. The relationship of the two worlds is most vividly evoked by memories and the use of Yiddish.

To Emanuel Litvinoff Yiddish was 'the language that to this very day speaks to me with the voice of mother'. It evoked home, religion, culture, family and generations stretching back to another land and another era. When he was growing up, 'the news came to us in Yiddish newspapers and it was usually bad', that is news about 'der haim'. Around the kitchen table, 'People spoke of Warsaw, Kishinev, Kiev, Kharkov, Odessa as if they were neighbouring suburbs'.[50] In less dramatic terms, to Gross Yiddish was associated with his father who travelled far to converse with fellow Yiddishists. Although John Gross could not speak the language he picked up fragments that were related to key aspects of life: religious terms, food, mood, Jewish values, nostalgia and curses – usually on non-Jews.[51] Berkoff's mother used to translate the subtitles at the silent movies for her mother who knew only Yiddish and attended the Yiddish theatre in the East End herself. She did not transmit much Yiddish to her actor son, but bequeathed him a sense of loss and inauthenticity. Berkoff was aware that 'when we spoke English and tried to sound posh' it was in opposition to or denial of another way of being.[52]

The awareness of spanning two worlds, today a cause for endorsement and celebration, was then a painful condition. Although parents wanted their offspring to succeed at school, learning involved the denial of one part of themselves – the part that linked to family, home and culture. Emanuel Litvinoff faced anti-Jewish taunts from his teachers who mocked his 'fine old Hanglo-Saxon name Levinskinoff'. Non-Jewish children just called him 'Pissoffsky'. 'Here I was', he recalled, 'facing my own test, surrounded by strangers and a long way from home.'[53] Kops first attended a Jewish elementary school, but went on to 'a Christian school' where crude anti-Jewish attitudes were common. He, and his mother, were soon engaged in running fights with playground bullies and teachers alike.[54]

Gross commenced his formal education during his enforced absence from London due to the war. In addition to the pedagogy of acculturation he experienced in reverse the mutual reinforcement of ethnicity and environment. 'It wasn't only in school that Englishness was instilled. The whole town offered a daily lesson in the subject, simply by being what it was.'[55]

By the time these youngsters entered adolescence and were on the cusp of independence they were unhinged from family, religion, and parental culture but they were not fully integrated into English society. Gross 'never felt quite at home' in synagogue. 'I had always known that a synagogue could never be the centre of my world, simply a centre. But was it even as much as that?'[56] Wesker lacked that option because his family was militantly atheistic. For a time he was involved with Habonim, the Zionist youth movement which offered a secular-national Jewish identity, but only briefly and mainly because of the contact with girls that it offered. Habonim was 'the closest I came to being a member of any Jewish community'.[57]

So does this litany of geographical and ethnic drift vindicate Sicher's conclusion that Anglo-Jewish writers and dramatists were 'by and large removed from a Jewish background' until 'moved by the Holocaust into re-examining Jewish identity'. In contrast to their New York cousins who turned marginality into a cult and a creed, did London Jewish intellectuals flee the margins until brought up short by a guilty awareness of the tragedy of Europe's Jews?[58] Is place significant in their work merely as a device to explore lost worlds and lost values?

This is a strange argument because almost every memoir attributes at least an inkling of the wartime catastrophe to the emerging youths, an awareness that persisted, rather than a sudden and late coming to consciousness that had an impact on their intellectual development. Gross recalls that he had only a 'fairly vague' awareness of the European Jewish disaster at the time it was occurring. More to the point, however, from the early 1950s he started reading voraciously about the persecution and mass murder of the Jews.[59] Berkoff admitted that 'I heard nothing, just felt this constant unease'. But he spent months in West Germany in the mid-1950s in pursuit of work and women and was inclined to take a jaundiced view of Germans through the lens of recent history.[60] Kops heard about the fate of the Dutch Jews directly from a cousin who survived. 'My hatred of Germans burned into my being. It consumed me and I cannot say I was ashamed of my hatred.'[61]

It is more reasonable to see the trajectory of London Jewish intellectuals following that of the New York Jewish intellectuals with uncanny precision. Place was an essential element in their self-formation and inculcated ethnicity into their being. Spatial experiences, from life in the inner city neighbourhood to resettlement in the suburbs, were measured as ethnic transitions too. If their terminus was different that may also be a consequence of location. Unlike the bulk of the New York Jewish intellectuals who had access to superb free institutes of higher education and the continuity to enjoy that privilege, war, evacuation and military service disrupted the lives and education of their London counterparts. Only Gross attended university and he was the son of a doctor. There was no GI Bill in England. Wesker and Berkoff eventually managed to study acting, drama and film, but paid their way with painful slowness.[62]

Having gained education, experience and served an apprenticeship, the New York intellectuals moved confidently into existing institutions or founded new ones: journals, publishing houses, universities. Hugh Wilford shrewdly observes that 'they were undoubtedly aided by the United States' lack of a cultural "establishment": that is, a single institutionalised intellectual formation capable of dominating high cultural discourse and regulating high cultural production like, say, Oxbridge and Bloomsbury in England'. On the contrary, in the 1950s their 'proximity to the metropolitan headquarters of the leading American publishing houses and other literary media enabled them to dictate a large portion of the national high cultural agenda'.[63]

As long as the location of culture in Britain was in Oxford and Cambridge, while the enclave in Bloomsbury was class and ethnically exclusive, London Jewish intellectuals were condemned to careers at the margins. It would not be until the transformation of the culture in the late 1950s and 1960s that they would enjoy recognition – and even then the price was a degree of ethnic self-effacement. It was not until the 1990s that place and ethnicity in London were finally brought together and celebrated.[64] By then the social and cultural milieu in which the London Jewish intellectuals had matured was long gone and nostalgia the only mode in which it could be explored.

NOTES

I would like to thank Professor Tony Kushner and Professor Nancy Foner for their comments on the first incarnation of this paper, delivered in Cape Town in January 2005, and members of the History Department, Royal Holloway, for many helpful observations when a revised version was given to the staff seminar. Professor Felix Driver and his colleagues in the Department of Geography, Royal Holloway, also made useful suggestions in the course of a lunchtime seminar based on an earlier version.

1. See Wayne Davies and David Herbert, *Communities Within Cities. An Urban Social Geography* (London: Belhaven, 1993), pp.34–60, 85–109. The classic text of the Chicago School is Robert Park, ed., *The City* (Chicago: Chicago University Press, 1925). See also K. Lynch, *The Image of the City* (Cambridge, MA: MIT Press, 1960), and T.R. Lee, 'Cities in the Mind', in *Social Areas in Cities*, ed. by D.T. Herbert and R.J. Johnston (Chichester: John Wiley, 1976), pp.253–81.
2. R. Relph, *Place and Placelessness* (London: Pion, 1976), cited in Davies and Herbert, *Communities Within Cities* (see note 1), p.101.
3. Yi-Fu Tan cited in Kenneth R. Olwing, 'Landscape as a Contested Topos of Place, Community and Self', in *Textures of Place. Exploring Humanist Geographies*, ed. by Paul C. Adams, Steven Hoelscher, Karen E. Till (Minneapolis: University of Minnesota Press, 2001), p.93. In the same volume Robert D. Sack gives a stimulating discussion of place with a different emphasis: 'Place, Power and the Good', in *Textures of Place*, ed. by Adams *et al*., pp.232–3. Space is commonly understood as enclosed areas, delineated by physical constructions within a given place. But space, too, has socially constructed meanings.
4. David Ley, *A Social Geography of the City* (New York: Harper and Row, 1983), pp.138, 143–70, 203.
5. See, for example, Duncan Timms, *The Urban Mosaic. Towards a Theory of Residential Segregation* (Cambridge: Cambridge University Press, 1971), pp.79–89, 98–106.
6. Karen E. Till, 'Reimagining National Identity. "Chapters of Life" at the German Historical Museum', in *Textures of Place*, ed. by Adams *et al*. (see note 3), p.275.
7. For examples see, Davies and Herbert, *Communities Within Cities* (see note 1), pp.87–8; Peter Dickens, *Urban Sociology. Society, Locality and Human Nature* (London: Harvester Wheatsheaf, 1990), pp.20–21; and Peter Jackson and Jan Penrose, eds., *Constructions of Place, Race and Nation* (London: University College London Press, 1993).
8. For instance, John Barrell, *The Idea of Landscape and the Sense of Place: 1730–1840* (Cambridge: Cambridge University Press, 1972); and Raymond Williams, *The Country and the City* (London: Chatto and Windus, 1973).
9. Several collections of essays published in the 1990s explored the relations between gender, ethnicity and place but at an extremely high level of abstraction and usually without reference to the Jewish experience: James Duncan and David Ley, eds., *Place/Culture/Representation* (London: Routledge, 1993); Michael Keith and Steve Pile, eds., *Place and the Politics of Identity* (London: Routledge, 1993); Steve Pile and Nigel Thrift, eds., *Mapping the Subject. Geographies of Cultural Transformation* (London: Routledge, 1995);
10. Alexander Bloom, *Prodigal Sons. The New York Intellectuals and Their World* (New York: Oxford University Press, 1986); Terry A. Cooney, *The Rise of the New York Intellectuals. Partisan Review and Its Circle* (Madison: University of Wisconsin Press, 1986); Alan M. Wald, *The New York Intellectuals. The Rise and Decline of the Anti-Stalinist Left from the 1930s to the 1980s* (Chapel Hill: University of North Carolina Press, 1987). See also Hugh Wilford, *The New York Intellectuals: From Vanguard to Institution* (Manchester: Manchester University Press, 1995).
11. For example, Alfred Kazin, *On Native Grounds* (New York: Harcourt Brace Janovich, 1942).
12. Bloom, *Prodigal Sons* (see note 10), p.4.
13. Ibid., pp.12–14. See Ronald Sanders, *The Lower East Side Jews. An Immigrant Generation* (New York: Dover, 1969); and Irving Howe, *World of Our Fathers* (New York: Harcourt Brace Janovich, 1976).

14. Bloom, *Prodigal Sons* (see note 10), pp.11, 18–20.
15. Cooney, *The Rise of the New York Intellectual* (see note 10), pp.10–13.
16. Wilford, *The New York Intellectuals* (see note 10), pp.1–5.
17. Juliet Steyn, *The Jew. Assumptions of Identity* (London: Cassell, 1999); Introduction, in *Passionate Renewal. Jewish Poetry in Britain Since 1945. An Anthology*, ed. by Peter Lawson (Nottingham: Five Leaves Publications, 2001), pp.1–20. See also Nils Roemer, 'Towards a Comparative Jewish Literary History; National Literary Canons in Nineteenth Century Germany and England', in *The Image of the Jew in European Liberal Culture, 1979–1914*, ed. by Nadia Valman and Bryan Cheyette, *Jewish History and Culture*, 6.1 (2003), 27–45, for a rare and an innovative attempt to construct such a cultural history. It is telling that unlike equivalent surveys of American Jewish history, there is *no* element of cultural history in Todd M. Endelman, *The Jews of Britain 1656 to 2000* (Berkeley: University of California Press, 2002) for the post-1945 era. For a pioneering effort that ranges beyond the confines of its title see Harold Pollins, 'Sociological Aspects of Anglo-Jewish Literature', *Jewish Journal of Sociology*, 2.1 (1960), 25–41.
18. Efraim Sicher, *Beyond Marginality. Anglo-Jewish Literature After the Holocaust* (Albany: State University of New York Press, 1985), pp.ix and 23. I am grateful to Professor Bryan Cheyette for confirming, and shedding light on the reasons for, the absence of Anglo-Jewish cultural history.
19. Ibid., p.25.
20. Ibid., p.57.
21. Emanuel Litvinoff, *Journey through a Small Planet* (London: Michael Joseph, 1972), p.26.
22. Bernard Kops, *The World is a Wedding* (London: MacGibbon and Kee, 1963), p.7.
23. Litvinoff, *Journey through a Small Planet* (see note 21), p.29.
24. John Gross, *A Double Thread. A Childhood in Mile End and Beyond* (London: Chatto and Windus, 2001), p.16.
25. Steven Berkoff, *Free Association. An Autobiography* (London: Faber and Faber, 1996), pp.5–6.
26. Ibid., pp.6–7.
27. Arnold Wesker, *As Much As I Dare. An Autobiography (1932–1959)* (London: Century, 1994), pp.1, 15–17. See also, ibid., pp.20–22 and 128–9.
28. Ibid., pp.15–17.
29. Ibid., pp.128–9.
30. Kops, *The World is a Wedding* (see note 22), p.11.
31. Litvinoff, *Journey through a Small Planet* (see note 21), p.133.
32. Kops, *The World is a Wedding* (see note 22), pp.23–4.
33. Wesker, *As Much as I Dare* (see note 27), p.1.
34. Barnett Litvinoff, *A Very British Subject. Telling Tales* (London: Vallentine Mitchell, 1996), p.18.
35. Kops, *The World is a Wedding* (see note 22), p.11.
36. Wesker, *As Much as I Dare* (see note 27), p.128.
37. Gross, *A Double Thread* (see note 24), pp.116–18.
38. Berkoff, *Free Association* (see note 25), pp.12–15.
39. Ibid., p.42.
40. Litvinoff, *Journey through a Small Planet* (see note 21), p.30.
41. Wesker, *As Much as I Dare* (see note 27), p.137.
42. Gross, *A Double Thread* (see note 24), p.20
43. Ibid., pp.37–9.
44. Berkoff, *Free Association* (see note 25), pp.10–11.
45. Wesker, *As Much as I Dare* (see note 27), pp.65–6; Berkoff, *Free Association* (see note 25), p.6.
46. Berkoff, *Free Association* (see note 25), p.10.
47. Ibid., p.31.
48. See the evocative lists in Gross, *A Double Thread* (see note 24), pp.127–8.
49. Kops, *The World is a Wedding* (see note 22), pp.9, 35–6; Gross, *A Double Thread* (see note 24), pp.48, 137.
50. Litvinoff, *Journey through a Small Planet* (see note 21), pp.29–30.
51. Gross, *A Double Thread* (see note 24), pp.30–36.
52. Berkoff, *Free Association* (see note 25), pp.357–8.
53. Litvinoff, *Journey through a Small Planet* (see note 21), pp.93–5.
54. Kops, *The World is a Wedding* (see note 22), pp.30–32.
55. Gross, *A Double Thread* (see note 24), p.68.
56. Ibid., p.25.

57. Wesker, *As Much as I Dare* (see note 27), pp.149, 154, 158. See also, pp.162–5.
58. Sicher, *Beyond Marginality* (see note 18), pp.153–62, 163.
59. Gross, *A Double Thread* (see note 24), p.99.
60. Berkoff, *Free Association* (see note 25), p.80.
61. Kops, *The World is a Wedding* (see note 22), p.135.
62. Wesker, *As Much as I Dare* (see note 27), pp.455–7; Berkoff, *Free Association* (see note 25), pp.110–14.
63. Wilford, *The New York Intellectuals* (see note 10), pp.5–6. London had its fair share of publishing houses and other media, too, but until another wave of Jewish immigrants set up in business (such as Andre Deutsch, George Weidenfeld, Paul Hamlyn, Tom Rosenthal), there was indeed an old and very English establishment.
64. For example, Caryl Phillips, ed., *Extravagant Strangers. A Literature of Belonging* (London: Faber and Faber, 1997); Zadie Smith, *White Teeth* (London: Hamish Hamilton, 2001); Monica Ali, *Brick Lane* (London: Doubleday, 2003).

Memory at the Margins, Matter Out of Place: Hidden Narratives of Jewish Settlement and Movement in Britain

TONY KUSHNER

Introduction

It was tucked away 'back of the walls', the seedy, seamy side of a seafaring centre. Canal Walk reeked of danger – and, indeed, of unidentifiable smells – a darkened, bumpy, narrow street packed with tiny tumbledown stores: butchers, drapers, twine-sellers, a homemade-sweets shop, a stewed-eel-and-pie shop, a primitive amusement arcade. Many of the places were run by immigrants, especially European Jews. It was a subculture straight out of a Dickens novel, the kind of street that mothers forbade their children to visit. If you did go there, the word about town was that you had better make sure that the fingers on your wallet were your own.[1]

This melodramatic urban scene could have been drawn from a 1930s crime novel with a Sexton Blake-style hero 'slumming it' in the mean alleyways of the East End, uncovering the ethnic intrigue behind the brutal murder of a local girl of 'low repute'. In fact, it is taken from Mark Lewisohn's *Funny Peculiar: The True Story of Benny Hill* (2002) and describes an area in Southampton popularly known as the Ditches.

Whilst it is possible to criticise Lewisohn for the overly lurid image he conjures up which, as will be shown, borrows heavily from earlier descriptions of Canal Walk, much of the factual detail is accurate. Indeed, Lewisohn, in this one paragraph, has revealed, or, more tellingly, exposed a communal experience forgotten within the dominant narratives of both local and Jewish history. There is a much wider significance of such amnesia, confirming the analysis of Doreen Massey that 'The identity of places is very much bound up with the *histories* which are told of them, *how* those histories are told, and which history turns out to be dominant'.[2] First, however, it is necessary to explain how the Jewish presence in streets such as the Ditches emerged in the inter-war period before exploring the meanings and symbolism that were attached to them.

There have been particular places and times where the Jewish presence has been more conspicuous in their settlement and resettlement in England from the medieval period onwards. Such visibility was generally because of Jewish concentration in certain locations, often linked to their place in the local economy.

Until the early twentieth century, however, the Jews of Southampton were neither numerous enough nor sufficiently focused in particular occupations and residential areas to be a specific visual feature of the town's topography. Post-expulsion, for example, the memory of medieval Anglo-Jewry in Southampton was limited to a particular house, rather than a major street as was the case in Winchester.[3] Similarly, after the readmission of the Jews, Southampton differed from its neighbour Portsmouth and the associations frequently made in the eighteenth and nineteenth centuries between the Point and the Hard and the Jewish presence. In 1773, when Southampton was enjoying a renaissance as a fashionable spa town, the *Hampshire Chronicle* reported on a ball in a new hotel which featured a 'Jew pedlar, Tancreds, Spaniards, sailors, nosegay-girls and ballad-singers'.[4] In contrast, however, to this imagined cosmopolitanism, the reality was that there were very few Jews living or passing through eighteenth century Southampton. Their paucity of numbers in the town was marked in comparison to its neighbour Portsmouth, where the Jewish community was experienced and encountered on an everyday level. Even in the nineteenth century in Southampton, whilst East European Jewish transmigrants increased rapidly in numbers in the 1890s and 1900s, they were largely isolated in the port area and cut off from the rest of the town's residential and commercial districts. Their prominence was further obscured in this port town by being part of a wider population of transmigrants and other temporary residents such as foreign sailors and itinerant workers. In 1888, Amrit Lal Roy, an Indian 'student turned tourist', linked Southampton with London and Liverpool in its cosmopolitan atmosphere and outlook, but this was in reference to the docks rather than the town as a whole.[5] Before 1900, there was nothing approximating to a visible East European Jewish sub-community in Southampton as had been the case in Portsmouth from the mid-nineteenth century onwards. In Southampton, the Jewish-owned commercial enterprises were largely in the respectable shopping streets of the town and were dispersed. That spatial invisibility was, however, to change just before, during and after the First World War when a new Jewish trading community emerged, and one that was very different to its predecessors.

In the period from the 1900s until the later 1930s, the Jewish population of Southampton more than tripled. According to the *Jewish Year Book*, in 1905 there were 20 Jewish families in the town and in 1934 this had grown to 65 – a growth from around 100 individuals to over 300.[6] Most of this increase was due to inward migration from other parts of Britain, most notably the East End of London. It reflected, as a pull factor, the growth of Southampton whose population increased from just over 100,000 to over 175,000 from 1901 to 1931.[7] It also represented the push factor – the economic misery and intense competition within primary immigrant settlement areas such as the East End. Whilst the fledgling Jewish communities of Basingstoke and Aldershot struggled to survive in the inter-war period, elsewhere in Hampshire those in Portsmouth and Bournemouth followed Southampton in receiving further influxes of East European origin Jews, many of whom had initially settled in London. It was Southampton Jewry, however, because of the late settlement of these new arrivals, that was particularly and perhaps uniquely transformed in the inter-war years.

New Arrivals

David Cesarani has suggested that:

> The belief in upward social mobility is cherished in Anglo-Jewry today, but it is substantially a myth. The inter-war years saw some dramatic cross-class mobility registered unambiguously by occupational and geographical change. But for a more significant section of the Jewish population, the experience was one of stasis or sideways movement. Occupations and addresses changed, but this only gave an illusion of genuine social mobility.[8]

Cesarani points to migration from the East End to other London districts, and to similar processes in other major cities of settlement such as Manchester, Leeds and Liverpool, emphasising that the move to 'adjacent inner-suburbs such as Hackney, Chapletown and Hightown ... did not [necessarily] signify upward social mobility'. He concludes that the 'Jewish route to the [middle-class] suburbs was long, hard and devious'.[9] This contribution will confirm Cesarani's analysis but add to it another layer of evidence relating to the economic desperation and marginality of first and second generation East European Jews in Britain. These Jews were not simply in motion *within* the major cities of primary settlement – their mobility extended into other urban locations, including towns such as Southampton which are not, in popular memory, normally associated with having possessed an East European Jewish milieu. Indeed, it must be emphasised that the struggle to make ends meet led to a geographical restlessness that has yet to be fully understood in the existing historiography of twentieth century British Jewry.

On the surface, Southampton, as a fast-developing port, as well as an industrial and commercial centre, would appear as an obvious magnet to those trying to move away from economically-depressed areas of Britain. In this respect, of particular relevance to the Jewish experience was the East End of London where, contrary to widespread contemporary assumptions, Jewish poverty was at a higher level than the local population as a whole. *The New Survey of London Life and Labour* estimated that, at the end of the 1920s, 13.7 per cent of Jewish East Enders were in poverty, compared to 12.1 per cent for the area as a whole.[10] And, as Harold Pollins points out, 'this was before the depression was at its deepest'.[11] The classic Jewish immigrant trades such as tailoring, shoe-making and furniture-making were particularly vulnerable to seasonal and long-term decline through increasing global competition and thus many Jews, especially the younger generation, either tried their luck in these trades in new locations or in different occupations, especially those involving self-employment.

But Southampton's image as a prosperous gateway to a more affluent south was deceptive. Indeed, its mixed economic and social reality surprised J.B. Priestley as he embarked from the port on his classic *English Journey* (1934).[12] Whilst escaping the worst ravages of inter-war depression, Southampton was still a poor town with major problems of overcrowding and seasonal labour with its main sources of wealth coming from outside.[13] Many of the Jewish newcomers to Southampton eked out a living in the lock-up shops of Canal Walk. Jim Bellows, who grew up a few streets away, remembers them clearly:

Along the top right-hand side of 'The Ditches' was a line of small shops built against the old town wall. These shops were just three or four feet deep and displayed their wares on shutters which, when lowered, turned into counters. They sold a variety of clothes, towels, curtains and such. These shops were kept by Jewish people and were the only shops open on a Sunday.[14]

These lock-ups were, in reality, closer to market stalls than shops and required minimal capital and were cheap to rent. Business concerns came and went and most disappeared without leaving much trace. One of these was a dress shop run by two women, Rachel Solomons and Sophie Noah, both of families of East European origin. Their story was perhaps typical of those who settled in Southampton in the inter-war period, consisting of frequent movement and the requirement of entrepreneurial risk-taking to make a living. It also reflected the economic activity of Jewish women, in spite of huge family commitments. Sophie was born in the East End in 1892 and married a Russian-born widower, Abraham Noah. Abraham had three children from his first marriage and a son and daughter with Sophie. With these five children Abraham and Sophie moved to Southampton in 1925. Abraham had not gone through the laborious and relatively expensive task of gaining naturalisation and thus Sophie, on marriage, lost her British citizenship. On 16 June 1925, therefore, she registered with Southampton Borough Police as an alien – under the Aliens Order, 1920, all permanent changes of residence had to be officially recorded.[15] Sophie's daughter, who was a small child when her parents moved to Southampton, recalls that the dress shop was 'not particularly successful' and it soon closed down.[16] Sophie's certificate of alien registration indicates that they left Southampton on the *SS Andes* in 1927 before returning to the port 14 months later. It must be assumed that the family had tried their luck abroad and had returned to England, this time moving to Stoke Newington in the north-east of London. Her business partner, Rachel, born in 1900, was married in Southampton in 1928 and she and her husband moved to Manchester shortly after.[17] In these cases scraping a living, even in the cheap and basic premises of Canal Walk, had proved impossible and both women, with their husbands, were forced eventually to try their luck elsewhere in Britain, especially in other areas of Jewish settlement.

In 1983 the Southampton Hebrew Congregation celebrated the 150th anniversary of its formal establishment with a visit of the Chief Rabbi, Immanuel Jakobovits. Sidney Weintroub, its President, marked the occasion by producing a short hand-written history of Southampton's Jewry. Contained within it were two sentences relating to the Jewish trading community of the inter-war years: 'Before World War II most of the members of the Congregation were private shopkeepers, many in Canal Walk and the lower part of the town. The blitz of 1940 destroyed most of their shops and they, like others, left the town.'[18] Weintroub, who came to Southampton in the early 1930s, was right to highlight the finality brought by German bombing to the commercial premises of Canal Walk. Yet the blitz was only the final part of a process of decline – failed businesses and slum demolition in the later 1930s had already altered the dynamics of Canal Walk and diminished the size of the local Jewish community. By the Second World War, the population of the Southampton Hebrew Congregation had fallen to 250 and would decline thereafter.[19]

It is significant in itself that contemporaries referring to Weintroub's narrative of Southampton Jewry in 1983 failed to mention his comments on the Canal Walk-linked community. Lacking permanence of presence, or the reassuring motif of Jewish economic success, they were difficult to place in official memory and thus subject to the active process that is amnesia. To Weintroub, however, as a committed second generation Jew born in Manchester of East European origin, they would have been the essence of Southampton Jewry in the inter-war period. As we will see, to many local non-Jews, too, memory of the Canal Walk community was still vivid as late as the last decades of the twentieth century.

In his 1980s history, Weintroub commented that in contemporary Southampton only one shop now bore the name of that inter-war Jewish trading community – Millet's.[20] In contrast to the lock-up shops of Canal Walk, in the inter-war years Millet's, a drapery business, was large and in a prominent and prestigious position in Above Bar. The premises were destroyed in the blitz in 1941 and the business did not return to Southampton until 1958.[21] The Millet family were of Galician origin and came to Southampton in the 1890s having first settled in London. The company that still bears the family name is now a major retailer and 'one of the high street's best-known names, offering quality [outdoor] products ... in over 280 stores nationwide'.[22] Yet rather than fundamentally query the model of Jewish economic marginality as exemplified by the Canal Walk business of Rachel Solomons and Sophie Noah, the experiences of the Millets shows that for every success there were, at least initially, many more failures. By the turn of the twentieth century there were four inter-related Millet families within Southampton, and most of the businesses they set up, almost all in the poorest parts of town, including Canal Walk, lasted only a few years. Itinerant hawk peddlers in the first instance, the Millet siblings and their partners set up enterprises as drapers, haberdashers and second-hand clothes dealers. These businesses depended on the poorest of customers and were thus particularly prone to bankruptcy. Indeed, it seems that the only Millets that were successful in Southampton most likely came to the town with some capital – as early as the 1901 census the family was listed as employing a servant.[23] They thus would have represented the small number of East European Jews who were not largely penniless. These were the so-called *alrightniks*, the most famous of whom was Michael Marks of Marks and Spencer fame.[24]

The Millet families consisted of 11 siblings. Their patterns of movement can be traced through the census which reveals the transient nature of the Jewish experience before the First World War. The children of these siblings were born in London, Dublin, Bristol, Southampton and Le Havre.[25] Three Millet brothers initially came to England and the other siblings followed in classic chain migration fashion. It was within Southampton that the pattern of economic marginality and business failure – their earlier ventures in London, Dublin and Bristol had failed – was partially overcome. The end of the Boer War provided the opportunity of selling government surplus uniform and kit and, in the words of a descendant, 'Max [one of the brothers], the commercial genius of the family, had the vision to see that he could sell it on on civvy street at a tremendous profit'.[26] East European Jewish immigrants, with their strong connection to the clothing and boot trade, were ideally and fortunately situated for this business opportunity. In Portsmouth as well, and in other provincial communities, army surplus shops provided the possibility of economic mobility for the new Jewish arrivals and their descendants, a form of entrepreneurship that has not yet received attention in the existing historiography.[27] Even then, the limited opportunities in Southampton, as well as sibling rivalry, meant that only one branch of the Millet family would remain in Southampton. Peter Millet's haberdasher's shop in Canal Walk, for instance, first appeared in the local trade directory in 1901. It then reduced in size and had disappeared by the end of 1909, thus conforming to the general pattern of business failure and marginality in this singular street.[28] Indeed, almost all the Millet siblings, continuing their pattern of restlessness, left Southampton before 1914 and settled across England in towns including Bristol, Nottingham, Leicester, Birmingham and Croydon as well as Portsmouth and Gosport in Hampshire.[29]

Constructing the Ditches

Whether economically successful or otherwise, Southampton Jewry, including its Hebrew Congregation, was transformed both in numbers and in nature by this East European influx. The religiosity of the community was changed, marked by a greater orthodoxy reflecting the recent roots of the newcomers. For example, in 1919 it was decided to build a *mikveh*, which was, in the words of the Polish-born religious leader of the community, Reverend Gordon, 'a most essential thing to our community'.[30] In the secular sphere, size and commitment enabled a flourishing of cultural Jewishness including literary events and sport – in 1921 the Southampton Jewish Cricket Club was formed.[31] Such activities extended into the political realm with a stronger Jewish diasporic identity emerging and manifest through support of Jews in distress abroad.[32] The importance of Zionism was reflected in 1919 when it was resolved to merge the local Zionist Society with the synagogue.[33]

It would be misleading to present this vibrant Jewish community as being without conflict. Some of the older, more anglicised members clearly were uneasy about the direction the expanded community was taking and, as elsewhere in Britain, tension existed between first and second generation Jews, the latter being drawn to the attractions of the secular world. In 1925, when discussions about building a *mikvah* were still ongoing, one committee member of the Southampton Hebrew Congregation wondered whether social facilities for the youth of the community might not be more useful, 'as our younger children only loiter about the town, and have nowhere that they can come and meet and get more sociable and know what we are'.[34] Nevertheless, such friction reflected the dynamism of the community during the 1920s. Whilst the transformation of Southampton Jewry through the arrival of East European Jews followed the general pattern of British Jewry as a whole, it was a metamorphosis which notably occurred later than the major points of migrant settlement such as London, Manchester, Leeds and Glasgow, or even Southampton's south coast rival, Portsmouth, which had experienced an influx of East End Jewish tailors as the pre-war naval race escalated.[35] And relatively small though it was compared to the larger Jewish communities in Britain, the new migrant Jewish community in Southampton became particularly prominent through its visibility in a singular street in the town.

Portsmouth Jewry in the Napoleonic era and beyond developed a notoriety linked to crime and violence in this roughest of seaports. In literature and popular discourse they were connected to particular places – the Hard and the Point – which now gentrified were then infamous for prostitution and disorder.[36] In a twentieth century context, the Ditches brought forth similar associations within Southampton. Just as the East End was both a geographical area and a symbol of London's dangerous 'other', so the Ditches was to Southampton as much an imagined place as a physical reality. What makes it intriguing as a site of contested collective memory is that it had a direct connection to all major developments in Southampton's history from the medieval period onwards. Rather than simply a small street in the heart of a major town, the Ditches had many layers of meanings attached to it. The naming and renaming of this street involved inclusion and exclusion, remembering and forgetting. The Ditches/Canal Walk was a place of evocation, bringing to mind Walter Benjamin's musings on Paris in his *Arcades Project*:

> Being past, being no more, is passionately at work in things. To this the historian trusts for his subject matter. He depends on this force, and knows things as they are at the moment of their ceasing to be. Arcades are such monuments of being-no-more ... And nothing lasts except the name: *passages* ... In the inmost recesses of these names the upheaval is working, and therefore we hold a world in the names of old streets, and to read the name of a street is like undergoing a transformation.[37]

In the inter-war period, 'Townsman', or E.A. Mitchell, was the leading populariser of Southampton's history. Theatre critic of the local paper, the *Southern Daily Echo*, he used his literary skills to produce intriguing vignettes of the town's past.[38] Canal Walk featured prominently in his publications. The street became a test case through which Mitchell could explore the relationship between Southampton 'then' and 'now'. The excitement as well as the dilemmas of flux in Mitchell's narratives of Southampton through the ages could be explored with reference to Canal Walk/the Ditches. Ultimately Mitchell's search for a usable and rejuvenating past by constructing a sense of continuity and tradition were realised through his topographical imaginings of this particular and peculiar place.

The Ditches were linked to the fortifications of the medieval town and had the dual function of defence and acting as the town's rubbish dump. Rather than dwell on its less savoury function, which by the sixteenth century had become a public nuisance,[39] Mitchell only connected the Ditches to its more illustrious role in helping to protect from invasion what was one of the major medieval ports in England.[40] In the late eighteenth century a canal, attempting to connect Southampton to Winchester, was partially built and ran through the Ditches. Unsuccessful and abandoned as a commercial venture, as early as 1800 it was parodied in the *Gentleman's Magazine*:

> Southampton's wise sons found the River so large,
> Tho' 'twould carry a ship, 'twould not carry a barge
> But soon this defect their sage noddles supply'd,
> For they cut a snug *ditch* to run close by its side.[41]

Business failure though it was, the abandoned canal nevertheless provided a pleasant walk connecting the docks to the south with the semi-rural outskirts of the Georgian spa town to the north. Its role as a pathway to an idyllically imagined pastoral Southampton was highlighted by Mitchell by including a sketch from the first half of the nineteenth century drawn by the prominent local artist, Thomas Gray Hart. Hart portrayed the Ditches literally as a romantic bridge to the countryside of old times complete with ruined medieval towers and walls.[42] Neighbouring Canal Walk was Orchard Lane, which, as was noted in the *Civic Survey* of Southampton in 1931, through its nomenclature, 'preserve[d] the memory of a rural past'.[43]

In the early nineteenth century the canal was filled in and by the 1850s 'respectable' businesses with dwellings above them were built in what became a street, Canal Walk. It was only at the turn of the twentieth century that the lock-up shops developed fully and the nature of Canal Walk was transformed. In the process of development from the late eighteenth century onwards, almost all physical traces of the medieval origins and spa town evolution of this area of Southampton were removed. It was a loss that clearly upset Mitchell. The critic/historian was one of the first to actively campaign for the saving of Southampton's physical historical heritage, a frustrating and lonely pursuit in a town that had little interest and put few resources into preserving and representing its past. Indeed, the landmark Southampton Civic Survey of 1931 commented that the 'state of affairs [with regard to museums] can only be described as "backward" for a city of such importance'.[44]

The social transformation and 'decline' of what became Canal Walk was symptomatic to Mitchell of the deterioration of Southampton as a whole and its lack of interest in its own history. As late as the 1860s, he reflected, 'it was [still] an attractive quarter'. He quoted a man brought up in Canal Walk who could remember 'watching the fashions go by' and his mother picking fruit in the back yard. Mitchell was dissatisfied with its current status and took refuge in its perceived Elysian past: 'It is a curiously challenging panorama that one sees with the mind's eye if one traces back in imagination the history of Canal Walk'. To emphasise the point further, and thereby not needing to make explicit his contemporary distaste, he stressed that 'There is no doubt that at one time Canal Walk was one of the pleasantest parts of Southampton'. He emphasised the point further by including a sketch of Canal Walk which, whilst drawn in 1915, reflected its more salubrious commercial past in the mid-nineteenth century, with the background dominated by two tall and flourishing trees.[45]

Mitchell was constructing a somewhat romanticised past for Canal Walk and Southampton as a whole. A later appreciation of Mitchell referred to his full identification with Southampton although he was born in London and only came to the town in 1913.[46] The same, however, cannot be said of those who made the street economically viable. In spatial terms, both physically and metaphorically, Canal Walk was situated in between worlds. The old dock area of Southampton to the south of Canal Walk was in many ways self-contained, especially as they were privately owned and had no public access. Here there were some shops catering specifically for the docks and the floating maritime population. The writer Laurie

Lee, as a young man coming from the Gloucestershire countryside, was disappointed not to see the sea in the Hampshire port, but instead 'a muddy river which they said was Southampton Water'. In contrast,

> Southampton Town ... came up to all expectations, proving to be salty and shifty in turns, like some ship-jumping sailor who'd turned his back on the sea in a desperate attempt to make good on the land. The streets near the water appeared to be jammed with shops designed more for entertainment than profit, including tattooists, ear-piercers, bump-readers, fortune-tellers, whelk-bars and pudding-boilers.[47]

Further up town was the main shopping area of High Street and East Street, with the tendency in both these thoroughfares since the First World War towards larger concerns. Shops in these major streets catered for a wide range of people from both inside and outside the town. Canal Walk's shops had a different constituency, firstly consisting of those living in the district, secondly adjacent working class districts such as Northam with its strong dock and seafaring connections, including streets that were literally decimated by the sinking of the Titanic in 1912, and finally the floating population of Southampton, the sailors, and an important category in any port, prostitutes.[48] It is here that the Benny Hill connection is made – his father had a shop selling surgical appliances and rubber goods in Canal Walk offering contraceptive devices to sailors and prostitutes.[49]

Canal Walk was undoubtedly cosmopolitan in inter-war Southampton – aside from the Jews, there were Italian shops, Chinese laundries, Lascars and many other foreign sailors. Violence and drunkenness were also not unknown. Its various attractions made it a colourful place to visit, especially on a Saturday night. Yet for many, its importance was more mundane. Maie Hodgson was, in her words, a 'child of the ditches'. To Hodgson, Canal Walk was home, a place she felt safe in and the various shopkeepers were people she grew up with: 'With this mixture of Jewish and Italian neighbours combined in later years with a sort of fair-ground element then added together with family businesses like ours, the Ditches certainly exuded a real cosmopolitan atmosphere.'[50]

The Jewish shops of the Ditches also served an important function as an alternative to the expensive and increasingly standardised shops of High Street and East Street. The oral testimony of Mrs G, an elderly lady brought up a docker's daughter in Chapel, provides an account that whilst not without its racialisation, also highlights the crucial economic role played by the Canal Walk shops:

> [It was] lined with Jew shops with all the latest tip-top clothes. They'd be at the door and well, floggin' the stuff you know. I think you could get a beautiful suit there for about sixpence, if you'd stay long enough to argue with 'em ... We all used to buy our clothes there. You'd go one week and perhaps buy the one part of yer rigout. You'd buy it bit by bit. As much as you could afford ... It was threepence down on it ... We all used to buy our clothes like that.[51]

Similarly, Jim Bellows recalled how for 'eleven pence and three farthings I could buy a pullover there and go to Sunday School looking tidy'.[52]

The Jewish shops of Canal Walk, therefore, were economically marginal businesses catering for economically marginal customers. The Southampton Council rate books show that, as a whole, the shops in Canal Walk were paying a fraction of the rateable value of those in Below Bar and East Street. Even then, the Jewish lock-up shops were paying half the rates of other shops in Canal Walk.[53] Survival was borderline, and, as we have seen in the case of Rachel Solomons and Sophie Noah, many went to the wall. Indeed, whilst the neighbourliness of Canal Walk should not be dismissed, nor should its poverty and violence be forgotten. John Arlott, later the voice of cricket in England, recalls the reality of policing the street in the 1930s: 'Colourful it was, but not always salubrious.'[54] In 1931 Southampton Civic Society sponsored a survey of the town. A pioneer study of urban development and planning, it highlighted two inner city slum areas. One was within the Town Ward with Canal Walk at the heart of it. Congested and unhealthy, most of the buildings were condemned as 'not really fit for human habitation at all' and partly cleared in the later 1930s.[55]

Although J.B. Priestley does not specifically name Canal Walk in *English Journey*, one of the most important pieces of social commentary in inter-war Britain, he clearly had visited its neighbourhood. First, however, Priestley remarked that:

> We hear a good deal about Southampton's comparative prosperity; and [High Street] is the symbol of it ... The pavement on each side was crowded with neat smiling people ... and the mile of shops seemed to be doing a brisk trade. Here at last was a town that had not fallen under the evil spell of our times.[56]

But Priestley's England was full of complexities and contradictions,[57] and two pages later in *English Journey* he turned off High Street to find himself 'in some very poor quarters'.[58] These were the Town Ward slums and Priestley was even more disgusted by the shops that serviced them. Priestley is hard to categorise – a man of the people capable of intense snobbery, a radical with international sympathies but also an English nationalist.[59] There is also a strong racialisation to *English Journey* and within it Priestley's ambiguities are exposed further. There was a deep sympathy towards persecuted German Jewry and a sense of nostalgia for the German Jews of his hometown Bradford. Alongside these, however, was at best a patronising attitude and often irritation towards East European Jews and other less 'desirable' immigrants. His class-racial snobbery and prejudices are blatant when describing what with little doubt was Canal Walk:

> The small shop flourishes in this quarter ... Even after you have given yourself the strongest dose of individualistic sentiment, it is hard to look at these small shops with anything but disgust or to find good reasons why they should not be promptly abolished. They are slovenly, dirty and inefficient.[60]

What slum clearance had not finished was completed by the blitz in 1940. By the end of the war there was little physical trace left of Canal Walk. Nevertheless, it has been noted that the street featured prominently in Sotonian autobiographical practice, whether written or oral. For those from working class backgrounds, Canal Walk was remembered as a place where everyday goods could be purchased (or had on credit) from its cosmopolitan shopkeepers far cheaper than the rest of

Southampton. For others, perhaps of a more prosperous background, it offered goods not available elsewhere and a place, in daytime at least, that was excitingly different with a frisson of danger adding further spice to the experience of a visit. For Eric Gadd, a 'tram-ride with Mum from the suburbs' to shop in the Ditches was 'a treat' enabling a sampling of its 'teeming cosmopolitan buzz'.[61] Recalling, over half a century later, such trips during and after the First World War, Gadd remembered vividly the entrance to Canal Walk:

> with its tiny shops and booths, its picturesque traders, its wide variety of merchandise and its cosmopolitan customers, many strolling in from the ships in nearby dockland. Here one saw sallow skins, brown skins, black skins, yellow skins; flashing eyes and gleaming teeth; turbans and fezzes; earrings and gaudy sashes. Often the air was filled with a babble of strange tongues.[62]

In contrast to those like Maie Hodgson who grew up in the Ditches and took its diversity for granted, for middle class outsiders the street provided an enticing otherness, representing the fear and fascination resulting from an orientalist discourse. Brian Lawrence was older than Eric Gadd when he visited the Ditches before the First World War. Like Gadd, the memories remained with him powerfully many decades later, although his testimony closes by revealing a greater self-reflexivity of his earlier responses to its 'strangeness':

> A picturesque touch was often added by the lascars from the troopships, who did much of their shopping here; they seemed to like these haunts, perhaps reminiscent of bazaars back home. Their often odd mixture of oriental and accidental costume, and the occasional overheard snatches of unintelligible speech, could add an exotic note which almost suggested, to the young imagination, a visit to 'foreign parts'.[63]

Both Gadd and Lawrence regretted the passing of this world within a world and wrote, during the 1970s, nostalgically of Canal Walk. To Gadd, 'Sadly, though the name may still be read upon a side wall, most of this thoroughfare and all of its vibrant, earthy character have long disappeared. Here were constant chatter, endless movement. Here the wise shopper made sure that the fingers on his wallet were his own'.[64] Lawrence went further and perceptively noted that the street and all it stood for was now subject to increasing amnesia: 'Those of us who saw and remember may regret the passing of these symbols of an earlier way of life; it is hard to realise that to the younger generation who have succeeded us they are not even a memory.'[65] It was left to an exceptionally talented local historian, Elsie Sandell, to ensure that the memory of Canal Walk/the Ditches was not totally forgotten at a collective level in Southampton.

After 1945, Elsie Sandell replaced 'Townsman' or E.A. Mitchell as the popular historian of Southampton. In her *Southampton Cavalcade* (1953) she commented that 'Many thousands of Southampton folk remember the Ditches, or Canal Walk, of pre-war days. It had closely packed little shops leaning forward on the narrow stone flagged footwalk'.[66] Sandell shared Mitchell's desire and enthusiasm to preserve the physical remnants of Southampton's past. Both were internationalist in outlook, although it manifested itself religiously in the case of Mitchell, and politically with Sandell and her work for, amongst others, the United Nations. Sandell, however, was a far more progressive interpreter of the past and had the foresight and confidence to confront contemporary history, as well as the experiences of marginalised groups such as minorities and women. As was said of her at her funeral, 'She knew that history is never past and that life to be lived to the full must be lived in the past and the future as well as the present'.[67] Sandell, like Mitchell, connected Canal Walk to Southampton's spa days and related how in the late eighteenth century it was 'fraught with many elegant and picturesque views'.[68] Yet she also relished its re-flourishing in the inter-war period when 'There was something almost continental in the look of it all and many a foreign name was written over the doors'. In stark contrast to Priestley, she listed positively the various outlets – there were 'confectioners, public houses, fruiterers, music dealers, fried fish shops, cats' meat purveyors, butchers, mouse-trap makers and many another trader' – and concluded that 'Canal Walk was, in fact, an epitome of the shopping life of a busy port'.[69] She, like Gadd and Lawrence, felt its loss in post-war Southampton which to her made 'one realise yet again the wholesale devastation of so much of our town'.[70]

Sandell, in her prolific writings on historic Southampton, could best be described as a cautious cosmopolitan. Since her death 30 years ago she has been largely forgotten and neglected, paralleled by a similar amnesia at a collective level of Southampton's past diversity. This has included the Jews of Southampton, especially at their most numerous around Canal Walk in the inter-war period. For example, although the Southampton contribution to the national 'Port Cities' web-based archive is a rich source of many aspects of its past, it is relatively weak in illustrating past ethnic diversity. There is, unfortunately, no material directly relating to its Jewish community and only five entries under the heading 'immigration' of any type.[71] Rather than a case of special pleading, inclusion of the Jewish presence in Canal Walk would not just show the diversity of Southampton but also reveal the process of identity formation in a modern port town. A sense of place, space, and concepts of 'home' are all crucial in memory work whether individual or collective. As Doreen Massey highlights:

> The description, definition and identification of a place is ... always inevitably an intervention not only into geography but also, at least implicitly, into the re(telling) of the historical constitution of the present. It is another move in the continuing struggle over the delineation and characterisation of space-time.[72]

In this particular case study of Southampton, the importance of shops and businesses, which often connect the global, national and local, has been particularly emphasised.[73] In this respect, it will be useful to return to Benny Hill who, through his father's business, grew up amongst the Yiddish-speaking East European Jewish shopkeepers of Canal Walk and came to love their culture, whether articulated through food, language or humour. In early career he changed from Alfred to Benny, wanting 'a stage name with a kosher ring to it'.[74] The particular reference point was the American comedian, Jack Benny, and his principal biographer suggests that Benny Hill believed that it 'would do him no harm to be thought of as Jewish'.[75] Many argue that Benny Hill produced offensive and outdated humour which relied on essentialised and stereotypical characters. It is for this reason that one of the most successful television comedians of the twentieth century at a global level has been deliberately marginalised since his death in the 1980s and has become 'the forgotten man'.[76] There is, as yet, no memorial to him in Britain, not even in Southampton, the place in which he grew up and spent much of his life: the 'city fathers seem embarrassed by the association'.[77] I would like to suggest a different reading of Benny Hill, one informed by the cosmopolitanism of Canal Walk and the cultural hybridity and fluidity that it reflected. His brother relates how in an early theatre performance Benny Hill provided a spoof of 'two popular tenors of the time. One was so Jewish you could not believe it; the other so Irish he was practically green all over. Benny combined the Yiddisher schmaltz and the Irish blarney to hilarious effect'.[78] Playing with 'ethnic' categories continued throughout his career – here is Benny Hill as his Chinese character, Chow-Mein, feigning exasperation at fellow comic, Des O'Connor: 'Oy vey, we got a right meshuggenah here.'[79] There is a serious final point to be made. The dismissal of Benny Hill, the most famous, or infamous resident of Canal Walk, is at one with the amnesia concerning the street's migrant past, including its vibrant Jewish community. Anthropologist Mary Douglas has suggested that 'if uncleanness is matter out of place, we must approach it through order. Uncleanness or dirt is that which must not be included if a pattern is to be maintained'.[80] Benny Hill and the diversity typified by Canal Walk have become, in the world of memory and the desire for homogeneous purity, such 'matter out of place'.

NOTES

1. Mark Lewisohn, *Funny Peculiar: The True Story of Benny Hill* (London: Sidgwick & Jackson, 2002), p.7.
2. Doreen Massey, 'Places and their Past', *History Workshop Journal*, 39 (Spring 1995), 186.
3. John Davies, *A History of Southampton* (Southampton: Gilbert, 1883), p.456.
4. *Hampshire Chronicle*, 20 September 1773.
5. A.L. Roy, *Reminiscences England and America* (1888), quoted by Rozina Visram, *Asians in Britain: 400 Years of History* (London: Pluto Press, 2002), pp.113, 116.
6. Figures from *Jewish Year Book 5668–9* (London: Greenberg, 1907), p.196; and *Jewish Chronicle*, 1 June 1934.
7. Percy Ford, *Work and Wealth in a Modern Port: An Economic Survey of Southampton* (London: George Allen & Unwin, 1934), p.25.
8. David Cesarani, 'A Funny Thing Happened on the Way to the Suburbs: Social Change in Anglo-Jewry Between the Wars, 1914–1945', *Jewish Culture and History*, 1.1 (1998), 5.
9. Ibid., pp.9, 22.
10. H. Llewellyn Smith, ed., *New Survey of London Life and Labour*, 6 (London: P.S. King, 1934), p.287.
11. Harold Pollins, *Economic History of the Jews in England* (East Brunswick, NJ: Associated University Presses, 1982), p.185.
12. J.B. Priestley, *English Journey* (London: Heinemann, 1934), chapter 1 'To Southampton'.
13. Ford, *Work and Wealth in a Modern Port* (see note 7), p.23.
14. Jim Bellows, *My Southampton in the Twenties and Thirties* (Bradford on Avon, Wilts: ELSP, 2001), pp.66–7.
15. Copy of Sophie Noah's Certificate of Registration, Aliens Order, 1920, in the possession of the author.
16. Letter of Frances Jacobs (nee Noah), to the author, 13 May 2002.
17. Family information provided by Frances Jacobs, 13 May 2002.
18. Sidney Weintroub, unpublished manuscript history of the Southampton Hebrew Congregation (SHC), SHC archives.
19. See *Jewish Year Book 1945–6* (London: Jewish Chronicle, 1945), p.193.
20. Weintroub, unpublished history, SHC archives.
21. *Southern Evening Echo*, 21 November 1958.

22. Taken from its website, http://www.leeds-uk.com/shopping/millets.htm, accessed 15 December 2006.
23. 1901 census; *Kelly's Trade Directories for Southampton*, 1898 to 1939.
24. For the *alrightniks*, see Bill Williams, '"East and West" in Manchester Jewry, 1850–1914', in *The Making of Modern Anglo-Jewry*, ed. by David Cesarani (Oxford: Blackwell, 1990), pp.24–6.
25. 1901 census entries for Southampton: 38, 45 and 102 Northam Road and 26 Derby Road.
26. Email communication to the author from Richard Cooper, 5 December 2006.
27. There is no mention, for example, in Pollins, *Economic History* (see note 11).
28. *Kelly's Directory* for Southampton, 1901–10.
29. Email communication to the author from Richard Cooper, 8 December 2006.
30. See SHC minutes, 12 January 1919 and 22 February 1925. Due to financial restraint and the opposition of the town authorities, the mikveh was never constructed. More generally see Sharman Kadish, *Building Jerusalem: Jewish Architecture in Britain* (London: Vallentine Mitchell, 1996), pp.105–33.
31. *Jewish Chronicle*, 29 July 1921.
32. See, for example, SHC minutes 8 June and 6 July 1919 concerning relief for and protests on behalf of victims of Polish massacres.
33. SHC minutes, 6 April 1919.
34. SHC minutes, 22 February 1925.
35. Aubrey Weinberg, *Portsmouth Jewry* (Portsmouth: Portsmouth City Council, 1985), p.17; and Ian Mikardo, *Back-Bencher* (London: Weidenfeld & Nicolson, 1988) for a family perspective on this inward migration to Portsmouth.
36. Tony Kushner, 'A Tale of Two Port Jewish Communities: Southampton and Portsmouth Compared', in *Port Jews*, ed. by David Cesarani (London: Frank Cass, 2002), pp.93–4; and Geoffrey Green, *The Royal Navy and Anglo-Jewry 1740–1820* (London: Geoffrey Green, 1989), passim.
37. Walter Benjamin, *The Arcades Project*, trans. by Howard Eiland and Kevin Mclaughlin (Cambridge, MA: Harvard University Press, 1999), p.833.
38. See his obituary in *Southern Daily Echo*, 1 November 1939.
39. Davies, *A History of Southampton* (see note 3), pp.107–8.
40. 'Townsman', *Southampton: Occasional Notes* (Southampton: Southern Newspapers, 1938), pp.70–71; and *Southern Daily Echo*, 1 July 1939.
41. *Gentleman's Magazine*, LX (September 1800), p.877.
42. Townsman, *Southampton: Occasional Notes*, p.70.
43. Elisabeth Withycombe, 'Some Southampton Street – and Place – Names', in *Southampton: A Civic Survey*, ed. by Percy Ford (London: Oxford University Press, 1931), p.17.
44. F. Stevens, 'Museums and Libraries', in *Southampton*, ed. by Ford (see note 43), p.83.
45. Townsman, 'Occasional Notes', *Southern Daily Echo*, 1 July 1939.
46. A.G.K. Leonard, 'The Man Who Was "Townsman"', *Southern Evening Echo*, 15 April 1953.
47. Laurie Lee, *As I Walked Out One Midsummer Morning* (London: Andre Deutsch, 1969), p.18.
48. O.H.T. Rishbeth, 'Land Utilization', in *Southampton*, ed. by Ford (see note 43), pp.33–5; and Ford, *Work and Wealth in a Modern Port* (see note 7), pp.48–56.
49. Lewisohn, *Funny Peculiar* (see note 1), pp.7–8.
50. Maie Hodgson, *Child of the Ditches* (Southampton: [no publisher], 1992), p.16.
51. Southampton City Heritage Oral history collection, 'Chapel and Northam', C0008.
52. Bellows, *My Southampton* (see note 14), p.67.
53. Southampton City Archive, SC51/144 (2), Rent Book, April 1922-March 1923.
54. John Arlott, 'Yesterday in Southampton', *Hampshire*, 3.6 (April 1963), p.16.
55. F.W. Cuthbertson, 'Housing', in *Southampton*, ed. by Ford (see note 43), p.65.
56. Priestley, *English Journey* (see note 12), pp.12–13.
57. See John Bexandale, '"I Had Seen a Lot of Englands": J.B. Priestley, Englishness and the People', *History Workshop Journal*, 51 (2001), pp.87–111.
58. Priestley, *English Journey* (see note 12), p.16.
59. Baxendale, '"I Had Seen a Lot of Englands"' (see note 57), passim.
60. Priestley, *English Journey* (see note 12), p.17.
61. Eric Gadd, 'Beside the Park...', *Hampshire*, 26.4 (February 1986), pp.47, 48.
62. Eric Gadd, 'Happiest Days?', *Hampshire*, 22.2 (December 1981), p.55.
63. Brian Lawrence, 'Southampton's Edwardian Barrow Boys', *Hampshire*, 12.1 (November 1971), p.47.
64. Eric Gadd, *Southampton in the Twenties* (Southampton: Paul Cave, 1979), p.18.
65. Lawrence, 'Southampton's Edwardian Barrow Boys' (see note 63), p.47.
66. Elsie M. Sandell, *Southampton Cavalcade* (Southampton: G.F. Wilson, 1953), p.67.
67. Rev. John Williams quoted in *Southern Evening Echo*, 17 July 1974.
68. Elsie Sandell, 'Old East Street and Its People', *Southern Daily Echo*, 11 June 1954.
69. Sandell, *Southampton Cavalcade* (see note 66), p.67.

70. Ibid.
71. The PortCities website is http://www.portcities.org.uk, accessed November 2004.
72. Massey, 'Places and Their Pasts' (see note 2), p.190.
73. See Russell King, 'Migrations, Globalization and Place', in *A Place in the World? Places, Cultures and Globalization*, ed. by Doreen Massey and Pat Jess (Oxford: Oxford University Press, 1995), p.30.
74. Leonard Hill, *Saucy Boy: The Life Story of Benny Hill* (London: Grafton Books, 1990), p.117.
75. Lewisohn, *Funny Peculiar* (see note 1), p.105.
76. Ibid., pp.436–9.
77. Ibid., p.438.
78. Hill, *Saucy Boy* (see note 74), p.156.
79. Lewisohn, *Funny Peculiar* (see note 1), pp.422–3.
80. Mary Douglas, *Purity and Danger: An Analysis of the Concepts of Pollution and Taboo* (London: Routledge, 1996 [orig. 1966]), p.41.

'A Slice of Eastern Europe in Johannesburg': Yiddish Theatre in Doornfontein, 1929–49

VERONICA BELLING

With hindsight it seems inevitable that Yiddish, the language of the majority of Eastern European Jews before 1939, would disappear as a language of the street, except in certain ultra-orthodox communities, as is the current situation.[1] The internal forces of enlightenment, integration and acculturation, combined with the external forces of political emancipation initiated in the late eighteenth and nineteenth centuries, would gradually have eroded its hold on the community, even without the Holocaust which destroyed over half of its speaker base, and the Zionist movement which attempted to obliterate it in order to facilitate the revival of the Hebrew language. Yiddish was transported to the various lands of Eastern European immigration, where its fortunes varied, dependent on an interrelationship of factors, such as country of origin, timing, numbers, as well as the prevailing economic and political situation, both in the country of origin and in the country of destination. A comparative examination of the fate of the Yiddish language in its various diasporic locations is one that has never really been attempted, yet it is one that could serve as a useful tool to highlight differences between Jewish communities.

I was first made aware of differing attitudes to the Yiddish language and the fate of Yiddish culture while attending the Weinreich Yiddish Summer Program, sponsored by the Yivo Institute for Jewish Research and Columbia University, in New York, between 1998 and 2000. In contrast to the consistently negative attitudes to Yiddish which were entrenched in South Africa's main Jewish communities of Cape Town and Johannesburg, Buenos Aires in Argentina, Montreal in Canada, and Melbourne in Australia, have all been strongholds of Yiddish culture. Montreal with its Dora Wasserman Yiddish Theatre[2] and Melbourne with *Kadimah*, the Jewish Cultural Centre and National Library, Australia's premier Yiddishist Organisation,[3] continue to this day. All these communities were constituted primarily by immigrants from Eastern Europe and, except for Australia, the main wave of immigration occurred between 1890 and 1914. Similarly in the latter communities, a strong sense of group identity was promoted by feelings of alienation from the host society by virtue of religion, nationalism and race – Spanish and French Catholicism and English Protestantism, in the case of Buenos Aires and Montreal respectively, and race and Dutch and English Protestantism in the case of South Africa. How then did one account for the contemptuous attitude to Yiddish culture which took root in South Africa at such an early stage.

The character of the Jewish community in South Africa was determined by two significant waves of immigration from Eastern Europe before and after the First World War. The main formative wave occurred between 1890 and 1914, when the small community of approximately 4,000 Jews of English, German, and Dutch origin, swelled to 49,926.[4] The immigrants were fleeing conditions of dire poverty and discrimination, and were only a small fraction of the approximately three million Jews who left Eastern Europe between 1880 and 1914. The majority of the migrants who made their way to South Africa came from a cluster of small towns and villages in Lithuania and White Russia, making South African Jewry unique in its homogeneity. The Zionist historian, Nahum Sokolov, characterised it as 'a colony of Lithuania'.[5] The Jews were known as *Litvaks*, a term referring exclusively to Jewish (never gentile) Lithuanians.[6] The immigrants were traditional, with only rudimentary education in the Hebrew religious texts from *heder* [Hebrew elementary school], artisans and small tradesman by profession. As this immigration pre-dated the establishment of the Yiddish *Folkshuln* [Folk Schools], although they spoke Yiddish they knew nothing of the new Yiddish literature. Ideologically they were influenced by the *Hibbat Zion* [Love of Zion], the movement in Russia and Romania which preceded the emergence of the Political Zionism of Theodor Herzl, which was committed to the establishment of a Jewish homeland in Palestine and to the revival of the Hebrew language. Thus the South African Zionist Federation, established in 1898,[7] only a year after Herzl called the first Zionist Congress at Basle, was the first inter-provincial communal body to represent the immigrants with the local authorities.[8] It was not until 1912 that the South African Jewish Board of Deputies began to take over this function.

On the negative side, this early defined communal structure with its accompanying strong South African Jewish identity, based on common origins and on the Zionist ideology, did not allow for diversity. The *Bund*, the General Jewish Workers' Union in Lithuania, Poland, and Russia, established in Vilna in 1897, promoted Yiddish rather than Hebrew as the national language of the Jewish masses.[9] However the *Bund* had far less influence than the Zionist movement on those Lithuanian Jews who found their way to South Africa at the turn of the century. This was because the secular nature of *Bundist* ideology was anathema to Jews in the small Lithuanian town and villages, where the *Hibbat Zion* movement was strong, and the Jews were still deeply rooted in religious tradition.[10] Very few Jews came to South Africa from Poland, the stronghold of the *Bund* until the outbreak of the Second World War. In addition the relatively rapid upward mobility of the immigrants in South Africa's pre-industrial and racially divided society, where unskilled and semi-skilled work was done by Blacks, mitigated against the formation of a Jewish proletariat.[11] Moreover unlike the situation in the United States and Britain, Zionism in South Africa never had to contend with the religious reform movement and its concomitant ideology of denationalised Judaism.[12]

In contrast to South Africa, the almost three times larger Jewish migration of 112,614 to Argentina at this time was more diverse in origin, emanating from Russia, Romania, Austrian Galicia and Poland as well as from Lithuania and White Russia.[13] Like the immigrants to South Africa they were petty traders and artisans. However, in Argentina they were more readily absorbed into light industry. They were among the founders of the Unions and of the Argentine Socialist Party, while also founding their own Socialist organisations.[14] From the outset Yiddish, the language of the Jewish proletariat, was a central element in the construction of identity of the Argentinean Jewish community. By 1916 two Yiddish theatre companies were performing twice weekly in Buenos Aires, and by 1929 three theatres were presenting Yiddish plays daily.[15]

The early Jewish community of Montreal, consisting of 45,846 souls in 1921,[16] like South Africa, was dominated by *Litvaks*. Yet between 1911 and 1920 a unique Yiddish–Hebrew synthesis was achieved. At a time when the *Bund* was committed exclusively to Yiddish and the *Poale Zion* movement in Palestine exclusively to Hebrew, the *Poale Zion* in Montreal sought to maintain an internal Jewish bilingualism of Hebrew and Yiddish in a unique effort to reinvent the internal cohesion of *shtetl* culture. It is stressed that this was not a reaction to environmental influences, but 'a cognitive and ... ideological construct, the work of a tiny group of secular Zionists intellectuals'. Beginning in 1913 they established Yiddish secular schools, a Yiddish library, the first Yiddish day schools anywhere in North America, a Yiddish theatre, and a Jewish Community Council.[17]

Australian Jewry's formative years as an immigrant Eastern European diasporic community occurred much later than either South Africa, Argentina or Canada because of its anti-Jewish immigration policy. In 1921 Melbourne, the second largest Jewish community in Australia, numbered only 6,927.[18] The initial reception to Zionism was mixed[19] and a Zionist Federation was only established in the 1920s.[20] With the reversal of the anti-immigration policy after the Second World War, by 1947 the Jewish population of Melbourne had doubled, the increase made up of Polish, Russian, Palestinian, German and Austrian Jews, refugees from Hitler's Europe.[21] This late immigration meant that the life span of Yiddish culture was extended. *Kadimah*, the Jewish National Library and Cultural Centre, Australia's premier Yiddishist cultural organization, was founded in 1911.[22] The oldest Yiddish supplementary school was founded in 1935.[23] Despite small numbers, Yiddish theatre was first performed in Melbourne in 1909 and before and during the First World War Melbourne had two theatre companies.[24] In 1925 two companies were formed which eventually amalgamated.[25] In 1939, with the arrival of the famous Polish theatre director, Jacob Waislitz, who had spent seven months in South Africa in 1937 in an unsuccessful attempt to establish a Yiddish theatre, the company was renamed the David Herman Theatre Company.[26] It was sponsored by *Kadimah* and lasted until as late as 1992.[27]

The second significant wave of Jewish immigration to South Africa occurred in the 1920s before the introduction of the 1930 Quota Act which severely curtailed immigration from Eastern Europe.[28] Between 1926 and 1936 the Jewish population of the Transvaal increased by 15,000 to 53,924,[29] making Johannesburg the largest Jewish centre in South Africa. The immigrants of the late 1920s were better educated and more politically conscious than the immigrants of the early 1900s. Imbued with Zionism and Socialism, they included graduates of the new Lithuanian Hebrew schools as well as of the Yiddish *Folkshuln*, who had participated both in the Zionist movement and in the *Bund*. During this period the political scene favoured the leftist orientated Yiddish speakers, with the small multi-racial Communist Party of

South Africa, established in 1921, including a disproportionate number of Jewish members.[30] English-speaking liberal white South Africans lauded the Soviet Union and looked to it to save them from the threat of Fascism in Nazi Germany. The South African Friends of the Soviet Union, and the Left Book Club were established and Medical Aid for Russia was regarded as a *cause célèbre*. Once Russia entered the war on the side of the Allies, diplomatic ties were established and in 1942 a Russian Consulate was dispatched to Pretoria.[31]

At this time the centre of Jewish immigrant life in Johannesburg shifted from Ferreirastown in the city centre to the eastern suburbs of Doornfontein, Bertrams and Jeppe.[32] The Jewish presence in Doornfontein originated around 1903 when a number of Jews, following in the footsteps of the Randlords, the rich mining magnates, moved out there from the city centre. By 1905 there was a significant Jewish community and the first synagogue, the Doornfontein Jewish Congregation, was established.[33] However, by the 1930s the Randlords had moved on to mansions in Parktown, leaving Doornfontein as the hub of Jewish immigrant life, the most ethnically Jewish neighbourhood in South Africa, where Jewish life was said to throb 'with a vitality that is seldom found outside eastern Europe'.[34] In 1936, the first time that home languages were surveyed in the census, Yiddish, the home language of 21 per cent of the Jews in the Transvaal, emerged as the third largest language group, after English and Afrikaans, amongst the White population of the Transvaal.[35] In Doornfontein Yiddish was spoken on every street corner, and not only by Jews but also by some non-Jews, Africans and Coloureds. Many shops had Yiddish signs on their windows. There were at least six or seven Shuls with excellent attendances on a Friday night. People flocked to the Alhambra Theatre to hear a speaker from the Communist Party of South Africa or to see the Yiddish talkies,[36] such as Maurice Schwartz in Sholem Asch's *Uncle Moses*, Molly Picon in *Yidl mitn Fidl*,[37] and the cantor with the golden voice, Moishe Oysher, in *Dem Hazens Zundel* [The Cantor's Son].[38] Old Doornfontein had many nicknames: Ormfontein, Little Lithuania, Texas, Schnorrerfontein, Yiddelfontein. In the 1930s Doornfontein was described as 'a slice of eastern Europe in Johannesburg'.[39]

The Jewish immigrants transplanted the network of societies and ideologies from their hometowns in Eastern Europe to Johannesburg. They included the Zionist *Zeire Zion*,[40] the Soviet-orientated Jewish Colonisation Fund, which aimed to settle Jews in the Crimea on the Black Sea,[41] which was succeeded by the *Afrikaner Gezerd*, which advocated Jewish settlement in Birobidjan in Siberia in Russia,[42] the *Bundist* Group,[43] the Johannesburg Jewish Workers' Club, the Workmen's Circle,[44] the Yiddish Literary and Dramatic Union,[45] succeeded by the Yiddish Cultural Union,[46] and between 30 and 40 *landmanschafts* [Fraternal societies].[47] To quote the *Afrikaner Idishe Tsaytung* "...in Doornfontein we never slept every night there was another meeting."[48] A Yiddish *Folkshul* was only established on a permanent basis in 1937.[49]

This was the most active period for amateur Yiddish theatre, and the call to establish a permanent Yiddish theatre was reiterated in the press at frequent intervals.[50] During this period several overseas actors, Paul Braitman and Vera Kanevska,[51] Boris Abramov and Mary Einhorn,[52] and Ossip Runitsch, a Russian star of stage and screen,[53] found refuge in South Africa, enriching the local Yiddish stage. Two eminent visiting actor-directors, Simche Nathan[54] and Jacob Waislitz,[55] from

Poland, at different times tried to form a dramatic studio with a view to establishing a permanent theatre. Visiting German directors Kurt Baum and Leo Kerz directed innovative Yiddish productions.[56] Sarah Sylvia, South Africa's premier Yiddish actress[57] returned from Buenos Aires to produce seasons of Yiddish theatre.[58] They worked with a core of committed and able amateurs, recent immigrants, several of whom had had training in the Yiddish theatre studios of Eastern Europe.

Mendl Tabatznik[59] and Shleyme Rubin[60] had directed amateur dramatic groups in Mir in Belarus and Rakishok in Lithuania, respectively. Dovid Dancig had been a member of Mendl Tabatznik's amateur dramatic group in Mir.[61] Benny Ozynski studied dramatic art in Vilna,[62] and Leib Galvin was a graduate of the Dnyepera Petroysker Theatre School in Russia.[63] Faivl Zygielbaum, from a large family of Yiddish actors, had performed with the experimental *Yung Teater* in Warsaw and studied at the Government Producing School.[64] The music for the productions, which were always accompanied by an original orchestral score, were written by Hirsch Ichilcheck from Nova Alexandrosk in Lithuania, orchestral conductor for the Tsarina's uncle for 20 years.[65] Ichilcheck was the father of the popular Johannesburg band leader, Dan Hill. Rene Shapshak, a well known French-Jewish sculptor, painter and Socialist, designed costumes and sets.[66] Shapshak was the driving force behind the attempt to rescue Jewish artists from Nazi Europe.[67]

While the early 1930s saw a proliferation of different societies producing Yiddish theatre, by the mid-1930s the Marxist, anti-religious and anti-Zionist, Johannesburg Jewish Workers' Club, established in Doornfontein in 1929, began to overshadow them. Theatre had long been a tradition of leftist radical societies, as evidenced by the vibrant Yiddish theatre of the studios of the *Bund* in Poland, and also in *Artef* the Jewish Workers' theatre troupe which existed in New York between 1925 and 1940.[68] The Jewish Workers' Club dominated the political, social and cultural life of Doornfontein and its surroundings for two decades. Although at its height there were only 300 paid up members, the influence of the club extended to all sections of the Jewish immigrant population.[69] In 1944 a large celebration to mark its fifteenth anniversary was attended by the Consul General of the Soviet Union.[70] By 1948, however, with the rise of the South African Nationalist government, Communist sympathising organisations became increasingly threatened. On 8 October 1948 the premises of the Workers' Club were burnt down together with all its documents and membership lists, in what seemed to have been a deliberate attempt to destroy all incriminating traces of its activities.[71]

The Yiddish Dramatic section was only one of the many activities of the club which included lecture series, debates and discussions on leftist topics, table tennis, chess, a gymnastics club, dances and picnics.[72] Bertha Englander, the only member still alive today, described it as much more than an amateur dramatic society, but 'a very close group of friends who helped one another in every capacity'.[73] Mrs Skikne, the mother of the famous film star Lawrence Harvey, was a regular performer on the stage and in the choir.[74] For their productions the club utilised its impressive choir, conducted by Nathan Bell (Natie Belyeikin), choir master of the Berea Synagogue and militant atheist,[75] occasionally accompanied by Shlomo Mandel, the popular *chazen* [cantor]. The choir was on occasion heard performing the Red Flag in Yiddish on the South African Broadcasting Corporation.[76]

The repertoire of the Dramatic Section reflected its close identification with political and social conditions in the Soviet Union, emphasising Marxist ideology, denigrating capitalism, religion and Fascism. Typical productions of this nature were Halper Leivick's *Shop*,[77] which depicts Jewish factory workers, recent immigrants from Eastern Europe, in the New York garment industry,[78] Avraham Vieviorka's *Af der Grenets* [On the Border], a Soviet comedy which pokes fun at the religious Jews who are smuggling diamonds across the border hidden in their *tefilin* [phylacteries],[79] and *Gelt* [Money], the Yiddish adaptation of Ben Jonson's *Volpone*, which illustrates the destructive force of money on men's lives.[80]

Between 1936 and 1940 the Dramatic Section of the Workers' Club, together with the United Yiddish Culture Front,[81] and the Yiddish Cultural Union, produced a variety of full-length productions. The repertoire ranged from the classics of Yiddish literature to translations from English, American and European literature. Yiddish comedies with strong social messages, included *Luft Parnoses* [Jewish Occupations], based on Sholem Aleichem's Menachem Mendl stories.[82] Menachem Mendl was the quintessential *shtetl* Jew, a *luftmensch* [person with no fixed occupation], pursuing various hairbrained schemes in his attempt to get rich quick. Another popular favourite was *Dos Greyse gevins* [The Great Windfall], the story of one of Sholem Aleichem's *kleyne menshlekh* [little people] who wins a lotto ticket,[83] as well as the famous folk comedy about the trickster *Hershele Ostropolyer*, which the Workers' Club received as a gift from the Moscow Yiddish Art theatre.[84] One of the best known tragedies of the Yiddish repertoire, which was performed on more than one occasion, was Leon Kobrin's *Der Dorfsyung* [The Village Youth]. This is the story of a simple Jewish youth, who, when he marries a Russian peasant girl, is tormented with guilt and commits suicide.[85] To commemorate the death of Sholem Schwartzbard, the assassin of the Ukrainian *pogrom* leader Simon Petlyura, who died in Cape Town in 1938, Alte Kacyzna's play *Shvartsbart*, about his Paris trial, was staged.[86]

Translations of topical American anti-Fascist plays pertinent to contemporary events included Clifford Odets' *Till the Day I Die*, which deals with underground Communist activity in Nazi Germany,[87] and Irwin Shaw's powerful anti-war play, *Bury the Dead*.[88] However, the play that made the greatest impression in 1936 with the deteriorating situation of the Jews in Nazi Germany, and with the Greyshirts, a group of Nazi sympathisers active in South Africa, was German Jewish playwright and member of the Communist Party Friedrich Wolf's *Professor Mamlock*, also known as *Di Gele Late* [The Yellow Patch]. The play is set in a hospital in Germany where the position of the director, Professor Mamlock, an assimilated Jew, is made untenable when one of his subordinates is placed over him. He eventually breaks down and commits suicide. Bertha Englander recalls that when as Mamlock's daughter Ruth she had to run through the auditorium on to the stage chased by Nazis, some of the audience became terrified thinking that it was real. Moreover, during the performance, when Dr Helpach was abusing the Professor, someone in the audience jumped up and shouted, '*Foetzak*, you bloody Nazi'.[89]

Besides the productions of the Jewish Workers' Club, another attempt to establish a Yiddish Art Theatre was made in 1939 by Ossip Runitsch, the Russian movie star and director, with a series of five productions from the Yiddish and

European repertoire.⁹⁰ In 1942 he also contributed to the short-lived Yiddish Forum, a literary, musical and dramatic society.⁹¹ Besides these more serious productions, several seasons of light musical comedies were produced by Boris Abramov⁹² and Vera Kanevska.⁹³ Sarah Sylvia brought out Meyer Tzelniker's London company in 1938,⁹⁴ and the American stars, Miriam Kressyn and Hymie Jacobson, who produced a season of plays with the local amateurs in 1939.⁹⁵ Thus the essential ingredients for establishing a Yiddish theatre were present in Johannesburg. These were talented Yiddish actors and directors, productions which on occasion equalled those in Warsaw and Vilna, and audiences as warm and enthusiastic as anywhere else in the world. In addition local Yiddish authors wrote several plays on South African themes, such as *Tsurik aheym* [Homeward Bound] by Abel Shaban⁹⁶ and *Fun Fordsburg biz Mayfair* [From Fordsburg to Mayfair] by South Africa's foremost Yiddish poet, Dovid Fram.⁹⁷ The plays dealt with the upward mobility and snobbishness of the immigrants. Yet despite all these factors a permanent Yiddish theatre group was never established. The reason is obscured by the fact that the main English-language Jewish newspaper in the Transvaal, the *Zionist Record*, virtually ignored the existence of the anti-Zionist Jewish Workers' Club. The *S.A. Jewish Chronicle* was published in Cape Town, and the *South African Jewish Times* was only established in July 1936. The only source therefore is the Yiddish weekly, *Afrikaner Idishe Tsaytung*.

At the time it seemed that the reasons for the failure to establish a permanent Yiddish theatre group stemmed from personality clashes and petty rivalries such as that between Yitskhok Charlash,⁹⁸ the cultural elitist⁹⁹ from the Yiddish Cultural Union, who was jealous of the great visiting Polish director, Jacob Waislitz, who seemed to be usurping his place in the community.¹⁰⁰ In 1938, after a season of four very successful plays, Waislitz left South Africa and in 1939 settled in the much smaller Jewish community of Melbourne in Australia. There he immediately became co-director of the existing Yiddish Theatre Group, the David Herman Yiddish Theatre, which lasted until 1992. Hostility between the Zionists and the anti-Zionists was one of the reasons for the break-up of the Yiddish Forum. After a very successful concert in Milner Park in 1942, the musical director, Jerry Idelsohn, brother of the famous musicologist, A.Z. Idelsohn,¹⁰¹ resigned, ostensibly on account of the singing of *Hatikvah*.¹⁰²

These conflicts were reinforced by the extremely negative attitude of the community to Yiddish education, demonstrated in the attitude of the S.A. Jewish Board of Education to the small Yiddish *Folkshul*.¹⁰³ An earlier Yiddish *Folkshul*, that had existed between January 1929 and March 1931, had been closed down by the Zionists because of its avowedly secular and radical programme, which was regarded as a threat to the Hebrew *Talmud-Torah* school system.¹⁰⁴ When it was re-established in 1937, it was simply ignored and barely supported.¹⁰⁵ In 1942 the S.A. Board of Jewish Education declined to participate in the school's fifth anniversary celebrations¹⁰⁶ and a questionnaire that was sent out to all Jewish pupils by the Jewish Board of Deputies as part of a campaign to raise funds and to promote consciousness of Hebrew education did not even refer to the existence of Yiddish education.¹⁰⁷ The attitude of the Board was embodied in the words of Rabbi Kossowsky, the head of the Beth Din, who claimed that, 'although he was one hundred percent in favour of Yiddish, he was one hundred percent against the Folk

School. It was anti-religious. A school that did not teach religion was against religion. It was anti-national because it neglected the Bible'.[108] It was not until 1949 when the *Folkshul* was finally recognised by the S.A. Board of Jewish Education that it received any type of communal support.[109]

This bitter hostility has been attributed to South African Jewry's exclusively *Litvak* origins. Yet in Montreal in Canada, a community also dominated by *Litvaks*, a unique synthesis was reached between Hebrew and Yiddish culture, and a Yiddish theatre still exists there to this day, the Dora Wasserman Yiddish Theatre. Similarly in Buenos Aires, Zionism and Socialism, Hebrew and Yiddish, have always co-existed harmoniously side by side.

Faivl Zygielbaum attributes the obstacles to Yiddish theatre in South Africa to the lack of a large Yiddish-speaking proletariat as existed in New York or Buenos Aires. As there was no grassroots support for Yiddish theatre it had to be promoted from above, by the *intelligentsia* and by the rich Jews. However, although the rich Jews enjoyed Yiddish theatre, they were quite happy to live without it and were loath to invest money in it. Nor did Yiddish theatre enjoy communal support and it was seldom even mentioned in minutes or proceedings. Reviews were non-committal and uncritical and potential audiences were not being educated. There was no financial backing and therefore no suitable venue for Yiddish theatre.[110] Visiting companies and actor-directors, such as Simche Nathan and Jacob Waislitz, soon sensed the indifference, quickly staged their best pieces and left.

Whilst these were the immediate reasons, deeper factors were at work. Firstly the Yiddish theatre enthusiasts of the late 1920s and 1930s encountered a community with a robust Jewish identity developed in its formative years between 1890 and 1914. This identity included Judaism and Zionism whilst Yiddish culture, stigmatised by its association with Jewish poverty and persecution, was discarded and marginalised at a very early stage. It was not within the capabilities of this relatively small and economically weak group of newcomers to change the values of the establishment. Moreover the small Yiddish cultural organisations of the time were allied with leftist politics and were anti-Zionist, which was anathema to the Anglo-Jewish establishment and to a great number of the East Europeans. The introduction of the Suppression of Communism Act in 1950 simply served to entrench these attitudes. Secondly, by 1947 17 years had gone by without any sizeable immigration from Eastern Europe to keep the Yiddish language alive and to replenish the fervour for Yiddish theatre. By 1936 it was estimated that over 78 per cent of all Jews under 30 years of age were South African born.[111] While between 1931 and 1940 the number of Yiddish productions per year varied between approximately five and eleven, after 1940 this was reduced to between one and three, and gradually began to peter out.

In the wake of the Holocaust, a *rapprochement* occurred between the majority of the Zionist establishment and the small leftist Yiddish societies, which resulted in the establishment of the non-politically affiliated South African Yiddish Cultural Federation. Under its aegis in the 1950s a revival of Yiddish theatre took place, facilitated by a record number of visiting artists in search of a stage.[112] However with no post-Holocaust renewal of Jewish immigration from Eastern Europe, by 1960 the percentage of Yiddish speakers in the Transvaal had shrunk to approximately five per cent,[113] the language was not being transferred to the second generation, and the interest in Yiddish theatre was waning worldwide. Ultimately the spectacular revival was artificial and could not be sustained. By 1960 the Dramatic Section of the South African Yiddish Cultural Federation in Johannesburg had disappeared.

NOTES

This paper is based on a Masters dissertation, 'The History of Yiddish Theatre in South Africa from the Late Nineteenth Century to 1960', supervised by Prof. Milton Shain.

1. For the current status quo of the Yiddish language as well as its history, see Dovid Katz, *Words on Fire: The Unfinished Story of Yiddish* (New York: Basic Books, 2004).
2. Jean-Marc Larrue, *Le Theatre Yiddish a Montreal* [Yiddish Theatre in Montreal] (Montreal: Editions Jeu, 1996); Dora Wasserman Yiddish Theatre, Montreal, http://www.saidyebronfman.org/theatre/t_y_hom.html.
3. http://home.iprimus.com.au/kadimah/.
4. Gideon Shimoni, *Jews and Zionism: The South African Experience, 1910–1967* (Cape Town: Oxford University Press, 1980), p.5.
5. Gustav Saron, *The Jews of South Africa: An Illustrated History to 1953* (Johannesburg: Scarecrow Books, 2001), p.5.
6. Shimoni (see note 4), p.5.
7. See Marcia Gitlin, *Vision Amazing* (Johannesburg,: Menorah Book Club 1950), pp.30–37.
8. Ibid., pp.84–99.
9. For a history of the Bund see Henry Tobias, *The Jewish Bund in Russia from its Origins to 1905* (Stanford, CA: Stanford University Press, 1972).
10. See Masha Greenbaum, *Jews of Lithuania* (Tel Aviv: Geffen, 1995), pp.127–45.
11. According to Leibl Feldman, an additional cause of the lack of formation of a Jewish proletariat in Johannesburg was the fact that Eastern European Jewish immigrant artisans were excluded from membership in certain White trade unions that were controlled by British immigrants. Feldman bases his observations on the oral testimony of Z.D. Fox, who also cites reluctance on the part of the Anglo-German Jews to employ their own Eastern European co-religionists. These circumstances forced them into various forms of petty trading, as peddlers, shopkeepers and middlemen. Leibl Feldman, *Yidn in Yohanesburg biz Yyunyen, 31 May 1910* (Yohanesburg: Kayor, 1955), pp.61–2.
12. Shimoni (see note 4), p.50.
13. J. Lestschinsky, 'Jewish Migrations, 1840–1956', in *The Jews of Latin America*, ed. by J. Laikin Elkin, rev. edn (New York: Holmes & Maier, 1998), p.52.
14. Elkin (see note 13), pp.52–7.
15. V.A. Mirelman, *Jewish Buenos Aires, 1890–1930: In Search of an Identity* (Detroit: Wayne State University Press, 1990), p.173.
16. *Encyclopedia Judaica* (Jerusalem: Keter, 1972), vol.12, p.286.
17. David G. Roskies, 'Yiddish in Montreal: A Utopian Experiment', in *An Everyday Miracle: Jewish Culture in Montreal*, ed. by I. Robinson, P. Anctil and M. Butovsky (Montreal: Vehicule Press, 1996), pp.22–38; David G. Roskies, 'A Hebrew–Yiddish Utopia in Montreal: Ideology in Bilingual Education', in *Hebrew in America: Perspectives and Prospects*, ed. by A. Mintz (Detroit: Wayne State University Press, 1993), pp.155–67.
18. Daniel J. Elazar with Peter Medding, *Jews in Frontier Societies: Argentina, South Africa and Australia* (New York: Holmes & Maier, 1983), p.262.
19. Ibid., pp.270–71.
20. Ibid., p.284.
21. Ibid., p.279.
22. S. Rutland, *Edge of Diaspora: Two Centuries of Jewish Settlement in Australia*, 2nd rev. edn (Rose Bay, NSW: Brandl & Schlesinger, 1997), p.92.
23. F. Klarberg, 'Yiddish in Melbourne', in *Never Say Die: a Thousand Years of Yiddish in Jewish Life and Letters*, ed. by Joshua A. Fishman (The Hague: Mouton Publishers, c.1981), pp.619–33 (p.623).
24. Rutland (see note 22), pp.91–2.
25. Ibid., p.152.
26. Ibid., p.211.
27. See Arnold Zable, *Wanderers and Dreamers: Tales of the David Herman Theatre* (South Melbourne: Hyland House, 1998).

28. Shimoni (see note 4), pp.97–108.
29. Union of South Africa, *Sixth Census of the Population of the Union of South Africa, Enumerated 5th May 1936* (Pretoria: Government Printer, 1941), vol.6, 'Religions', p.4.
30. See M. Israel and S. Adams, '"That Spells Trouble": Jews and the Communist Party of South Africa', *Journal of Southern African Studies*, 26.1 (March 2000), 145–62.
31. K.M. Campbell, *Soviet Policy towards South Africa* (Boston Spa: British Library, Document Supply Centre, 1984), p.124.
32. In 1935 the highest percentage of people engaged in manual labour was to be found there H. Sonnabend, *Statistical Survey of Johannesburg's Jewish Population 1935* (Johannesburg: [s.n., 19-?]), Table 19, p.22.
33. *Afrikaner Idishe Tsaytung*, 7 August 1931.
34. Jacob Waislitz, quoted in the *Zionist Record*, 16 October 1936.
35. Union of South Africa, *Sixth Census of the Population of the Union of South Africa, Enumerated 5th May 1936* (Pretoria: Government Printer, 1938), vol.4, 'Languages', p.62. 11,438 out of a total Jewish population of 53,924 gave Yiddish as their home language. It has been speculated that this number was far too low considering the large number of recent immigrants and it is possible that many were too embarrassed to admit that Yiddish, because of its low status, was their home language.
36. L. Hill, 'Remembrance of a Shtetl in Johannesburg', *Jewish Affairs*, 36.12 (December 1981), 24–7.
37. *Afrikaner Idishe Tsaytung*, 4 February 1938.
38. Ibid., 24 March 1939.
39. Hill (see note 36), p.24.
40. Shimoni (see note 4), p.59.
41. Ibid., pp.56–7.
42. Ibid., pp.57–8.
43. The *Bundist* Group's memorial evening for the executed leaders, Henryk Erlich and Viktor Alter, on 9 December 1943, was advertised as 'closed' with entry only 'by invitation', indicating that it was a small and exclusive group, *Afrikaner Idishe Tsaytung*, 3 December 1943.
44. The Workman's Circle was primarily a sick relief society modelled on its American counterpart, *Der Afrikaner*, 13 February 1931.
45. Gideon Shimoni (see note 4), pp.55–6.
46. *Afrikaner Idishe Tsaytung*, 31 May 1935.
47. *Der Afrikaner*, 16 July 1918.
48. *Afrikaner Idishe Tsaytung*, 7 August 1931.
49. 'Yidisher Kultur Fareyn: Barg-aruf', *Forois*, 1.1 (June 1937), 22.
50. See review of *Der Vilder Mentsh*, *Afrikaner Idishe Tsaytung*, 15 July 1932; 'Oyfn Veg fun a Hign Yidishn Teater', *Afrikaner Idishe Tsaytung*, 9 December 1933; Letter to the Editor, *Afrikaner Idishe Tsaytung*, 27 October 1936; F. Zygielbaum, 'Di Meglekhkeytn tsu Shafn a Yidishn Teater in Dorem Arike', *Afrikaner Idishe Tsaytung*, 9 December 1938.
51. Paul Breitman and Vera Kanevska first came to South Africa with visiting troupes from London in the 1920s and settled in South Africa in 1938. For Paul Breitman, who became a popular *chazen* [cantor] in Johannesburg, see Zalman Zylbercweig, *Leksikon fun Yidishn Teater* (New York: Elisheva, 1931–69), vol.1, p.244. For Vera Kanevska, see her obituary in the *Afrikaner Idishe Tsaytung*, 7 September 1945.
52. Mary Einhorn and Boris Abramov came to Johannesburg in 1928. For Mary Einhorn, see *Zionist Record*, 7 September 1928. For Boris Abramov, see *Afrikaner Idishe Tsaytung*, 29 April 1932.
53. Ossip Runitsch (1899–1947), who came to Johannesburg in 1939, had been a member of the Moscow State Theatre and was one of the founders and stars of the Russian cinema. He worked for the German film company, UFA, in Berlin for nine years. When Hitler came to power he left for Riga, where he worked with the Yiddish Minorities Theatre, *Afrikaner Idishe Tsaytung*, 9 June 1939: In South Africa he produced opera as well as Afrikaans theatre *South African Music Encyclopedia*, ed. by J.P. Malan (Cape Town: Oxford University Press, 1979–86), vol.4, p.201.
54. Simche Nathan came to South Africa in 1933 with a troupe brought out by Vera Kanevska and Paul Breitman. He stayed on to establish an experimental theatre studio which staged only one production, *Afrikaner Idishe Tsaytung, Erev Rosh ha-Shone* 1933; *Zionist Record*, 5 December 1933.
55. Waislitz, who was brought out by the United Yiddish Culture Front, formed an experimental theatre studio which staged four productions. *Afrikaner Idishe Tsaytung*, 8 October 1936, 29 January, 7, 11, 14, 28 May 1937.
56. Baum directed the Yiddish adaptation of Ben Jonson's *Volpone*, *Afrikaner Idishe Tsaytung*, 29 October 1937. Kerz directed the Yiddish production of Irwin Shaw's *Bury the Dead*, *Afrikaner Idishe Tsaytung*, 21 April, 1938.

57. Sarah Sylvia was born Serke Goldstein in London on 18 May 1893, but came to South Africa as a child. She began acting on the Yiddish stage in Cape Town when she was only 12 years old. In the 1910s she was taken to London where she joined Moscovitch's Yiddish Company at the Pavilion Theatre, and became a star both in London and later in Argentina. From the 1920s she returned to South Africa on occasion bringing out visiting companies and directing the local amateurs, Zalman Zylbercweig, *Leksikon fun Yidishn Teater*, vol.2, p.1486; R. Zygielbaum, 'The Darling of the Theatre: Sarah Sylvia', *Jewish Affairs*, 33.2 (February 1978), 26–8.
58. *Afrikaner Idishe Tsaytung*, 9 July 1935, 23 March 1936.
59. Tabatznik, who came to Johannesburg in 1929, directed Yiddish theatre, folk choirs, taught, lectured, and wrote six Yiddish books. Mendel Tabatznik, *Shtaplen in Mayn Lebnsveg* (Johannesburg: Kayor, 1973); 'Mendel Tabatznik', in *From a Land Far Off: South African Yiddish Stories in English Translation*, selected and ed. by Joseph Sherman (Cape Town: Jewish Publications, 1986), pp.160–66 (pp.160–61).
60. 'Shleyme Rubin', *Dorem Afrike*, 6.11 (July 1954), 32.
61. Dovid Dancig came to South Africa in 1929 and established a Yiddish theatre group in Benoni, 'Fun der D.A. Yidishe Kultur-Federatsye: Benoni', *Dorem Afrike*, 2.4 (December 1949), 31.
62. *Merchant of Venice*, programme notes, Bertha Englander Yiddish Theatre Collection (Johannesburg: South African Jewish Board of Deputies Archives). Ozynski was the chairman of the Dramatic Section of the Jewish Workers' Club.
63. *Afrikaner Idishe Tsaytung*, 7 October 1932.
64. *Afrikaner Idishe Tsaytung*, 22 December 1936; *Merchant of Venice* programme notes (see note 62); Z. Levi, 'Avrom un zayne brider', *Dorem Afrike*, 12.9 (September 1959), 28–9.
65. B. Sachs, *South African Personalities and Places* (Johannesburg: Kayor, 1959), pp.109–10.
66. *S.A. Jewish Times*, 22 August 1947.
67. J. Sachs, 'Rene Shapshak', *Jewish Affairs*, 2.5 (May 1947), 32–5 (p.32).
68. See Edna Nahshon, *Yiddish Proletarian Theatre: The Art and Politics of the Artef: 1925–1940* (Westport, CT: Greenwood Press, 1998).
69. T. Adler, 'History of Jewish Workers Clubs', in *Papers Presented at the African Studies Seminar* (Johannesburg: University of the Witwatersrand, 1977), pp.1–66 (pp.19–20).
70. *Afrikaner Idishe Tsaytung*, 21 July 1944.
71. Ibid., 8 October 1948.
72. Adler (see note 69).
73. Interview with Bertha Englander, 3 November 1999.
74. Ibid.
75. J. Slovo, *Slovo: The Unfinished Autobiography* (South Africa: Ravan Press, 1995), p.21.
76. Taffy Adler, '"Lithuania's Diaspora": The Johannesburg Jewish Workers' Club, 1928–1948', *Journal of Southern African Studies*, 6.1 (1979), 70–92 (p.77).
77. *Der Afrikaner*, 8 April, 7 May 1932.
78. See H. Leivick, 'Shop', in *God, Man, and the Devil: Yiddish Plays in Translation*, transl. and ed. by N. Sandrow (Syracuse, NY: Syracuse University Press, 1999), pp.16–20, 139–83.
79. *Afrikaner Idishe Tsaytung*, 21 December 1934; Interview with Chaim Klein, 21 November 2000.
80. Ibid., 29 October 1937.
81. The United Yiddish Culture Front was established in April 1936 to fight against Fascism and to promote Yiddish culture. It consisted of the Yiddish Cultural Union, the *Gezerd*, the Jewish Workers' Club, the *Bundist* Group, the Youth *Gezerd*, the United Latvian Society, the Polish Club and by the Vilna Society, *Afrikaner Idishe Tsaytung*, 19 April, 5 June 1936.
82. *Afrikaner Idishe Tsaytung*, 9 April 1936.
83. Ibid., 8 October 1936, 29 January 1937.
84. Ibid., 28 July 1939, 17 May, 21 June 1940.
85. See Nahma Sandrow, *Vagabond Stars: A World History of Yiddish Theater* (Syracuse, NY: Syracuse University Press, 1996), pp.172–75.
86. 'Far der Oyfirung fun Sholem Shvartsbard', *Forois*, 3.6 (June 1939), 18; *Afrikaner Idishe Tsaytung*, 9, 16 June 1939.
87. *Afrikaner Idishe Tsaytung*, 23 March 1937.
88. Ibid., 21 April 1938.
89. Interview with Bertha Englander, 3 November 1999.
90. *Afrikaner Idishe Ttsaytung*, 28 July, 27 September, 17 November, 8 December 1939.
91. Ibid., 10 April 1942.
92. Ibid., 6 June 1935.
93. Joel Myerson opera boy [scrapbook, 1939] (Johannesburg: S.A. Jewish Board of Deputies Archives).
94. *Afrikaner Idishe Tsaytung*, 15 June 1938.

95. Ibid., 9 June 1939
96. Ibid., 8, 29 July 1932.
97. Ibid., 8 September 1933.
98. Charlash came out from Poland in 1935 as a Yiddish cultural emissary to raise funds for the Tsisho network of Yiddish day schools in Poland. He dominated the Yiddish Cultural Union, until his departure from South Africa in 1948, Z. Tabachovitch, 'Yitskhok Charlash iz Shoyn Nito?', *Dorem Afrike*, 25.8 (March/April 1973), 22–3.
99. Charlash lambasted the popular musical comedies staged by Meyer Tzelniker's London company, *Afrikaner Idishe Tsaytung*, 15 June 1938.
100. After his production of the musical comedy, *Parnose* [A Living], it was unfairly reported that Waislitz was more interested in making money than in producing good theatre, *Afrikaner Idishe Tsaytung*, 24 August 1938.
101. *South African Music Encyclopedia* (see note 53), vol.2, pp.260–61.
102. *Afrikaner Idishe Tsaytung*, 5 June 1942.
103. See letters to the editor in the *S.A. Jewish Times*, 20 November, 11 December 1942.
104. Shimoni (see note 4), p.56; Tabatznik (see note 59), vol.2, pp.83–4.
105. *Yidishe Folkshul in Yohanesburg Finf Yor, 1937 – September – 1942* (Yohanesburg: Yidishe Folkshul un Kindergorten baym Yidishn Kultur Fareyn, 1937), pp.3–5. Although 200 pupils were registered at one time or another between 1937 and 1942, only 60 attended for a year or more.
106. Myer Katz, 'The History of Jewish Education in South Africa, 1841–1980' (Ph.D. diss., University of Cape Town, 1980), vol.2, p.621.
107. Letters to the Editor, *S.A. Jewish Times*, 20 November, 11 December 1942.
108. *S.A. Jewish Times*, 2 July 1943.
109. Katz (see note 106), vol.2, p.621.
110. F. Zygielbaum, 'Vegn Yidishn Teater in Dorem Afrike', in *Dorem-Afrikaner Zamlbukh* (Yohanesburg: Literarishn Krayz, 1945), pp.96–8.
111. Shimoni (see note 4), p.59.
112. See Veronica Belling, 'A Short-lived Revival: Yiddish Theatre in South Africa, 1945–1960' *in Yiddish after the Holocaust*, ed. by Joseph Sherman (Oxford, UK: Boulevard, 2004), pp.92–116.
113. Total number of Yiddish speakers was 3,468 out of a total of 74,221 Jews in the Transvaal. Republic of South Africa, *Population Census*, 6 September 1960, vol.7, no.1, 'Characteristics of the population in each magisterial district and economic region, age, marital status and home language' (Pretoria: Government Printer, 1968), p.135; *South Africa, Bureau of Statistics, Statistical Year Book 1964*, compiled by the Bureau of Statistics, (Pretoria: Bureau of Statistics, 1963), p.A–28.

Abstracts

Foreigners in their Own City:
Italian Fascism and the Dispersal of Trieste's Port Jews
MAURA E. HAMETZ

After the First World War, despite the decline of liberalism and the collapse of the Habsburg empire, the community of port Jews in Trieste continued to thrive. For much of the inter-war period, Italy recognised port Jews' economic utility to schemes for economic expansion in Central Europe and the Mediterranean. Political transformation, embodied in Italy's adoption of racial legislation, not economic decline, caused the Jews' dispersal after 1938. Yet it was port Jews' flexibility, their international contacts, wealth, and influence that enabled them to escape Italy, fascist persecution, and, ultimately, the Nazi Holocaust.

'Lost Worlds': Reflections on Home and Belonging
in Jewish Holocaust Survivor Testimonies
MICHELE LANGFIELD

This article draws upon Holocaust survivor testimonies to explore the interaction between place and displacement in the formation and evolution of local, Jewish and ethnic identities. In particular, the ways in which the personal experiences of interviewees have affected their notions of 'home' and 'belonging' are addressed. Relationships with former homelands vary and have been significantly affected by pre-war, wartime and post-war experiences. Connections with home and family have frequently been severed and are more likely to exist in diasporic communities than in countries of origin.

Constructing a Usable Past:
History, Memory and South African Jewry in an Age of Anxiety
RICHARD MENDELSOHN and MILTON SHAIN

Three seminal studies published between 1930 and 1955 played a critical role in defining a received version of South African Jewish history. All three helped towards a self-definition of a community looking for a usable and respectable past in an age of anxiety and vulnerability. Shaped in significant measure by these texts, a collective memory emerged which incorporated a questionable understanding of the community's origins, development and character. Critical dimensions of the South African Jewish experience were ignored or distorted in this drive towards acceptance and respectability.

Comparing the Jewish and Irish Communities in Twentieth Century Scotland

WILLIAM KENEFICK

When examining 'place and displacement in Jewish history and memory' it is clear that the notion of 'displacement' is too pejorative and unhelpful in the Scottish historical context. In examining Jewish relations with the Irish this study demonstrates that while the Jews settled in the Gorbals area of Glasgow's south side a generation after the Irish, they 'broke free' of the 'Glasgow Ghetto' a generation and more before them. The Jewish experience of settlement in modern Scotland was thus a positive one and their relations with host community much less problematic than that of the immigrant Irish.

On Burial, Boundaries and the Creolisation of the Surinamese Jewish Community

WIEKE VINK

A central theme in the history of the Surinamese Jews is the persistent tension between the creolisation of the local community and a continued belonging to the Jewish diaspora. This field of tension is manifested by the way community boundaries were created, negotiated and recreated throughout Surinamese Jewish history. The cemetery reflects this history of changing cultural identifications of the Surinamese Jews by its changing style of gravestones and by the various conflicts surrounding death, burial and cemetery space. Based on a study of the shifting position of 'coloured Jews' in the Surinamese Jewish community from the late eighteenth to mid-nineteenth century, as displayed both at the cemetery and in cemetery-related stories, I will argue that this transformation of cemetery space should be understood as a case in point of a creolising Surinamese Jewish community.

Memory, Place and Displacement in the Formation of Jewish Identity in Rangoon and Surabaya

JONATHAN GOLDSTEIN

In nineteenth and early twentieth century Rangoon, Burma, and Surabaya, Dutch East Indies, 'memory' [*zachor*], 'source' [*makor*], and 'location' [*makom*] were important determinants of Jewish identity. Jews lived in alien contexts but tolerant surroundings. Immigrant Jews were civically included and could organise freely. Each city was a tranquil location where Jews could deepen their commitment to Rabbinic Judaism and/or Zion. But precisely the same conditions enabled Jews to intermarry and/or convert. This process began well before World War II. A brutal wartime Japanese occupation and post-war economic trauma and political upheaval in both places ultimately destroyed the peaceful environments Jews once knew. By 1960 virtually all Burmese and Indonesians who had remained Jews had moved on to other places of refuge, notably to the reborn State of Israel. A handful of stalwarts remained in both locations to tend their respective synagogues and cemeteries.

Jewish Identity in Two Remote Areas of the Cape Province: A Double Case Study

JOHN SIMON

This article examines two important and somewhat picturesque centres of Jewish life in (then) remote areas of the Cape Province, namely Namaqualand in the North Western Cape and Oudtshoorn in the South Western Cape. The Namaqualand Jews featured prominently in the shipping and mineral industries and in the subsidiary commercial activities which emerged from them. Oudtshoorn Jews became deeply involved in the two principal industries with which the area's prosperity waxed and waned, namely ostrich farming and tobacco. Both brought the Jews more closely into contact with their mainly Afrikaans neighbours than was the case in other areas and yet the Oudtshoorn community at its peak was so Jewishly robust that it earned the soubriquet 'Jerusalem of South Africa'. The article examines those features which characterised the two communities and their relationship with their neighbours.

Migration, Location and Memory: Jewish History through a Comparative Lens

NANCY FONER

This article is based on the premise that a comparative perspective can enrich our understanding of the role of location in the lives of Eastern European Jewish migrants and their descendants. It explores, through a comparative lens, how the context or place where Eastern European Jews moved 100 years ago shaped their lives in their new homes at the time of initial settlement. It also considers issues concerned with memory, including how the historical experience of migration in specific locations influenced memory of it.

Putting London Jewish Intellectuals in their Place

DAVID CESARANI

The extensive cultural histories of New York's Jewish intellectuals have made much of the ethnic and spatial dimension in their formation as individuals and as a group. Over the same time span that New York Jews threw up a galaxy of creative figures, from the 1920s to the 1950s, London witnessed the emergence of a stunning concentration of Jewish intellectuals. Many came from London's East End which performed a similar function to New York's Jewish immigrant districts. Yet cultural historians have not delineated a prototypical London Jewish intellectual and there is little cultural history of Jewish intellectuals in London. This article is a tentative attempt at a sociological analysis of London Jewish intellectuals investigating the relationship between place, ethnicity and memory in the emergence of a distinctive intellectual cadre.

Memory at the Margins, Matter Out of Place: Hidden Narratives of Jewish Settlement and Movement in Britain

TONY KUSHNER

This article explores the memory and history of a Jewish shopkeeping community in the south coast English port of Southampton during the first half of the twentieth century. By focusing on the marginality of these Jews, it highlights the fluidity of Jewish migration within countries of immigration such as Britain and questions assumptions of Jewish economic success and mobility. It then explores why this community has been subsequently subject to amnesia in both local and Jewish collective memory, suggesting that these Jews and their cosmopolitan neighbours have been regarded as 'matter out of place'.

'A Slice of Eastern Europe in Johannesburg': Yiddish Theatre in Doornfontein, 1929–49

VERONICA BELLING

This article explores how location influenced attitudes to the preservation of Yiddish language and culture and hence the construction of historical memory. Between 1929 and 1949 the Johannesburg Jewish Workers' Club, had a thriving Dramatic Section which produced Yiddish theatre with a leftist slant. It was situated in Doornfontein, the suburb east of Johannesburg, that from the early 1930s was the focus of the Eastern European immigration. Based on an examination of the Yiddish weekly newspaper, the *Afrikaner Idishe Tsaytung* [African Jewish Newspaper], this paper will examine why a permanent Yiddish theatre group never emerged, and why this rich and lively episode was 'forgotten' and erased from the collective memory of South African Jewry.

Notes on Contributors

Veronica Belling is the Jewish Studies Librarian at the University of Cape Town Libraries and the Kaplan Centre for Jewish Studies and Research. She is the author of *Bibliography of South African Jewry (1997)*, *The Jews of Johannesburg (2007* - translation of Leibl Feldman's *Yidn in Yohanesburg)*, and *Yiddish Theatre in South Africa (2008)*. Her forthcoming book, co-authored with Mendel Kaplan, is a translation of the writings of the Yiddish journalist, Yakov Azriel Davidson.

David Cesarani is research professor in History, Royal Holloway, University of London. His most recent book is Major Farran's Hat. Britain's War against Jewish Terrorism *1945-48* (Heinemann, *2009)*.

Nancy Foner is Distinguished Professor of Sociology at Hunter College and the Graduate Center of the City University of New York. She is the author or editor of more than a dozen books, including *From Ellis Island to JFK. New York's Two Great Waves of Immigration (2000)*, *In a New Land: A Comparative View of Immigration (2000)*, and the forthcoming edited volume *Across Generations: Immigrant Families in America (2009)*.

Jonathan Goldstein is a Research Associate of Harvard University's Fairbank Center for East Asian Research and a Professor of East and Southeast Asian history at the University of West Georgia. His books include *China and Israel* (1999), *The Jews of China* (2000), *America Views China: American Images of China Then and Now* (1991), and *Philadelphia and the China Trade, 1682–1846* (1978).

Maura E. Hametz, an Associate Professor of history at Old Dominion University, Norfolk, VA, received her Ph.D. at Brandeis University in 1995. Her research on Trieste's Jewish population has appeared in *Holocaust and Genocide Studies* and *Names*. Her forthcoming book *Making Trieste Italian, 1918–1954* explores Italian identity.

William Kenefick lectures in Scottish and British history at the University of Dundee. He completed his monograph *Rebellious and Contrary: The Glasgow Dockers, c.1853 to 1932*, in 2000, and has published widely on Scottish maritime labour history and Scottish political and industrial radicalism between the 1880s and the 1930s.

Tony Kushner is Professor of Jewish/non-Jewish relations in the Parkes Institute and History Department, University of Southampton. His recent publications include *Remembering Refugees: Then and Now (2006)* and *Anglo-Jewry since 1066 (2009)*

Michele Langfield is Associate Professor in the School of History, Heritage and Society, Faculty of Arts and Education, Deakin University, Australia. She publishes in the fields of migration, ethnicity, identity and cultural heritage. Much of her work utilises oral histories and video testimonies, particularly in the field of Jewish and Holocaust studies.

Richard Mendelsohn teaches in the history department of the University of Cape Town. He is the author of *Sammy Marks: 'The Uncrowned King of the Transvaal'*, and has published extensively on various aspects of the history of late nineteenth and early twentieth century South Africa. In 2002 he co-edited *Memories, Realities and Dreams: Aspects of the South African Jewish Experience* with Milton Shain and they are currently completing a history of the Jews in South Africa.

Milton Shain is Director of the Isaac and Jessie Kaplan Centre for Jewish Studies and Research at the University of Cape Town. He is the author of numerous books, including *The Roots of Antisemitism in South Africa*. In 2002 he co-edited *Memories, Realities and Dreams: Aspects of the South African Jewish Experience* with Richard Mendelsohn and they are currently completing a history of the Jews in South Africa.

John Simon practises law in Cape Town. He has an MA from the University of Cape Town where he is a part-time lecturer in the Department of Jewish Studies. He has contributed chapters to several books and has numerous articles published in refereed journals, mainly on early South African Jewish history and also on legal topics.

Moshe Terdiman is completing his Ph.D. dissertation at the University of Haifa. It is entitled 'The Maritime Power of the Mamluks in the Eastern Mediterranean and in the Red Sea'. He was awarded BA and MA degrees in Middle Eastern Studies from the Hebrew University. His main areas of interest are the Middle East, Islam in Africa, Jews under Arab and Islamic rule, Jews and the sea.

Wieke Vink is a Ph.D. student at the Faculty of History and Arts (Department of Non-Western History) of the Erasmus University Rotterdam in the Netherlands since 2001. The working title of her dissertation is 'Surinamese Jews: Creolisation and Changing Group Identities, 18th to 20th Century'.

Index

abjuration 24
Abrahams, Israel 43, 45, 47–8
acculturation 15, 16, 149
Afrikaner Idishe Tsaytung 175
Agron, Gershon 93
Algiers 6, 7, 99
  governance of 100–1, 108–10
  Jewish communities in 103–6, 111
  Livorno Jews 6, 99, 106–12
  population 101–3, 105–6
  Spanish Jews in 103, 104–5, 107–8, 109–11
antisemitism 3, 4, 17, 18
  Glasgow 54, 56–9, 66
  Indonesia 93–4
  Italian 20–5,
  South Africa 45, 125, 126
Argentina 2, 23, 170–1
Arlott, John 163
Ashkenazi Jews 71
assimilation 2, 15, 16, 24, 46–7, 134–5
  in Glasgow 63–5
  in South Africa 126
Australia 2
  personal histories 32–9
  postwar migration to 29, 36–9, 171

Bacri-Busnach merchant family 110, 111–12
Beadle 122–3
Bellows, Jim 156–7, 162
Bendix, Reinhard 132
Berkoff, Steven 145–50
Beyond Marginality: Anglo-Jewish Literature after the Holocaust 144
Beyond the Melting Pot 134
Birth of a Community 45, 47
Bloom, Alexander 143
Bloomburg, Michael 134
Buenos Aires 169
Bund 170, 171, 173
burial practices 4–5
  Surinam 73–84
Burma 5
  see also Rangoon

Canal Walk, Southampton 154, 166
  Jewish commerce in 157–8, 159, 162–5
  see also Ditches Southampton
Cape Town 44, 114
Cape Town Hebrew Congregation 44, 47
cemeteries 4–5
  identity and 72, 73
  Surinamese Jewish 74–8, 85
Cohen, Israel 89, 91, 92
Congregants 5, 75, 79–82, 84
Cooney, Terry 143

cosmopolitanism 16, 25
creolisation 4, 5, 7, 71–2, 73, 82–4
  definition 72

Darhe Jessarim 82–3
David Herman Theatre Company 171, 175
De Pass, Aaron 115
Diner, Hasia 137
Ditches Southampton 154, 160–1
  see also Canal Walk Southampton
Doornfontein 172
  Jewish education 175–6
  Jewish identity 176
  Yiddish theatre 172–5, 176–7
Dora Wasserman Yiddish Theatre 169, 176

East End London 9, 11, 145, 156
  Jewish community 146–50
  see also London
Englander, Bertha 173, 174
English Journey 156, 163
ethnicity 142–3, 145–51

Feldman, Leibl 124
Finneston, Monty 62–3
Fredrickson, George 132
From Ellis Island to JFK 138
Funny Peculiar: the true story of Benny Hill 154

Gadd, Eric 164
Ginzburg, Nicola 24
Glasgow 53, 54, 136
  antisemitism 56–9, 66
  assimilation 63–5
  Irish/Jewish relations 55–7, 65
  Jewish occupations 60–2
  personal histories 55–65
  sectarianism 57, 65–6
Glasgow Jewish Institute 55, 63
Glazer, Nathan 134
Goffman, Erving 141
Gorbals 3
  see also Glasgow
Gourgey, Percy 92
Gross, John 145–50
Gvishon, Avraham 104

Habsburg Empire 16–18
Haedo, Diego de 104, 105
halakha 5, 75, 81–2, 84
Hart, Thomas Gray 161
Herrman, Louis 43–5, 47
Herzl, Theodor 170
Hibbat Zion 170
Hill, Benny 154, 162, 165–6

Hirschbein, Peretz 124
historiography 3, 43–8
History of the Jews in South Africa 43–5
Hodgson, Maie 162, 164
Hotz, Louis 43, 45–7,

identity 4, 5
　place and 30–1, 40
　cemeteries and 72, 73
Into Kokerboom Country 118
Irish immigrants 53, 65
　Jews and 55–9

Jager, Jannie de 124
Jakobovits, Immanuel 157
Java 88
　see also Surabaya
Jewish intellectuals London 143–51
Jewish intellectuals New York 142–3, 150
Jewish mulattoes 5, 78–84
Jews *for Jews in particular places see the place, e.g. Algiers, Trieste*
　'Christian' 99, 105–6
　coloured 4, 73, 78–84
　commerce and 6, 155–8, 162, 165
　Eastern European 9, 44, 71, 115, 121–4, 131, 132–6, 146, 155–6, 159, 169–72
　High German 5, 71–85 *passim*
　intermarriage 5, 65, 89, 71, 133–4
　Lithuanian 170, 171, 176
　peddlers 60–1, 116–17, 132
　'port' 15–19, 25, 53, 54
　Portuguese 5, 71–85 *passim*
　Spanish 71, 103–11 *passim*
Jews in South Africa 45–7
Jodensavanne 72–3, 74–6, 84–5
Johannesburg 8, 10, 44, 172
Johannesburg Jewish Workers Club 10–11, 173
　Yiddish theatre productions 173–5
Jowell, Joe 7, 118–19

Kadimah 169, 171
Kops, Bernard 144–50

Langenhoven, C.J. 124–5
Lawrence, Brian 164
Le Roux, S.P. 125
Lee, Laurie 161–2
Lee, T.R. 141
Leighton, Lilian 59–60, 64
Lewisohn, Mark 154
Ley, David 142–3
Lithuanian Jews 170, 171, 176
Litvinoff, Barnett 145, 147
Litvinoff, Emmanuel 144–7, 149,
Livorno 6, 106–7
London 8–10
　Jewish intellectuals 143–51
　see also East End London
Lower East Side New York 9, 133–4, 143

　memory and 137–8
Lower East Side Memories 137
Lynch, Kevin 141

Maisel, Phillip 39–40
Manasseh, Charles 90
Mankowitz, Wolf 144
marxism 173–4
Melbourne 35, 171
memory 8, 10, 32, 39–40, 48
　identity and 5
　Lower East Side and 136–8
Miller, Jack Elias 57–8, 64 also Elius, Elais
Millet family 158–9
Mitchell, E.A. 160–1
Montreal 169, 171
Mordecai, Eliyahu 90
Morpurgo, Alma 23
Morpurgo, Elena 24
Moynihan, Daniel 134
muqaddam 6, 99, 108–9, 111
mulattoes 5
　Surinamese 75–6, 78–84
Müller, Geza 21, 23
Mussolini, Benito 18–19, 21
Mussry, David 94

Naftalin, Leslie 62–3, 64, 65
Namaqualand 6–7, 114
　Jewish community in 115–19, 126
Nassy, David Cohen 74–5
Nassy, Joseph de David Cohen 82–3
New Survey of London Life and Labour 156
New York 8–9, 131, 138, 143
　Jewish communities in 133–6
　see also Lower East Side New York
Noah, Sophie 157

oral history 39, 54–5
　see also personal histories
ostrich feather trade 7, 119–20, 122, 123
Oudtshoorn 6, 7, 114–15
　Jewish community in 119–26
Oudtshoorn Jewish Museum 125
Out of the Ghetto 66

Paramaribo 71, 76–8
Paris 136
Park, Robert 141
peddlers 60–1, 116–17, 132
personal histories 3–4
　Australian migrants 31–9
　Glasgow 55–65
　London intellectuals 145–50
　methodology 39, 54–5
　Southampton 162–5
piracy 101, 110–111
port cities 4, 99, 155, 156, 160
place 1, 2, 3, 7, 11
　belonging and 30, 35, 141–3

INDEX

comparative approach to 131–2
ethnicity and 145–51
identity and 30–1, 40
migration and 8, 10
social construct 141–2
Poale Zion 171
Popovich, Eugenio 18
Port Jews 15, 17, 23
Portsmouth 155, 158, 159–60
Preziosi, Giovanni 20
Priestley, J.B. 156, 163
Prodigal Sons: the New York Jewish Intellectuals and their World 143

Rangoon 5, 88
    Jews in 89–90
Read, Peter 30, 35
Relph, Edward 141
Remaking the American Mainstream 134–5
Rose, Max 7, 123, 125
Runitsch, Ossip 174–5

Sachete, Salomon 111
Sandell, Elsie 164–5
Saphir, Ya'akov 91
Saron, Gus 43, 45–7
Scotland 3–4
    see also Glasgow
Scotland's Shame 66
Scottish Jewish Archives Centre 54
sectarianism 57, 65–6
Segrè Sartario, Salvatore 21
Sephardi Jews 71
Sicher, Efraim 144
Simon, Michael 59
Smith, Pauline 122–3
Sokolov, Nahum 170
Solomons, Rachel 157
Sorkin, David 15
South Africa 3, 6–7, 114, 169
    antisemitism in 125, 126
    Jewish communities in 170, 171–2, 176–7
    see also Namaqualand, Oudtshoorn
South African Jewish Sociological and Historical Society 45
South African Zionist Federation 170
Southampton 8–10, 154
    Jewish community in 155–60, 162–5
Southampton Cavalcade 164–5

Southampton Civic Society 163
Southampton Hebrew Congregation 157, 159
Southern Daily Echo 160
Surabaya 5, 88–9
    Jewish community in 91–3
Surinam 4–5, 7
Surinamese Jews 71
    burial practices 73, 84
    cemeteries of 73, 74–8
    coloured Jews 75–6, 78–84
    creolisation concept 72, 78, 83–4

Till, Karen 142
Trieste 1–2,
    emigration from 22–5
    'foreign' Jews in 19–21, 23
    Jewish commerce 16–18
    port history 17–19
    racial laws 2, 15–16, 21–5

Uberti, Corrado 21, 25

Vassilikou, Maria 54–5
Völker und Länder 124

Waislitz, Jacob 171, 172–3, 175, 76
Weintroub, Sidney 157–8
Wesker, Arnold 145–50
Wilford, Hugh 143
Wirth, Louis 141
World Zionist Organisation 92

Yachidim 5, 73, 76, 79, 81, 84
Yerusheloyim b'drom Afrika 124
Yi-Fi Tuan 8, 11, 141–2
Yiddish 3, 11, 55, 124, 149, 169–72, 175–6
Yiddish theatre 10–11, 133, 171, 172–5, 176–7

Zionism 3, 5, 19, 20
    Australia 171
    Glasgow 63
    South Africa 123, 170, 171, 172, 176
    Southampton 159
    Surabaya 91–3
Zionist Organisation of Indonesia 93
Zionist Record 175

Hebrew Writing of the First World War
Glenda Abramson

Almost one and a quarter million Jewish soldiers took part in the First World War, spread through the armies on both sides of the conflict. Their numbers were more or less in proportion to the Jewish populations in the countries involved, and sometimes even greater. There is comparatively little writing about this experience in Hebrew. Those who did write novels, poetry, stories, memoirs and diaries in Hebrew were either serving soldiers on the Eastern Front and in Palestine, or civilians who were caught up in the war in one way or another. Their work reflected not only the tribulations of the trenches, but also the hardship suffered by civilians. For example, during and after the war the situation for Jewish civilians throughout the Russian Empire was dire. The Czarist army's campaign of brutalisation of the Jews resulted in approximately 600,000 Jews thrown out of their homes and almost a quarter of a million Jewish civilians slaughtered. Most of the Hebrew writers in Europe, including Saul Tchernichowsky, U.Z. Greenberg and Yehuda Ya'ari, confront these pogroms in their work. Starvation, illness and banishment were the lot of the Jews in Jerusalem and the Lower Galilee, and the appalling situation of the Jewish refugees was represented by memoirists, journalists and fiction writers such as Aharon Reuveni, L.A. Orloff and Y.H. Brenner, all caught up in the trials of the wartime *yishuv*. Woven into their views of the war is a portrait of the major transition taking place in Jewish political culture at the time, and their growing identification with Zionism.

Interesting aspects emerge from these texts: Jewish nationalism became a crucial theme in view of what the Jews considered to be the permanent setting of Europe's sun. The texts raise the question of genre: fiction in relation to autobiography. Also the trauma of the war led to an abandonment of the prevailing literary styles and structures, and the Hebrew writers adopted some of the new modernist trends, Expressionism in particular.

2008   448 pages
978 0 85303 770 5 cloth   £45.00/$75.00
978 0 85303 771 2 paper £19.50/$30.00

His Majesty's Loyal Internee: Fred Uhlman in Captivity

Charmian Brinson, Anna Müller-Härlin and Christine Winckler

In May and June 1940, when the war seemed to be going badly for Britain, thousands of German and Austrian refugees from Nazi oppression were rounded up and put into internment camps on the Isle of Man and elsewhere. Fred Uhlman, a Jewish refugee from Stuttgart, a lawyer and an artist, was one of them. Uhlman, who was deeply affected by the experience, set out to record it in word and image. This volume reproduces his original internment diary from 1940 alongside another version of the same text from 1979, compiled retrospectively. These texts are complemented by sixteen haunting drawings and linocuts that Uhlman produced during internment. The volume also contains the letters, highly moving personal documents, exchanged to and from the internment camp between Uhlman and his wife Diana; correspondence between Uhlman and his disapproving aristocratic father-in-law Lord Croft; and documents from the daily life of Hutchinson Camp, Douglas, Isle of Man, where Uhlman was held for seven months. Chapters on Uhlman's biography and on his artistic and literary output set his writings and drawings within the wider context of his life and work. In addition, a chapter outlining the internment crisis of 1940 also sets out to recreate the extraordinary cultural and intellectual life that the internees managed to make for themselves in Hutchinson Camp, in particular the activities of the sizeable group of artists, such as Kurt Schwitters, who happened to find themselves there.

2008   192 pages   2 x 8 page b/w plate sections
978 0 85303 930 3   cloth   £40.00/$69.95
978 0 85303 920 4   paper   £17.95/$32.95

Film and the Shoah in France and Italy
Giacomo Lichtner

Film and the Shoah in France and Italy is a uniquely comparative analysis of the role of cinema in the development of collective memories of the Shoah in these countries. The work follows a chronological structure of which three French documentaries - *Night and Fog, The Sorrow* and *The Pity and Shoah* - form the backbone. These three sections are linked by comparative case studies on famous and lesser-known fictional works, such as Roberto Benigni's *Life is Beautiful*, Louis Malle's *Lacombe Lucien*, Armand Gatti's *The Enclosure* and Radu Mihaileanu's *Train of Life*. The book tackles crucial themes, such as the politics of history and its representation, the 1970s obsession with collaboration and the ethical debate around cinema's ability adequately to represent the Shoah. The book adopts a parallel analysis of the text and its reception in order to demonstrate the historical relevance of film as a cultural artefact. In so doing, the book offers a highly innovative methodological approach to the controversial relationship between film and history.

The book fulfils three complementary purposes: to offer a detailed historical and textual analysis of key cinematic works on the Shoah; to firmly situate the popular and institutional reception of these works within the political and socio-cultural context of the time, so as to link cinema to society's attitudes towards the Shoah; and thirdly, to show how these attitudes have changed over time, in order to evince the role cinema has played in the transmission of history and memory. *Film and the Shoah in France and Italy* shows that cinema has both reflected and affected the dominant perceptions of history, contributing to the transition from recognition to representation of the Shoah. Yet the book also shows how this transition has been slow and uneven, and questions whether recognition and commemoration necessarily imply a deeper historical understanding.

2008   256 pages
978 0 85303 786 6 cloth   £45.00/$74.95

The Memory of the Holocaust in Australia

Tom Lawson and James Jordan (Eds)

This collection of essays considers the development of Holocaust memory in Australia since 1945. Bringing together the work of younger and more established scholars, the volume examines Holocaust memory in a variety of local and national contexts from both inside and outside of Australia's Jewish communities. The articles presented here emanate from a variety of different disciplinary perspectives, from history through literary, cultural and museum studies. This collection considers both the general development of Holocaust memory, engaging historically with particular moments when the Shoah punctuated public perceptions of the recent past, as well as its representation and memorialisation in contemporary Australia. A detailed introduction discusses the relationship between the Australian case and the general development of Holocaust memory in the Western world, asking whether we need to revise the assumptions of what have become the rather staid narratives of the journey of the Shoah into public consciousness.

2008   160 pages
978 0 85303 794 1   cloth   £45.00/$74.95
978 0 85303 795 8   paper   £18.95/$29.95

Arnold Daghani's Memories of Mikhailowka
The Illustrated Diary of a Slave Labour Camp Survivor

Deborah Schultz and Edward Timms

Arnold Daghani (1909-85) came from a German-speaking Jewish family in Suczawa, then in the Austro-Hungarian Empire, now Romania. His understated narrative of his experiences in the slave labour camp at Mikhailowka, south west Ukraine (1942-43), presented here in its first English book edition, provides a day-by-day account of the chilling experiences of Jewish slave labourers. It is written in a compelling style and illustrated by watercolours and drawings that Daghani made secretly in captivity and smuggled out of the camp and a Romanian ghetto. It includes an extraordinary account of the couple's escape and the shooting of over three hundred prisoners.

The uniqueness of Daghani's Holocaust testimony lies in his role as an artist which led to his (and his wife's) escape from the camp and their survival. The camps in Ukraine have been under-investigated and the diary provides significant material. It was used as the basis of investigations in the 1960s into war crimes in the slave labour camps in Ukraine, helping to bring attention to the region and providing some form of recognition for those who suffered there. This richly illustrated and scrupulously edited book is distinguished from more conventional Holocaust memoirs by focusing on fundamental questions of historical testimony and the problems of representation in both words and images. Daghani's diary is contextualized on the basis of wide-ranging new historical, archival and art historical research in essays that document the artist's attempts to achieve justice and reconciliation. They locate the diary in relation to contemporary issues on migration and statelessness, genocide and trauma, self-reflection and memory. The diary is both art and document, addressing how we understand and construct history. It enables readers to engage with the Holocaust via the viewpoint of an individual, making statistics more meaningful and history less distant.

2009   256 pages   2 b/w plate sections
978 0 85303 638 8   cloth   £45.00/$75.00
978 0 85303 639 5   paper   £18.95/$32.50

Jews in Glasgow 1879–1939
Immigration and Integration

Ben Braber

Foreword by Tom Devine

This is the first study of the integration of Jewish immigrants, from eastern and central Europe, into Scotland, and places Scottish Jewish history in context. The book looks at aspects of their immigration and integration into Scottish society, namely: the reaction of the native population and the Jewish responses; the education of immigrant children; the participation of Jews in the Glasgow economy; their participation in the political and the arts worlds; and changes in Jewish organisations, religious habits and lifestyle. A special chapter is devoted to post-1945 developments bringing the history of the Jews in Glasgow up to the present day. The final chapter compares the Jewish experience in Glasgow to that of other Jews in English cities, and to the experience of other immigrants in Glasgow such as the Irish, Italians, Germans and Asians, and brings out what was and is distinctive about Glasgow and Scotland.

2007   256 pages
978 0 85303 709 5   cloth   £49.50/$65.00
978 0 85303 710 1   paper   £19.95/$27.50